OKANAGAN COLLEGE LIBRARY
P9-BJM-989

RESCUE THE EARTH!

RESCUE THE EARTH!

Conversations with the Green Crusaders

Farley Mowat

An Adrienne Clarkson Book

CANADIAN CATALOGUING IN PUBLICATION DATA

Mowat, Farley, 1921–
Rescue the earth!

ISBN 0-7710-6684-8

1. Nature conservation – Canada – Societies, etc. 2. Nature conservation – Societies, etc. 3. Wildlife conservation – Canada – Societies, etc. 4. Wildlife conservation – Societies, etc. 5. Naturalists – Canada – Biography. 6. Naturalists – Biography. I. Title.

QH77.C3M6 1990 333.95′16′0922 C90-093445-X

Printed and bound in Canada

An Adrienne Clarkson Book

McClelland & Stewart Inc.
The Canadian Publishers
481 University Avenue
Toronto, Ontario
M5G 2E9

Acknowledgements

I am extremely grateful to the following people, who contributed their time, energy and enthusiasm to this book: Stephen Best, Michael Bloomfield, Ron Burchell, Brian Davies, Gerry Glazier, Paul Griss, Monte Hummel, John Livingston, Vicki Miller, Michael O'Sullivan, Peter Singer and David Suzuki.

I am particularly indebted to Elizabeth May for her special contributions, to my editor, Mary Adachi, and to Wade Rowland, my co-instigator in this project.

BOOKS BY FARLEY MOWAT

People of the Deer (1952, revised edition 1975)
The Regiment (1955, new edition 1973)
Lost in the Barrens (1956)
The Dog Who Wouldn't Be (1957)
Grey Seas Under (1959)
The Desperate People (1959, revised edition 1975)
Owls in the Family (1961)
The Serpent's Coil (1961)
The Black Joke (1962)
Never Cry Wolf (1963, new edition 1973)
Westviking (1965)
The Curse of the Viking Grave (1966)
Canada North (illustrated edition 1967)
Canada North Now (revised paperback edition 1976)
This Rock Within the Sea (1968, reissued 1976)
The Boat Who Wouldn't Float (1969, illustrated edition 1974)
Sibir (1970, new edition 1973)
A Whale for the Killing (1972)
Wake of the Great Sealers (1973)
The Snow Walker (1975)
And No Birds Sang (1979)
The World of Farley Mowat, a selection from his works
(edited by Peter Davison) (1980)
Sea of Slaughter (1984)
My Discovery of America (1985)
Virunga (1987)
The New Founde Land (1989)
Rescue the Earth! (1990)

EDITED BY FARLEY MOWAT

Coppermine Journey (1958)

THE TOP OF THE WORLD TRILOGY
Ordeal by Ice (1960, revised edition 1973)
The Polar Passion (1967, revised edition 1973)
Tundra (1973)

Contents

Preface

The Canadian environmental movement bears some resemblance to a tropical rain forest in that it encompasses a bewildering variety of inhabitants which together form a vigorous single organism devoted to the continuing survival and flowering of life on earth.

Individuals within the movement run the gamut from Prince Philip of Britain, in his role as patron of the World Wildlife Fund (Canada), to that ultimate activist, Paul Watson, who hunts down and sinks pirate whaling ships on the high seas. Some notion of their diversity can be gained by considering the names they call themselves. These include animal rightists and liberationists, naturalists, protectionists, conservationists, environmentalists, ecologists, preservationists and animal welfare workers.

The organizations they direct, or serve, are equally diverse. They range from bastions of respectability based mainly in Toronto office towers to radical cells of the Green Party dispersed in the most remote corners of the country. And they are proliferating with jungle fecundity. At the time of writing the Canadian environmental movement comprised *twelve hundred* identifiable groups.

The core of the movement consists of four major elements. One embraces the several national conservation and wilderness institutions which, for the most part, are involved with relatively "safe" environmental issues such as the preservation of threatened species, or of parklands and habitat. A second category includes high-pressure, high-profile organizations which focus on such thorny problems as nuclear dangers, toxic wastes and ozone depletion. A third category includes animal rights and welfare groups, which are chiefly concerned with defending and protecting non-human life whether it be domestic or in the wild. Finally there are the grass-roots groups which seem to spring up almost spontaneously wherever the well-being of the natural world is threatened by human stupidity, greed and arrogance.

There is also an assemblage of special-interest groups – mostly sport hunters, trappers and fishermen – who are essentially concerned with defending their own interests in nature. These refer to themselves as wildlife conservationists.

Unfortunately, there is no single Canadian organization which can claim to effectively represent the environmental constituency as a whole. There is nothing comparable to models in the United States, with branches in every state, huge paid memberships and powerful centralized structures. This seems odd when one considers how slavishly Canada tends to follow the U.S. lead. The explanation is probably to be found in the extraordinary difficulties encountered by Canadian groups in obtaining financial support.

Most Canadians seem to believe that organizations committed to good works or worthy causes will be automatically supported by government grants, charitable foundations, or wealthy and public-spirited corporations and individuals. None of these comfortable assumptions holds water. Overall funding of the environmental movement by our federal government consists of an annual grant of $150,000 which, if equally shared amongst the existing groups, would amount to $150 each! As for charitable foundations, corporations and wealthy individuals, these mainly prefer to support such prestigious causes as the performing arts, medical research or the construction of new mansions for higher education. Their contributions to the environmental cause have been miserly in the extreme.

The result is that almost all of our environmental rescue efforts depend heavily, and often exclusively, on financial support by the general public. But this has not been forthcoming at anything approaching the level needed to staunch the bleeding, let alone heal the wounds of a critically sick planet. Brave and true spirits alone do not have the power to put an end to the despoliation of this earth. Muscles are needed, and in our times it is *only* money that can provide sufficient muscle to empower those who are struggling on our behalf to rescue the living world.

The inadequacy of the public response is partly due to complacency, but it also owes much to the very multiplicity of environmental groups, and to a consequent confusion which clouds our perception of their identities, aims and methods. People cannot distinguish the trees in the forest from one another and so cannot decide which cause to espouse. Too often the result of this indecision is either to support none at all, or to send one's contributions to the (fortunately few) slick practitioners of direct-mail solicitation, which tend to plow most of the money they receive back into ever more importunate appeals for more funds.

Rescue the Earth! is not intended to serve as a guide to all of the manifestations of the environmental movement in Canada. Rather, it is designed to provide an introduction to a selection of people in the movement and let them tell you in their own words what they believe must be done to ensure the survival in good health of a living world.

In a forthcoming companion volume entitled, *Front Line*, Wade Rowland will examine and evaluate a number of organizations defending our common cause, and will also provide a comprehensive descriptive catalogue of the leading environmental groups.

It is my hope, and that of my publisher, fellow author and contributors to the two books, that *you* will respond by choosing a champion, or champions, and giving your generous support to what may well be our last chance to rescue life on earth . . . including human life.

Port Hope, Ontario
January 1990

Introduction:

Resisting the New Juggernaut

The last three decades of this century have witnessed the ignition of the most significant internal conflict ever to engage the human species. It is not the struggle between capitalism and communism or between any other set of "isms." It is not the contest between affluent societies and impoverished ones. It is not the conflict between warmongers and peaceniks.

It is the conflict between those who possess the means and the will to exploit the living world to destruction and those who are banding together in a desperate and last-ditch attempt to prevent the New Juggernaut from trashing our small planet.

If the right side wins, this combat may become known to future generations as the Crusade that Rescued the Earth. If the wrong side wins – there will *be* no future generations.

The struggle is an unequal one. The Big Battalions belong to and are commanded by some of the most powerful individuals and cabals history has ever recorded. Their battle cry is "Progress!" Their arsenals are supplied by Commerce and Industry. Their most fearsome weapon is Technology. Science is their supportive priesthood. Politics is their handmaiden.

They are now effectively masters of our species. They believe they can and will become masters of the planet, if not the universe. They at least purport to believe their dominance is benign. "What's good for General Motors is good for the world" is a thesis to which they give vigorous support.

Since it is so dominant, and since it also controls most means of communication, this master class is all too well known to us. However, we know all too little about the forces that oppose it. These are so new, so diverse in character and composition, and present such a confused and kaleidoscopic set of images that we bemusedly lump them into one amorphous aggregation which we vaguely refer to as the Environmental Movement.

This is not good enough. If we, the opposition, are to become united and effective in defence of animate creation, we need to know who *our* generals are; what forces they command; what principles they espouse; and how they plan to prevent the living fabric which clothes this earth from being ripped asunder.

This book is an attempt to meet that need. In the main it consists of conversations between myself and proponents of several of the most active and representative of the combat units currently engaged on behalf of the angels. They range from a self-styled environmental diplomat to grass-roots guerilla fighters, but they all share one thing in common. They are allies of the earth.

Since I count myself amongst them, I have chosen to begin the book with a one-sided conversation between me and you. I have tried to get my other subjects to explain how and why they felt compelled to take up arms, so I shall do the same.

Almost all young children have a natural affinity for other animals, an attitude which seems to be endemic in young creatures of whatever species. I was no exception. As a child I fearlessly and happily consorted with frogs, snakes, chickens, squirrels and whatever else came my way.

As a boy growing up on the Saskatchewan prairies, that feeling of affinity persisted – but it became perverted. Under my father's tutelage I was taught to be a hunter; taught that "communion with nature" could be achieved over the barrel of a gun; taught that killing wild animals for sport establishes a mystic bond between them and us.

I learned how to handle first a BB gun, then a .22 rifle, and finally a shotgun. With these I killed "vermin" – sparrows, gophers, crows and hawks. Having served that bloody apprenticeship, I began killing "game" – prairie chicken, ruffed grouse and ducks. By the time I was fourteen, I had been fully indoctrinated with the sportsman's view of "wildlife" as objects to be exploited for pleasure.

Then I experienced a revelation, which I described in *The Dog Who Wouldn't Be*.

It was in November of 1935 and my father and I were crouched in a muddy pit at the edge of a prairie slough called Wakaw Lake, waiting for daybreak.

The dawn, when it came at last, was grey and sombre. The sky lightened so imperceptibly that we could hardly detect the coming of the morning. We strained our eyes into swirling snow squalls and suddenly heard the sound of wings. Cold was forgotten. We crouched lower and flexed numb fingers in our shooting gloves.

My father saw them first. He nudged me sharply and I half turned my head to behold a spectacle of incomparable grandeur. Out of the storm scud, like ghostly ships, a hundred whistling swans bore down upon us on their stately wings. They passed directly overhead, not half a gunshot from us, and I was suddenly transported beyond time and space by a vision of unparallelled majesty and mystery. For one flashing instant I felt that they and I were one. Then they were gone and snow eddies obscured my straining vision.

After that it would not have mattered to me if we had seen no other living things that day, or fired a single shot. But the swans were only the forerunners of multitudes. The windy silence was soon pierced by the sonorous cries of seemingly endless flocks of geese that drifted, wraithlike, overhead. They were flying low that day, so we could see them clearly. Snow geese, startlingly white of breast, with jet-black wing-tips, beat past while flocks of piebald wavies kept station on their flanks. An immense "V" of Canadas came close behind. As the rush of air through their great pinions sounded in our ears we jumped up and in an action that was more of a conditioned reflex than a conscious one, we raised our guns. The Honkers veered directly toward us, and we fired. The sound of the shots seemed puny, and was lost at once in that immensity of wind and wings.

It was pure mischance that one of the great geese was hit for, as we admitted to each other later, neither of us had aimed at them. Nevertheless one fell, appearing gigantic in the tenuous light as it spiralled sharply down. It struck the water a hundred yards from shore and I saw with sick dismay that it had only been winged. It swam off into the growing storm, its neck outstretched, calling . . . calling . . . calling after the fast disappearing flock.

Driving home to Saskatoon that night I felt a sick repugnance for what we had done; but what was of far greater import, I was experiencing a poignant but indefinable sense of loss. I felt, although I could not then have expressed it in words, as if I had glimpsed another and quite magical world – a world of Oneness – and had been denied entry into it through my own stupidity.

I never hunted for sport again.

During the years that followed I tried to find my way back to that moment when I sensed a magical unity with other living beings, but I chose the wrong path. I was persuaded that science could gain me entry into the world that I had glimpsed on Wakaw Lake. So I set out to become a biologist. I did not realize that biology – the study of life – would have been more accurately defined in those days as necrology – the study of death. For the pursuit of biological knowledge then entailed (and to a large extent still does) the *killing* of animals in order to study their physical mechanisms.

Until 1940 I spent much of my time, as a neophyte, "collecting" specimens for graduate biologists to study in their laboratories. It was all done from the purest of motives, using the most exemplary procedures, and for the highest possible purpose – the amassing of scientific knowledge. In my case it mostly entailed killing birds and small mammals with traps and guns on a scale quite equal to the slaughter I had done as a sportsman.

After the Second World War, most of which I spent trying not to be killed by my fellow men (an experience which gave me considerable empathy with wild animals also trying not to be killed by men), I tried to continue as a biologist, but the scales were falling from my eyes. In 1947 I went to the Arctic as a student biologist charged with studying caribou and wolves for the federal government. I was equipped with a small arsenal of guns, traps and ampoules of cyanide. My instructions required me to use these to "collect" as many wolves as I could find, together with several scores of caribou, and then to dissect them all in order to ascertain their food habits, growth rates, rates of sexual development, parasitology and other recondite matters of the flesh.

I was unable to adhere to these instructions because I had experienced a second revelation shortly after my arrival in the north, this time under the tutelage of a man who was attuned to the living world as we can never be – an Inuit of an older time. In *People of the Deer* I recalled this remarkable event.

On an evening when the sun hovered above the horizon's lip I sat beside a man who was not of my race and watched a spectacle so overwhelming that I had no words for it.

Below us, on the undulating darkness of the tundra plains the caribou were moving, a tide of life flowing out of the dim south to engulf the world, submerging it so that it sank beneath a living sea. The very air was heavy with the breath of life. There was a sound as of the earth breathing and moving. It was as if the inanimate crust of rock below us had been imbued with the essential spark.

The man beside me stared out at the antlered hordes that swept in upon us and stretched his hands out to that living flood. He was no longer with me. He had gone from me into that all-embracing torrent. There was an ecstasy upon him as if his spirit had found union with the amorphous entity which was sweeping across his land.

And I, an alien in that place, knew him for what he was: an integral part of the profound spectacle I was beholding . . . and I envied him terribly.

Darkness had come full across the Barrens before he returned to me. The shadows still held the faint murmur of ten thousand vital pulses beating with indomitable power on every side. Although it was too dark to see, I knew he had turned toward me. He spoke, and his words might have been an echo of the divided voice of the visitation I had witnessed.

"*Tuktu-mie!* This is the heart's blood of the world."

During the rest of that Arctic sojourn I abandoned the blinkers of scientific attitudes and struggled instead to fathom the nature of the inter-species empathy and understanding which existed between the Inuit and the other creatures of the Barrenlands. I strove to overleap, or crawl under (it hardly mattered which), the barriers my own kind had erected between us and our non-human fellows. I was not markedly successful in these endeavours, but by the end of my second year in the land I had at least come to realize that my variant of mankind had somehow lost its way; was becoming increasingly isolated and alienated from its natural family.

I spent much of my final summer insinuating myself into the life of a family of wolves. Although I was initially fearful about the possible consequence of my invasion of their privacy, the wolves proved quite incredibly accepting of my presence. If they did not welcome me into their lives, they certainly did not exclude me. As my time with them drew to a close, the adults began taking the half-grown young of the year off on hunting trips, and I decided to satisfy my curiosity about the construction of the family den which had been dug into the bank of a sandy ridge, something that I had hesitated to do while the wolves were in close occupancy. And then I experienced a third revelation, which I described in *Never Cry Wolf*.

I was within half a mile of the den when there was a thunderous roar behind me. It was so loud and unexpected that I involuntarily flung myself down on the moss. A Norseman float plane full of prospectors came over me at about fifty feet then lifted to skim the crest of the wolves' ridge, sending a blast of sand down the slope with its propeller wash. I picked myself up and quieted my thumping heart, thinking black thoughts about the jokers in the now rapidly vanishing aircraft.

The den ridge was, as I had expected, wolfless. Reaching the entrance to the burrow I shed my heavy trousers, tunic and sweater and taking a flashlight whose batteries were nearly dead I began the difficult task of wriggling my way down an entrance tunnel which descended at a forty-five-degree angle. My mouth and eyes were soon full of sand and I was beginning to suffer from claustrophobia, for the tunnel was just wide enough to admit my body.

Then the tunnel took a sharp upward bend and swung to the left. I pointed the flashlight in that direction and pressed the switch. The batteries produced just sufficient light to reveal four glowing green orbs a few feet farther on.

In this case green was definitely *not* the signal to advance. I froze where I was, while my startled brain tried to digest the information that at least two wolves were with me in the den.

Despite my relative degree of familiarity with these wolves this was the kind of situation where deeply ingrained prejudices could completely overmaster reason, and I had been thoroughly conditioned from childhood to envisage wolves as vicious and merciless killers. Now I was deathly sure I would be attacked.

The wolves did not so much as growl. Save for the two faintly glowing pairs of eyes they might not have been there at all.

In a fit of blind bravado I shoved the torch as far forward as my arm would reach. It now gave sufficient illumination for me to recognize the female and one of her pups. They were scrunched hard against the back wall of the nest cavity, and they were as motionless as death.

As quickly as I could I wriggled back up the slanting tunnel, tense with the expectation that at any instant the wolves would charge. However, by the time I cleared the entrance I had still not heard or seen the slightest sign of movement from within.

I sat down on a stone and shakily lit a cigarette. An irrational rage possessed me. If I had had a rifle I believe I might have reacted in brute fury and tried to kill both wolves in revenge for the terror which had so unmanned me.

The cigarette burned down and a cold wind began to blow out of the sombre northern sky. My anger passed and I grew limp in the aftermath. I now began to be appalled at the realization of how readily I had denied all that the wolves had taught me about myself and themselves during the long summer sojourn together. I thought of the female and the pup cowering at the bottom of the den where they had sought refuge from the thundering apparition of the Norseman ... and I was shamed.

Somewhere to the eastward a wolf howled lightly, questioningly, sounding the wastelands for the missing members of its family; and the vibrant voice spoke directly to me of the lost world which had been ours before we chose the alien role.

These experiences, together with some others shared with the wolves, the caribou and the barrenlands Inuit, brought me to my first conscious awareness of just how far modern men have distanced themselves from the world that gave us birth, and which still nurtures other living beings who are indivisibly linked to us. I remembered reading one of Rudyard Kipling's stories in which Baloo, a wise old bear, tells the human child, Mowgli (who has been adopted into the jungle world by wolves), "We be of one blood, ye and I." I had felt that this was true when I read it at the age of eight or nine. Now I knew it to be true, and I became more and more anxious to bridge the abyss that yawned between.

During the early fifties I concentrated my efforts on trying to discover how the surviving handful of native peoples had managed to maintain their communion with the rest of animate creation. My particular interest lay with the Inuit. When I found that even these last connecting links were themselves being torn from their age-old certainties by the new technological tyranny, and were suffering not only psychic dislocation but were being physically destroyed, I was impelled to come to their defence. In so doing, and all unwittingly, I had begun to be an activist in the environmental movement which, at that time, did not even have a name, existing mainly as a sense of growing unease dimly perceived by those whose natural sensibilities had not been stifled by the machine.

When the 1960s began I was living in the remote Newfoundland outport of Burgeo. And there I had still another revelation.

During the early spring of 1967 a seventy-foot, female fin whale became trapped in a salt-water lagoon close to the settlement. By the time I heard about her presence in Aldridge's Pond she had become the target of a dozen or so rifle-wielding men shooting steel-jacketed bullets into her for sport. I came to her defence, hoping eventually to free her – and found myself enmeshed in a tangled skein which I described in *A Whale For the Killing*.

The whale was not alone in being trapped. We were all trapped with her. An awesome mystery had intruded into the closely circumscribed order of our lives with consequences from which we, in our self-imposed fetters of arrogance and stupidity, could not escape. This riddle from the deeps was to be the measure of modern man's unquenchable ignorance of life . . . it was a mirror in which we were to see ourselves for what we had become, strangers in paradise lost.

Not all of those who knew about the whale wanted her dead. In fact, as the days went on and her plight became internationally known, more and more people began rallying to her cause from all over North America. It began to appear that she would not only be permitted to survive but eventually would be returned to her own aquatic world. Meantime I spent days with her, in a small dory, accompanied by a fisherman friend.

Once she rose about fifty feet from our dory and instead of just breaking the surface, thrust her whole head out of the calm waters.

That gigantic head appeared to rear directly over us like a moving, living cliff. It might have been a moment of terror, but I felt no fear even when she altered course so that one cyclopean orb looked directly at us. She had deliberately emerged from her own element as far as she could in order to see us in ours and, although her purpose was inscrutable, I knew it was not inimical.

Then she submerged and a few seconds later passed directly under the dory, less than an oar's length below us. It seemed to take as long for the enormous sweep of her body to slip by as it does for a train to pass a railroad crossing. But so smoothly and gently did she pass that we felt no motion except when the vast flukes made the dory bob a little.

Then I heard her voice – a throbbing, sonorous moan, with unearthly overtones almost more felt than heard. It was a voice not of our world.

When the whale had passed, Onie sat as if paralyzed. Slowly he relaxed. He turned and looked at me with an anxious and questioning gaze.

"That whale . . . Sure, she spoke to we! I t'inks she *spoke* to we!"

I nodded, for I believed then, and always will, that she had purposefully tried to span the abyss between our species, if only to acknowledge that she knew we were on her side. So long as I live I shall hear the echoes of that haunting voice, and they will continue to remind me that life *itself* – not *human* life – is the ultimate miracle upon this earth, and that all of life reaches out to all of life.

In the end we could not save her. The bullet wounds, which in my ignorance I had thought might have meant no more to her than flea bites, gave rise to massive and virulent infections from which, one night, she died.

Not until Friday was the weather good enough to allow Claire and me in Onie's dory to pay our last visit to Aldridge's

Pond. Although a fine day for whale spotting, we saw none. There were no distant puffs of vapour hanging like exclamation marks above the dark-skinned sea. The remaining whales of the Finners family had abandoned their one-time sanctuary among the Burgeo Islands.

It would have been a lifeless scene except for three eagles soaring on an updraft over Richards Head. Like silent mourners they described their majestic arabesques in the void of air above the void of sea. When I dropped my gaze we were in the Pond and there before us floated what was left of her.

Even after the lapse of years it grieves me to write about her as I saw her then. She had been immense in life; now she was titanic, floating on her back, high out of the water so that the pallid mountain of her grossly swollen belly was like a capsized ship. From a being of transcendental grace she had been transformed into a grotesque abomination. She stank so horribly that, as we cautiously approached, we had to fight down nausea.

I do not know what Onie felt as we drifted toward that monstrous corpse, but Claire was crying quietly. We were all grateful for the distraction when the thumping of a big diesel engine announced the arrival of another boat.

This was a tow boat from the fish plant. Ignoring us, it went directly to the whale. Its crew had handkerchiefs tied over their mouths and noses. They worked quickly to secure a loop of wire cable around the small of the whale's tail just forward of her mighty flukes. Then the boat, dwarfed to insignificance by its tow, put its stern down and white water foamed under its counter. Slowly, ponderously, the whale began to move. The bizarre cortege drew abreast of us and turned toward the reef guarding the entrance to the channel.

The great fin whale who had been unable to pass over that barrier while alive floated easily over it in death . . . returning, now that there was no return, to the heart of mystery.

That evening I climbed to the lonely summit of Messers Head. It was already too dark to see clearly. I could barely make out the old stone beacon on Eclipse Island where, almost three centuries earlier, Captain James Cook had taken observations on a transit of Venus.

I sat there for a long time, locked in the confines of my mind and savouring the bitter taste of defeat. Then, slowly, I became conscious of the eternal sounding of the sea and my thoughts drifted away from myself and the world of man and his machines, turning outward to the world of whales.

Now I allowed myself to be overwhelmed by my rending sense of loss. It was full dark by then, and there was none to know that I was weeping . . . not for the whale alone, but because the fragile link between her kind and mine was gone.

I wept because I know that this fleeting opportunity to bridge, no matter how tenuously, the gulf that is increasingly isolating mankind from the totality of life had perished in a welter of human stupidity and ignorance – some part of which was mine.

I wept, not for the loneliness which would now be my lot amongst a people I had grown to love, but for the inexpressibly greater loneliness which modern man, having committed himself to becoming the ultimate stranger on his own planet, shall be doomed to carry into the silence of his final hour.

The death of the fin whale radically changed my life. I had to depart from Burgeo and from a community of people which had become dear to me. I had now to accept and learn to live with the sure knowledge that I was a member of the most lethal, murderous and un-natural species ever to run riot on earth. Like it or not, I had now become a full-fledged member of the conspiracy to save the planet.

Since 1967 I have served the cause. Shortly after the death of the fin whale I became the Canadian founding president of Project Jonah, an organization devoted to saving the remaining whales from extinction. Alas, I am not an organization man, and Jonah spent most of its short life just trying to keep itself alive. So I reverted to doing what I have always done best: to being a propagandist and a preacher. In that role I have written several books and scores of shorter pieces in defence of nature, and in explanation of man's true place in nature. I have been a spokesman for the other beings, who have no voice in how we treat them. I have not been entirely ignored. I have been sued by Canada's largest "conservation" organization – a consortium of hunters, trappers and fishermen called the Canadian Wildlife Federation. I have even been denied entry to the ultimate citadel of the Masters – the United States of America – because some of the environmental causes I have espoused are considered subversive there.

In 1984 I made what I think may be my most useful contribution – a book called *Sea of Slaughter*. It details five centuries of human destruction of life on the Atlantic seaboard. Its epilogue sums up what I believe to be the truth about the works of modern man – and the future of life on earth.

"I sit at the window of my home beside the Atlantic Ocean. This task is almost done. Having led me through so many dark and bloody chronicles, this book comes to its end. The question with which it began is answered.

"The living world is dying in our time.

"I look out over the unquiet waters of the bay, south to the convergence of sea and sky beyond which the North Atlantic heaves against the eastern seaboard of the continent. And in my mind's eye I see it as it was before our coming.

"Pod after pod of spouting whales, the great ones together with the lesser kinds, surge through waters everywhere a-ripple with living tides of fishes. Wheeling multitudes of gannets, kittiwakes and others such becloud the sky. The stony finger marking the end of the long beach below me is clustered with resting seals. The beach itself flickers with a restless drift of shorebirds as thick as blowing sand. In the bight of the bay, whose bottom is a metropolis of clams, mussels and lobsters, a concourse of massive heads emerges amongst floating islands of eider ducks. The walrus' tusks gleam like lambent flames . . . and then the vision fails.

"And I behold the world as it is now. In all that vast expanse of sea and sky and fringing land, one gull soars in lonely flight – a single, drifting mote of life upon an enormous and an empty stage.

"When our forebears commenced their exploitation of this continent they believed its animate resources were infinite and inexhaustible. The vulnerability of the living fabric which clothed the New World – the intricacy and fragility of its all-too-finite parts – was beyond their comprehension. So it can at least be said in their defence that they were mostly ignorant of the inevitable results of their dreadful depradations.

"We who are alive today can claim no such exculpation for our biocidal actions and their dire consequences. Modern man now has every opportunity to be aware of the complexity and inter-relationships of the living world. If ignorance is to serve now as an excuse, then it can only be wilful, murderous ignorance.

"The hideous results of five centuries of death-dealing on this continent are not to be gainsaid; but there are at least some indications that we may at last be developing the will, and the conscience, to look beyond our own immediate gratifications and desires. Belatedly, some part of mankind is trying to rejoin the community of living beings from which we have for so long a time been alienating ourselves – and of which we have for so long a time been the mortal enemy.

"Evidence of such a return to sanity is not yet to be looked for in the attitudes and actions of the exploiters who dominate the human world. Rather, the emerging signs of sanity are seen in individuals who, revolted by the frightful excesses to which we have subjected animate creation, are beginning to reject the killer beast which man has become.

"Banding together with ever-increasing potency, they are challenging the self-granted licence of the vested interests to continue plundering and savaging the living world for policy, profit or pleasure. Although they are being furiously opposed by the old order, they may be slowly gaining ground.

"It is to this new-found resolution to reassert our indivisibility with life, to recognize the obligations incumbent upon us as the most powerful and deadly species ever to exist, and to begin making amends for the havoc we have wrought, that my own hopes for a revival and continuance of life on earth now turn. If we persevere in this new way we may succeed in making man humane . . . at last."

1
Flag Carriers

Princes and Commoners:

Monte Hummel and the World Wildlife Fund

The World Wildlife Fund (recently re-named the World Wide Fund for Nature in some countries) is the ultimate class act of the conservation establishment. Boasting such luminaries as Britain's Prince Philip and Holland's Prince Bernhardt amongst its patrons, it commands enormous public attention and wields considerable political and financial clout.

Its Canadian operation is centred in a tastefully decorated suite of offices in one of Toronto's most prestigious business towers, and is presided over by a most persuasive youngish man who, in dress and manner, is virtually indistinguishable from the business executives who share the building with him. Monte Hummel is the antithesis of the long-haired, sneaker-wearing environmental activist of popular image. Witty and urbane, he is perfectly at home with the royal patrons who grace the WWF.

It was not always thus. Only after some years spent amongst radical activists did he move on to his current role as chief executive officer of the most powerful and the wealthiest conservation organization in Canada.

F.M. I'd like to know how a man who was a radical in his early years became the CEO of perhaps the most establishmentarian conservation group in the world. How did you, to quote one of your own phrases, become a "conservation diplomat"?

M.H. That'll cover a little history. My grandparents homesteaded in Saskatchewan and I used to work on my grandfather's farm up there. After Saskatchewan, I moved up north to a Hydro camp at White Dog Falls, Ontario – my dad worked for the Hydro.

There I spent my spare time walking around with a BB gun and a fishing rod, shooting song birds and catching fish. I spent half my time on the Indian reserve because I had a lot of Indian friends at school. We all had BB guns. I hate to think of how many pileated woodpeckers and robins and everything else paid the price for our having guns, but it was an environment in which people hunted and fished. I was a participant, and I still have what some people regard as some rather distorted and perverted views about a kind of appreciation you can get from wildlife from actually putting your hands on it and devouring it. I think there are ways of participating in natural systems. I think our society has developed a very distanced, platonic, non-offending, so-called non-consumptive appreciation of wildlife.

F.M. There may be good reason for that. During the generations that preceded us there were not that many human beings on the planet, and there was a hell of a lot more of animate creation. But today I think it's very short-sighted to be espousing the idea that we have to kill things in order to understand or appreciate them.

M.H. I agree with you. My idea of a great experience would be to ramble through a wilderness region with a shotgun and pot a couple of grouse, build a lean-to and a bed out of fir boughs, and eat the grouse. Then you think for a moment and wonder what would happen if everybody did that in a wilderness park. If the environment can stand it and if you are operating in a natural system where you've got only a few people and an abundance of natural riches, then that's a legitimate and rational way to behave. But back to my history.

I went to high school down in southern Ontario. I did very well. I was a keen athlete. I was valedictorian. I was draped with medals and prizes. Then I went into university. I studied philosophy. University was a very formative time for me. I basically rebelled. I was one of the first people to have hair down to my ass. I earned my way through school playing in rock-and-roll bands and hustling ping-pong – two things I did very well. My whole intellectual training was very anti-establishment. I was and still am a sort of existentialist phenomenologist, whereas the mainstream philosophy of the time was logical positivism and analytic philosophy. I was an argumentative son of a bitch. I never read the critics or the commentators on philosophical treatises. I would only read the treatises myself and give my own views. So I was a very smart-assed rebel.

F.M. Did you have the feeling then that something was going wrong with the world and that somebody was going to have to do something about it?

M.H. Sure – there was a whole crew of us who were campus radicals and totally dissatisfied with the system. I was a raging leftist. I mean Marxism wasn't nearly far enough left for me. I was an anarchist; I thought any system or hierarchy was repressive of the human personality and creativity; the whole system was fascist as far as I was concerned. So I had the whole vocabulary, the appearance, the hair, the pea jacket, the whole shebang and I was more than a follower; I was leading certain groups.

F.M. In the ecological movement?

M.H. Yes. I was one of the founders of Pollution Probe – Don Chant and I and a guy named Tony Barrett put the organization together, and Stanley Burke was involved, and it was an interesting gestation. That was 1969. Tony Barrett threw over Bay Street to put on an army helmet to work for Probe, and I did too, and Don Chant was our guardian angel.

That same summer, I took a trip back up to White Dog. The first things I saw up and down the river were *Fish for Fun Only* signs with a skull and crossbones in the background, right in the spots where I had been sitting and fishing as a kid. They'd discovered the rivers were full of mercury from the pulp mills.

I was profoundly shaken. The whole economy of the reserve had fallen apart. Some of the Indian kids I'd gone to school with were in jail in Kenora; others were banging around in taverns. The commercial fishery was gone. They were bringing in fish from outside to eat. This was like going from the glory days of youth, when everything was wonderful and we ran around happily fishing and having a great time, to this social and environmental disaster, and it really shook me and made me very angry. It solidified my whole feeling that things were going badly wrong, and there were wrongs that bloody well needed to be righted. So my motto when I worked for Pollution Probe was "Sue the bastards." Right above my desk I'd posted a cut-out bowling alley; the pins were made up of an assemblage of business and establishment heads snipped out of *The Globe and Mail*, and there was a ball rolling down the alley with all the long-hairs and all the activists on it heading at all those grey people who were screwing up the world. It was us versus them. As far as I was concerned, the whole world needed a total revolution.

I headed up the educational activities of Pollution Probe, which was really just a euphemism for propagandizing and spreading values that we believed in. We did this with very little modesty or tolerance of the views of others. If you didn't agree with us, you were one of "them," part of the problem; if you did agree with us, you were part of the solution.

It was fun; we were characters; we were the darlings of the press; we worked ninety hours a week on a pittance; we did some incredible schemes; pulled off some wonderful stunts – the way DDT was banned in Canada is a whole book in itself. But underlying it had to be an almost religious belief in the assuredness and rightness of our view, and it was like a self-perpetuating system in which you were allowed very few admissions that there was anybody on the other side who had anything to say for himself or herself.

As Probe got bigger, it needed money. My best friend, Tony Barrett, got to the point where he was drinking cases of the stuff you take for ulcers. Tony didn't take this by the tablespoon; he chug-a-lugged it trying to meet the payroll for Pollution Probe, and there were months when Tony himself went without being paid at all. It was a struggle to make ends meet. I believe I was paid in the neighbourhood of $4,000 a year when I took over as executive director of Pollution

Probe. We had a very egalitarian group; the process was as important as the goal; we had no hierarchies; we had no bosses. Titles were very sensitive, so we didn't have them; everybody was a "co-ordinator," and not a leader or president, or anything like that. And, of course, no corporate vocabulary creeping its way into the organization at all.

But we were also poor and there were a lot of things that were grinding to a halt because we just couldn't find the resources to do them. We'd do a terrific piece of research, then couldn't afford to publish it in booklet form or whatever, so finally in crept the necessary evil. I disappeared for a year up to a place called Quetico Centre and learned a little bit about how organizations work, business organizations, religious organizations, you name it. And I came back and brought all this gee-whiz new knowledge to Probe and decided I was going to help Tony on the fund-raising side of things because it was obvious that it was the grease for the wheels. If we didn't have some money coming in the door, the best efforts of our brethren weren't going to go ahead. So the first cracks appeared in the revolutionary Monte Hummel, and I started to learn the ropes of fund-raising, and had to buy my first suit, and started having lunches in the Toronto Club and whatnot. I had to learn how to present our case in a way that said what we were trying to do but toned it down to palatable stuff.

I was now working with chief executives, presidents and chairmen, and I soon learned my way around in these circles. I also worked with some of the people who were heading up the social and environmental programmes of various corporations, and certain government people. I started to realize that there were some people out there who actually had the potential to take a polluting bad-guy at least an incremental step in the right direction, and that maybe it was a mistake to totally write all these people off.

At the same time, we were spinning people through Probe. When I was there, I counted somewhere between four and five hundred people who worked for us, either for three or four years or maybe only a couple of months on a summer job. Some of them went off, crunching granola, and had hippie farms on the east coast; but others went into advertising and consulting and business and accounting and government.

During all of this I was teaching at the University of Toronto. I taught the whole undergraduate programme in environmental studies, and I was spinning students out into the system. They were becoming executive assistants to ministers and I was building a tremendous network of people – ex-Probers, ex-students – with whom I was in touch and still am, and I realized that we had an opportunity to parachute some people into some of the problem areas, whether it was political or corporate. I have never been convinced of the view that all power corrupts. I think there are some good people who can go in and exercise power benignly in the interests of an issue or social group. So I was starting to get whittled away and softened up. The old hard edge of how simple things were – it was black and white – was beginning to disappear.

I got more and more involved in organizational thinking; raising the money; the budgeting; working with people; realizing that so-and-so is a nice person but is totally ineffective; that Probe wasn't just a club, we had some sort of responsibility to our supporters to make progress on the issues. So I'm now becoming a boss; I'm hiring people, firing people. I've got an income statement to keep one eye on; I've got a fund-raising committee that I'm trying to keep alive; I'm phoning premiers and cabinet ministers and trying to lobby to get things done; I'm becoming a big wheel sitting at my desk.

I felt that in the interests of making progress on the issues it was legitimate to start building a few business principles into the organization. My views have only intensified in that respect. Now when you walk into my current offices – the World Wildlife Fund in Toronto – you might as well be walking into the head office of IBM. Absolutely everybody has a computer at his or her station. At the WWF we take a business-like approach in what I think is the good sense of business, which is channelling your energy efficiently and accountably and getting results.

So now I've compressed about ten years of my life, during which I got rid of the free-form "isn't this fun, we're all in it together, it doesn't matter whether you win or lose, it's whether you fought the good fight" approach. I have no room for that any more. I no longer have any time for "going down fighting." I want to win. So that accounts for having gone from the rock-'em-sock-'em-sue-'em radical at university level to channelling my efforts and time towards a specific organization and set of goals.

I've been involved in founding over thirty environmental organizations in Canada and I presently serve on the board of about fourteen. I'm invited to be there for my fund-raising skills and for the rather hard-nosed perspective I have. I think that often I am pressing too hard, and dehumanizing and desubjectivizing the organization in the interest of trying to get results. I am now over forty. I have a sense of my own mortality, which people older than me find humorous. I have a sense that I have only so many more years left in my life. I have a very definite mapped-out set of goals that I want to see chalked up and they are big goals.

F.M. What do you have in mind?

M.H. I am very interested in wilderness. I actually *believe* all this stuff you read about no habitat means no wildlife. You use the word biocide in your books a lot, and that's a term I like. I think what's happening to the earth transcends what's happening to individual species, and in fact is an assault on all of nature through natural systems. I am very keen on *systemic* level conservation. I see a lot of messing around at the individual animal welfare level as being cosmetic and almost an opportunity lost. I think Rome is burning. We are committing biocide. I believe that *nature* has rights, *natural systems* have rights, and I love Canada. I think I can make a contribution at a national level.

F.M. What's the contribution?

M.H. The contribution is to push the political and corporate sectors – to press Canadian society within the next ten years – to make the major decisions regarding reserving major blocks of wild country in Canada in the form of parks, wildlife reserves and that sort of thing. Wild country already is something which has been very diminished elsewhere, so I think it's good economics. I think in the year 2050 wilderness is going to be worth a bundle.

F.M. If it's worth a bundle, if all those people who've lost their wilderness areas start coming to *our* wilderness areas – Japanese, Germans, you name them – they will cease to be wilderness areas.

M.H. I am naive enough to think that we can control that. Wilderness will be visited and enjoyed by people but it will not be destroyed and trampled by people. I think that is controllable and that is one of the things that makes the value of it go up because there will be limited access. I think we have a very good crack at reserving major blocks of the country as wild Canada, as wild natural landscape. Not only is it good biology but it has become good politics to do things like that. You get terrific payback politically if you are seen to be doing something for the environment. You pay heavily if you're not.

We are drafting a conservation strategy for large carnivores in Canada, my argument being that cougars, bears, wolves need a big piece of country to roam around in. They serve as lightning rods for conserving large chunks of wilderness. We are working feverishly on several specific potential park areas – the Khutzeymateen Valley in British Columbia, Grasslands National Park in Saskatchewan, a marine park at the mouth of the Saguenay River in Quebec, Isabella Bay on North Baffin Island, and two contiguous parks – biggest sleeper in the country – Atikaki and Woodland Caribou – comprising a million acres of wilderness and boreal forest in Manitoba and Ontario joined at the border.

F.M. You seem to have decided the time has come when you don't mind making enemies amongst some of the people with whom the World Wildlife Fund in Canada has been associated.

M.H. Such as?

F.M. The hunting/fishing conservationists, including the Canadian Wildlife Federation and all its provincial affiliates.

M.H. No. I haven't decided that that time has come.

F.M. But they oppose the idea of wilderness preserves, unless they can hunt in them.
M.H. That's right.
F.M. And if they can hunt in them, then they're no longer wilderness.
M.H. I don't know that I agree with the second statement. We have certainly had our differences with our brethren in the hook and bullet crowd. I do not agree that hunting should be permitted everywhere, and have disagreed with the Canadian Wildlife Federation on that. I think there are definite big chunks of the landscape where there should be no hunting, where wildlife is left alone to the forces of nature. I think there are esthetic reasons for that; there are also good scientific reasons. So I have locked horns with the Ontario Federation of Anglers and Hunters, for instance, on whether or not hunting should be permitted in Ontario wilderness parks. However, I am not an anti-hunting person. I do not believe that hunting is the seat of all evil. I do not believe that sport hunting is a manifestation of some perverted, distorted personality that's gone awry and no longer relates to nature. I agree that it is by and large a frivolous and unnecessary activity as far as getting meat is concerned, at least for southern-based so-called sport hunters.

But I do not have the same distaste and problems in principle that the animal rights movement in general does with sport hunting. I would be prepared to sit down and strike a bargain with the hunting and fishing crowd regarding a grizzly reserve in British Columbia, for example, if in my judgment we might lose that reserve because the hook and bullet crowd will be against such a proposal if no hunting is permitted. If their opposition would make a difference in getting that habitat reserved, I would be open to negotiating some grizzly hunting in it.

If I could be persuaded that the safeguards were there, yes, I would let one or two grizzlies do it for their brothers every year.

That's my personal view. It's very much in keeping with the principles of the World Conservation Strategy. I quite appreciate some people's absolute repugnance at the thought of creating a grizzly reserve in which grizzlies are going to be killed like fish in a barrel. But I think it is a biologically and a politically strategically misplaced set of priorities, just as they think my judgment is misplaced and distorted, and that I am letting the boogey man in the back door. I think they are making a mistake and are not ensuring what is important, which is the system, the habitat, the wild country in which those bears are found.

F.M. Do you really believe that it is not possible to exert sufficient pressure, influence, whatever you want to call it, to establish large wildlife regions where the natural system is allowed to operate unhampered?

M.H. I do believe there are situations where we will not get that without allowing some sport hunting. The sport hunting fraternity has become powerful enough to give you all kinds of trouble. Why make enemies and create problems for yourself out of the hunting and fishing group which, in my view, is not the major problem. We have enough bona fide systemic rapers and gougers and system-wreckers to take on, without engaging in petty differences amongst ourselves.

I'm not at all suggesting that hunting can gaily go on everywhere, which tends to be the position of the hunting groups. One of the things that frustrates me about the animal rights protectionist side of the spectrum versus the old-time conservationist view that hunting is great is that both want their views to dominate the entire landscape. One side wants to hunt every square centimetre, and the other says we mustn't ever kill anything wild because hunting is barbaric.

F.M. These are extreme positions. It seems undeniable that hunting exerts a major predation pressure and animal populations world-wide can no longer tolerate that pressure on top of everything else we are doing to them and to the world in which they live.

M.H. Farley, I would agree with you there. If sport hunting is shown to be obviously a limiting factor on a population, or having a serious impact on a wildlife population, or even shows the potential of having such an impact, then I am sure that World Wildlife Fund would speak up.

We are not a front. Prince Philip enjoys shooting grouse on estates. I think Prince Bernhardt used to be a big-game hunter, so the public has the feeling that somehow, since this is the case, the WWF is in the back pockets of some elite sport-hunting group. That is totally untrue. Sport hunting can clearly be a problem or a potential problem as it is now on duck populations in south-eastern United States for instance. I can give you examples of native over-harvest of wildlife as well. There is nothing sacred about sport hunting within the World Wildlife Fund network.

There is very little division between the principles of the World Conservation Strategy and my personal beliefs about conservation. I have one qualifier in that I do not think that the World Conservation Strategy has a nearly strong enough preservationist view. I was responsible for launching the World Conservation Strategy in Canada. You have to understand why that document was drafted; that its basic purpose is to try to interest developing countries in the mission of conservation and to assure them that you can have some kinds of sustainable economic development that are compatible with conservation. Before, they saw conservation as being an albatross around their necks and something that was going to stop them from developing an economic base. What the World Conservation Strategy is trying to argue is that you can have your cake and eat it too. So it is very pro-development – it didn't want to come out strongly and espouse a preservationist view so it does have overtones of sending us on a mission of humanizing and developing almost every square centimetre on the planet.

But you wanted to know if I would allow hunting in a so-called wilderness area wildlife reserve. The answer is "yes," but only under a whole set of very careful "ifs" and circumstances.

F.M. Is that policy applicable to the World Wildlife Fund in general?

M.H. It's certainly very compatible with the World Conservation Strategy. WWF International, the whole world wildlife network now is looking very much at how protected areas can be an economic benefit to people who live around them or near them or even in them. Why shouldn't a community near a park benefit from its existence?

F.M. Isn't that dangerous? Once you introduce the economic element into any preservationist concept, you open the door to exploitation. You may only open it a crack, but once that door is open, it's almost impossible to ever close it again.

M.H. Yes, I agree. Therefore you open the door at your peril. I would be the first one to say, for instance, that our so-called fish management policies have been a total disaster. It's been one of totally wiping out by over-harvesting one population, switching to another, wiping that out, switching to another. And anybody who has looked at the data that you gathered in *Sea of Slaughter* would have a lot of difficulty believing that anybody will ever forgo an immediate economic advantage. That's probably the only reason why there is any major sport hunting left – because of the economic spin-off. I would differ from you though in that I believe the wildlife biologists do have relatively acceptable and reliable techniques for determining the relative abundance and distribution of the species which are going to be taken for sport or commercial exploitation.

F.M. They may have the techniques, yet wildlife management still operates largely by guess and by God. The guesses are perhaps a little better than they used to be, but they are still guesses.

M.H. I would accept that. I think the guesses are a little better and in some cases the guesses are good enough to know that it's safe for sport hunters to take a certain number of animals of a certain sex out of a population.

F.M. Instead of turning the so-called surplus population over to "recreational" hunters, why not control them, if you must, by using professional employees of the department involved. Biologists call that "culling," and it is a substitute for natural predation – it isn't done for fun – old, infirm and diseased animals are culled first.

M.H. Whether professionals take them or whether hunters take them, the animals are just as dead. Granted, there's a big difference because with hunters you have to control human predation that has a lot of power behind it, and the incentive to take more than is good for the species.

F.M. And they will be *allowed* to take more, so long as they have the requisite political clout. Whereas if the cull was an internal operation, there would be no such pressure.

M.H. I can't disagree with that, Farley. What it really boils down to is the ability of government to resist the pressure from groups who have a vested interest in promoting policies of over-harvesting.

F.M. What is your position on protecting wild animals from abuse at human hands?

M.H. I feel very strongly that inhumane forms of taking animals should not be permitted. For need, greed or whatever. Although animal welfare and the humane treatment of animals is not a mainline concern of World Wildlife Fund, we certainly recognize the issue and take it into account. I would have no problems with the animal welfare movement and the animal rights movement if they were using their debate about appropriate end use to lead people into an appreciation and concern about the more fundamental issues such as ecosystem conservation, but they do not.

F.M. They may not be leading the public towards objectives such as the preservation of habitat. What they claim to be doing is leading them towards a new attitude of mind. One that may be just as important in the long run.

M.H. I would agree with you that at best this focus develops a sensitivity to the natural world and starts sending messages about an appropriate way for humankind to relate to non-humankind. But I'm concerned that the whole conservation debate issue is about passing judgment on whether an end use is frivolous or not, because it isn't in my view.

F.M. You feel they are drawing support away from your objectives?

M.H. To a certain extent. Not my objectives, which I think are fundamental. I think that in some cases they cause diversions though. It's gotten to the point where Mr. Brynaert,* who also supports the World Conservation Strategy, looks at those people – and I've heard him say this – and calls them "the biggest threat to conservation that we have today" – not pollution, not acid rain, not raping the tropical forests, but the "anti-conservationists." I personally find this an incredible statement.

F.M. Dian Fossey, who spent nearly twenty years trying to preserve the mountain gorilla from extinction, distinguished between what she called "active conservationists" and "theoretical conservationists"; between the kind of people who go out and fight poachers by tearing up traps, as opposed to the World Wildlife Fund approach, which she epitomized as being of the theoretical conservationist variety.

M.H. I have great sympathy for her view, but I don't agree that WWF is always involved in theoretical conservation.

F.M. Do you think there is room for both?

M.H. I think there is relatively little room for the theoretical conservationist, and I am embarked in a continual battle to make my own organization as absolutely activist as possible. Conservation pieties and rhetoric, theoretical documents and planning concepts are a dime a dozen. Many conservationists become disgustingly institutionalized. I think we need many many more practical people who will get out there and put themselves on the line.

So I can understand that some people have been frustrated in their relationships with the World Wildlife Fund if they think we fight at too theoretical a level.

F.M. WWF seldom uses the word "preservation." You've used it today more than your printed material does. Almost invariably it's the word "conservation," a word that seems to have been largely co-opted by those who want to manage and maintain wildlife resources to satisfy their own requirements. What's wrong with the concept of *preservation*?

---

*Executive Director of the Canadian Wildlife Federation

M.H. In my view, absolutely nothing, but it depends on who you talk to. Preservation is often equated with protectionism, and protectionism equated with animal rights; so protectionists and preservationists and animal rights people are all put in the same bailiwick. When you let the spectre of preservation in the door, you are opening the door to the odours of protectionism and animal rights. Conservation, on the other hand, is a much more comfortable concept. Conservation can bring in business, it can bring in commercial interests, it brings in aboriginal peoples, it brings in users. Conservation fits the concept of utility and use. So it's not so much what's wrong with preservation, it's what's right and attractive with the term conservation. In truth, I think conservation can include the concept of preservation, but would never name something the World *Preservation* Strategy; it's the World *Conservation* Strategy. I think we have to balance the use of certain living things or systems with their *preservation* as well.

F.M. Let's look at the WWF Canada expenditure of funds. Most of your grants seem to go to scientific research projects. It is vital for the WWF to have the support of the scientific community, since this is one of your great selling points to the public. So you need a roster of scientists, but they all have their pet projects, and it's very easy to legitimize these and say in the long run this somewhat esoteric research is going to contribute to conservation.

M.H. We are sensitive to this problem and unsympathetic to research which is not leading to some practical result. I promise you that WWF of Canada will never become a victim to a scientist's pet project. I could never promise you in good conscience that we get a successful conservation result out of every project we support, since we support about two hundred a year.

F.M. What do you think about the proliferation of environmental organizations and structures and, your words, the institutionalization of the movement? How does the WWF fit in?

M.H. We are part of it.

F.M. But it worries you?

M.H. Yes, it does. I think my 1960s upbringing causes me to have a suspicion about anything when it becomes an institution. I have a very short fuse for big talkers. I like people who deliver.

F.M. Do you like big outfits?

M.H. No, not necessarily. But if you have a big problem you may need a big outfit for it.

F.M. But you keep your own outfit lean and mean?

M.H. Yes, I do, and I don't want to make it any bigger than it is. I am not sure I would be competent to manage it if it was much bigger, although I was recently offered a job to manage four thousand employees and a $350 million budget. I like trim, productive outfits that draw on donated services, resources and expertise. I think we have an obligation to people who give money to us to run that kind of an organization.

F.M. One of the criticisms of the conservation movement is that there are too many empire-builders in it. How do you react to that?

M.H. I think a question that should be asked with respect to empire-building and its self-perpetuating nature is how many conservation organizations are truly looking forward to the day when they are no longer in business because there is no longer a need for them. It troubles me that many conservation organizations have no end in sight.

F.M. WWF has recently changed its name to the World Wide Fund for Nature. What does this mean?

M.H. It means that some parts of our family thought the concept implied by the word "wildlife" was too narrow. Some of the WWF organizations, particularly in Europe, were having the problem of being perceived as strictly in the business of saving cute, cuddly, endangered species – elephants, tigers, lions, gorillas, pandas, etc. The mission is broader than that. It's not only the business of conserving wildlife *species* but wild living *systems*, and it's not only the business of conserving wildlife systems for themselves but for the benefit and welfare of people. I don't want it to be overemphasized that the whole goal is utility, but it's the broader concept that what's good for nature can be good for people. There is a relationship.

F.M. There certainly is an *essential* relationship. If nature goes, we go.

M.H. However, we in Canada still call ourselves World Wildlife Fund and so does the WWF U.S. The concept of wildlife in Canada and the United States is generally hunting and shooting, so we didn't feel we had the same problem that our brothers in Europe had in terms of public perceptions.

F.M. What degree of autonomy does World Wildlife Fund Canada have?

M.H. Absolute. We are under no legal or contractual obligation to provide any money whatsoever to our international headquarters in Switzerland. The Canadian organization totally determines where funds raised from Canadian sources are spent. To date that has been about a 90:10 percentage in Canada, though we intend to play a greater international role in the future.

F.M. What is the connection between the WWF and the International Union for the Conservation of Nature and Natural Resources?

M.H. IUCN was founded in 1947 by a number of people who decided that the world needed a body of scientific opinion that could sort out projects and priorities that needed to be undertaken to save the planet. It was a very far-seeing group – ahead of its time. It now includes about five thousand scientists around the world. In my view it's a somewhat bureaucratic, slow-moving organization, but, if nothing else, it's authoritative, and when IUCN comes forth and says the vicuna is or isn't in trouble, or the harp seal is or isn't a bona fide scientific conservation concern, there tends to be a good weight of scientific opinion behind it. If you've got IUCN on your side, it's a feather in your cap. If they are not on your side, you've got problems.

World Wildlife Fund was originally started by Sir Peter Scott, Prince Bernhardt and a few other people as a funding front for IUCN. Somebody had to raise the financial resources to translate all the IUCN programmes and priorities into action. World Wildlife Fund was founded to get out there, raise the money, provide some business know-how and management capability to actually get things going. So, in a way, World Wildlife Fund is the sister group to IUCN, but the Canadian Nature Federation is also a member of IUCN, as are the Canadian Wildlife Federation and Greenpeace. Altogether, world-wide there are over five hundred state and organizational members of IUCN, including the government of Canada.

F.M. Greenpeace had a lot of trouble getting in. Why was it important for them to join?

M.H. Because IUCN carries with it a great weight of scientific opinion and Greenpeace is often criticized for being lightweight. And because you can lobby within IUCN to get the scientific community on your side. It means that when somebody calls you a crackpot, you can say "On the contrary, we're a member of IUCN."

F.M. Where does your money come from? And what *is* your annual income?

M.H. Total income in Canada is about $4 million. We cover our fund-raising and administrative expenses from earned income, which permits all public donations to be spent directly on conservation activities. We are involved in two trust funds. One is called the 1001 Nature Trust, which is an international fund made up of 1001 people around the world who have each given $10,000 US in a single donation to the World Wildlife Fund. It was initiated in the late sixties, and the ante is now $25,000 US. There are about seventy members in Canada.

We also have our own trust called 200 Canadians for Wildlife, each of whom gives $5,000. This covers the lion's share but not all of our fund-raising and administration expenses. We have other sources of earned income, such as sales of conservation materials – books, stuff like that.

The bulk of our *project* money comes from donations. These include public donations from all sorts of people. Although some of the money for projects comes from corporate donors, our largest single source of support continues to be individuals.

F.M. If man continues to treat nature as he has being doing in the fairly recent past, how is the world going to look in the next century?

M.H. It will be disaster. There's no doubt about it. It's like being aboard the *Titanic*. We see the iceberg. Are we going to have the bloody sense to hang a left and get off this collison course and into something that makes a lot more sense? If not, it's going to be a disaster.

F.M. What do you personally think are the odds that we might change course in time?

M.H. I'd say 50-50. But I am not a pessimist about this. I see signs of hope. Most important, the environment has become good politics. It is now not only politically respectable to be pro-environment but, as I said, political suicide if you are perceived as being anti-environment.

F.M. But what about the attitudes of the *real* masters of our destiny – the business community?

M.H. In my view, the verdict is out on this one. I can't give you a definitive answer. I know many people in business who I think are committed to conservation principles; and I see younger generations of business people coming up who I think will transform business organizations – what I call third-wave managers – and make them much more harmonious with the environment. They already have think tanks; they're getting together and talking about environment and economy, and how they are halves of the same coin. There's no problem with business and environment going together, they say. And you've got the presidents of Inco, Noranda and Alcan saying a healthy environment and a healthy economy are linked; environmentalists saying the same thing; government ministers, unusual groupings of people all saying "We're going to bring business and the environment together; we are doing it; we will do more of it." There is a consequent wave of optimism and rhetoric.

F.M. Optimism and rhetoric are fine in their place. How about action?

M.H. I said the verdict was out. I fall back on my sixties upbringing. I am a sceptic and a doubter until I see what people are prepared to do as opposed to what they say. Right now we are too much involved in the kind of conservation Dian Fossey despised – theoretical conservation. The real test will come in terms of what the talkers, both environmentalists *and* businessmen, will deliver. I don't think we can afford to say that all of this will amount to nothing, that it's simply business co-opting the environmental movement, and that it's really going to go nowhere. I think we have to invest some hope and optimism in this. It's absolutely unrealistic to leave business out of the equation. It has to be brought in – if not coerced, then in a co-operative fashion. I think a little of both are called for. So we have this optimistic note on the horizon. Why not pursue it and see if it can be nourished into something? But the verdict is still out as to whether business means it, and is going to do what has to be done.

Protector of the Land:

Gerry Glazier and the Nature Conservancy of Canada

Although Gerry Glazier, in his capacity as executive director of the Nature Conservancy of Canada, qualifies for inclusion in the new managerial class of the conservation establishment, he personally does not fit the mould. For one thing, he is a professional biologist who fully understands how readily science can be co-opted to serve selfish interests and, for another, he has experienced first-hand the frustrations attendant on trying to protect the natural world while in the employ of government and commerce.

Soft-spoken, unassuming but determined, he combines a mature understanding of the way the world works with the conviction that the battle to save the planet can still be won. At any rate, if Glazier can't save it all, he and the Nature Conservancy intend to ensure that at least some patches of Canada will be protected from the destructive effects of our rapacity.

G.G. I first worked as a biologist with the federal government for a couple of years, mainly in the fisheries area. Following that I went north to Yellowknife and became Manager of Fisheries for the Northwest Territories. I did that for four years, then worked for Indian and Northern Affairs for three years as their director of water, forest and lands – everything from fire control through to managing the land and water resources in the north.

Through that I became involved with the oil industry which was drilling in the high Arctic and the Beaufort Sea. I chaired what were then quasi-public hearings for offshore drilling, then along came Petro-Canada as a new crown corporation with a lot of acreage in the north and attracted me into its fold as manager of environmental affairs.

The question that kept bothering me was: Which am I, an environmentalist, or a civil servant or industry manager? The two kinds of careers were definitely in conflict. I felt I had to make a decision about that and I decided that environmental work must take precedence. At that point the Nature Conservancy of Canada was looking for an executive director, so I took the job.

F.M. I'm told that you also took a severe reduction in income. But tell me more about why you felt you had to make the switch.

G.G. Well, an environmental bureaucrat ought to be in a position to work *for* the environment. If you are far enough away from the command centres, you *can* sometimes do that. The Northwest Territories in the days when I was there were a unique challenge because there was a lot happening and, quite frankly, the bureaucracy didn't have time to put many constraints on me. I was given a lot of freedom and used it, I think, judiciously. But eventually the organization began to close in. You are pressured to climb the ladder, and ultimately get to Ottawa, which true civil servants view as Mecca but which can be appallingly frustrating to people who want to change things.

Whenever you start a new job in conservation or the environment, you have all sorts of hopes that you can change things, until you discover that you are just part of a big system. I really wanted to get into a job where some positive things could happen, and to get a feel for the non-profit sector and for the people who, in my opinion, are doing a heck of a lot for the environment with very little.

F.M. But you're not an activist?

G.G. I just like to do something positive, and I think the type of work the Nature Conservancy does is something that society and most people can relate to. The acquisition, maintenance and protection of natural habitat is something everyone can understand and most people can support.

F.M. The Nature Conservancy seems to be very low-keyed. In fact, it seems to have such a low profile as to be almost invisible.

G.G. That's just about right. A lot of people think we have a large endowment fund set up by governments or industry, and it keeps us in business. We don't. We lead almost a hand-to-mouth existence. One of the problems we've had is we are so quiet that we haven't built up the broad base of support that keeps a lot of conservation organizations in business.

F.M. So you don't do a dozen fund-raising mailings a year out of a vast computer system, with pretty little stamps of birds and animals as a come-on?

G.G. We did our very first mailing in May 1988, of twenty-five thousand pieces, with a message that you'll get a kick out of because it says "Help us celebrate 25 years of sneaking around." It's true. We've been literally sneaking around buying land to conserve for the future. Not many people have heard about us, yet we are a quarter-century old. In celebration of that we would like to get a lot more Canadians into the fold. So we have started a programme where people can take out a membership in the Conservancy. The problem has been that though the Conservancy does good work, it's not the type of work that gets a lot of press.

F.M. Why don't you sink a few pirate whaling ships, or fly some banners from INCO's giant smokestack?

G.G. Because we are not an advocacy group. We work with all parties. For example, we'll work with developers because we realize that development *will* take place. If we can get a piece of the action for conservation, or quietly steer development away from areas that are environmentally important, we'll do that; but we don't do it in the headlines. We leave that to other groups. It's important that other groups *do* that job, but I think that we must stay away from radical actions.

F.M. Where and how did the Conservancy begin?

G.G. It was incorporated in 1963 as the Nature Conservancy of Canada with the task of acquiring and protecting as much ecologically significant habitat as we could get. It is not part of any larger network. There *is* a nature conservancy in the

United States with which we work very closely, but we are a one hundred per cent Canadian organization.

F.M. What does it consist of?

G.G. It's trustee-governed. We have a board of twenty-four trustees from across the country and a full-time staff of four and a part-time staff of three or four.

F.M. So you are not spending an unseemly proportion of your income on administration.

G.G. We are pretty proud of the low level of money we spend on administration versus what we spend on conservation. In 1988 we spent, on all administration including the fund-raising side of it, about $331,389, and we spent over one and a half million dollars preserving natural areas in this country. We are running a pretty tight ship.

F.M. Clearly you're not a rich outfit.

G.G. No. Last year our general fund was heavily in debt. We have no back-up fund. All the general fund and all the money we spend on land we raise in a given year. We are actually buying land without having all the money in place, on the assumption that we will somehow raise the money. Quite often, if you wait too long, the land price will go up, so on several projects we've had to move ahead of the financial resources. It took a little convincing at the board level to do that. It's some risk, but you have to take risks.

F.M. How are the trustees selected?

G.G. A lot of them find out about us through various means – either other trustees or perhaps because they have heard of a piece of land we have bought. Some are lawyers involved in the real-estate business, and there are some fairly well known academics, together with business people and naturalists. We are looking for people with a lot of business connections, well-respected members of the community who can pick up the phone and say, "The Conservancy is here; they need some money; this is what they are doing; will you give the executive director a half-hour of your time?" They all donate a lot of their professional talents.

F.M. It's still unclear to me just *who* you are. How did you get together? Who initiated all of this?

G.G. It was actually the Federation of Ontario Naturalists who decided it would be useful to have a Canadian organization for land acquisition. Four individuals affiliated with the FON actually put it together. Aird Lewis, Bill Gunn, Dave Fowle and Anton deVos. John Livingston was involved too. At first it was a part-time thing but three years later they hired Charles Sauriol as projects director, and then executive director. He's really been the heart and soul of the Conservancy until recently. He built up the donor base that still, to a large extent, supports our activity.

F.M. You don't have an open membership?

G.G. We didn't have, but as of now, anybody who wants to can become a member at an annual fee of twenty-five dollars. Our objective is to get two thousand new members a year for the next five or so years. At first, they probably won't feel they're getting a lot for their money, but one area that I am really stressing we should be more involved in is the actual *management* of the land we buy. I am not satisfied that a lot of the land we have acquired is being properly managed. Some has been transferred to government agencies or to conservation groups with no set standards of management. I think the Conservancy is going to have to take on some of the management itself. To do that requires a lot of income, but as you get into land management, you can offer your members site tours that aren't open to the general public, and make them feel a little more part of the organization. Belonging to the Conservancy will then become a tangible thing. We've already got three management programmes in the gestation phase. One of the most exciting is in Alberta. It's only six miles from the city limits of Calgary, and is two thousand acres! The individual who donated it wanted to give it direct to the Conservancy but his tax advisers said, "If you can gift it to the Crown, do it," which he did, but he required that the Crown have an agreement in place where the Conservancy would take it for a dollar a year and manage it. It was a two-million-dollar land donation and he is donating another half-million dollars' worth of adjacent land to us, which we will then sell to form a trust fund to manage the main piece. It's not going to be a public park; it's just going to be a big piece of prime habitat kept in a state of nature. There will be an emphasis on getting school kids out there to learn something about what the natural environment really is all about. About forty per cent of it is virgin prairie that's never been broken. We are going to keep it that way and try to restore the rest to the way it was.

F.M. You're probably going to be trampled to death by people who want to see virgin prairie.

G.G. That's right, but we are going to control it very closely. People who go there will have to have a reason other than entertainment or they won't be allowed in. But members of the Conservancy will have no problem getting through the gate.

F.M. Tell me about the Brier Island land project.

G.G. Brier Island is at the very southern part of Digby Neck in Nova Scotia and it's about six square miles. We own a little less than a third of the island. We bought it because it's prime bird habitat, and also the sea around it is frequented by whales, including the very rare right whales, and we were concerned that there would be an increasing amount of development for summer homes and cottages. This land was owned by an American who had bought it on spec. He'd never, in fact, visited the property. We had been after it for years but he wanted quite a ridiculous price for it. So we worked with our American counterparts to structure a deal whereby he would be able to get considerable tax relief on his American income by having the American Nature Conservancy buy it, and then sell it to us. He still wanted too much, so we waited until just after the stock market crashed – not that we knew it was coming. The crash did do some good for the conservation cause because I think he must have taken a bit of a beating, and the price dropped dramatically. We closed about a week later, at half of the original appraised value.

Our original intent was to hand it over to the province of Nova Scotia, which was going to establish an ecological reserve. They may in fact still want to do that, but I like the idea of managing it ourselves. I met with the mayor of Westport, the little town on the island, and she is very interested in having the community get behind the management. It's rather littered right now and needs a good clean-up. We also have to do something about damage being done by all-terrain vehicles, but I think the people on the island will themselves decide it should be posted and, hopefully, peer pressure will control it. It will be good for the community because it will attract people who want to enjoy nature. They can go out whale watching in local boats for four or five hours, then wander through the Nature Conservancy preserve, bird watching and seeing the unique plants.

F.M. It's one of the best bird migration places in Canada. In spring and fall they just stream through Brier Island. Practically the whole land bird population of Nova Scotia – plus those going to, or coming from, as far north as Labrador – land at or jump off from Brier Island in spring and fall migration.

G.G. We still owe a little money on it so we need some visibility and some more donations. It was a good acquisition. I'm pretty proud of that one.

We also did one in Ontario which we are proud of too. For years conservationists have been trying to protect the Alfred Bog – the largest remaining bog in southern Ontario. It's close to Ottawa, and it's huge. We managed to get 3800 acres of it. We bought it from a food company that had bought it thinking it was a great place to grow carrots. We went through one of our trustees who had some connections into the senior management of the company, and we put together a pretty good package and got it. We'll give that one to the local conservation authority to manage.

F.M. Isn't there some danger in that? Local conservation authorities tend to become dominated by the hunting/fishing people.

G.G. There is some risk to it. Part of the reason we are giving it to the conservation authority is that there's a fair amount of provincial government money in it. Also, Alfred Bog is hunted now and it's not our intention to stop the hunting. It's got a fair moose population, and as long as it's properly managed, I don't think hunting is really a problem. The main thing is really to protect that piece of habitat. Some local conservation authority lands get a lot of logging, but this area doesn't lend itself to logging. It just needed protection so we didn't get peat farming and sod farming encroaching on it, and eventually just eliminating most of the prime bog habitat.

F.M. So essentially your organization is about habitat protection, not species protection?

G.G. I think that's a fair description right now. We feel if we can protect the habitat, the plant and animal species will at least have some place to live.

F.M. If they are getting beaten up, then some other organization can take up the cause of looking after them. Meanwhile you are protecting the base, the habitat, without which no living things can exist.

G.G. That's right. Very much so.

F.M. As it happens I've got a large piece of land I'm interested in preserving. I thought of deeding it to government but none of the authorities seem very interested. Some of them would rather see it turned into a subdivision, or logged, or opened up to hunting. What happens if I go to the Nature Conservancy?

G.G. If you come to us, we'll arrange to have somebody with good sound biological training make sure it is habitat we think is worth protecting. People have a lot of personal attachment to their properties – particularly if it's cottage country which may be very beautiful but doesn't make a whole lot of sense for us to hold in the long term. In such cases we have to be pretty honest; we still would like to receive it as a donation, but we make it very clear that at some point we may sell it if we think we can use that money to get better habitat somewhere else. The one thing we will guarantee is that the value of it will go into purchasing land that's as good or better than that which is donated.

However, if we are really keen on it from a conservation standpoint, then we'll accept it and give guarantees to the donor that we will either hold on to it or make sure it passes into the hands of a like-minded organization who will manage it for its ecological value. After that, it's very simple – you can offer to sell it to us, and if we are interested enough, we'll raise the money to buy it. Naturally that's the least preferred approach from our standpoint, because raising money is hard work. Or you can donate it to us and get a tax receipt; or you can do a combination of both.

F.M. How does the tax receipt work?

G.G. We need an appraisal for Revenue Canada's purposes, and let's say that the appraisal comes out at $200,000. If you made the donation to us, you would then have a receipt from the Conservancy for $200,000. This can be written off against taxable income at a rate of twenty per cent of income per year. If you do not have sufficient income to write it off in the first year, the remainder can be carried forward for up to five years for write-off against future income. So if you are in the top bracket, you basically get $90,000 back, or close to it. It's changed a little bit with tax reform, but you would still get back pretty close to half of it. Or you can decide that you would like to get $100,000 cash for a $200,000 parcel of land, then we could structure it so that the $100,000 value you donated would be a charitable donation. Another alternative is to bequeath it to us. Or donate it with the right of life tenancy, if you want to continue to use it while giving the Conservancy the chance to get some visibility from it while you are still alive. That's fairly common actually. A lot of people want to do that. They hate to give it to us and then have to move off, and we'd rather that not happen, and, in some cases, it makes it good from our standpoint because the person can manage it for us.

F.M. The property then has official status and so can be protected with some authority?

G.G. That's right, and here's an example. Freeman Patterson, the photographer, has offered to donate 120 acres on the Kingston Peninsula, near Saint John, New Brunswick. He's got two parcels of land separated by about 80 acres. The deal that we have structured with Freeman is that the Conservancy is going to buy those 80 intervening acres; he'll then donate his parcels, and we'll have a 200-hundred-acre-plus parcel of land which will be protected in perpetuity. And Freeman is going to continue to live there. He'll get life tenancy, and be involved in the management of it. We're going to manage it primarily for conservation education. We've got the local school board interested, and they've offered to help put some funding together to put a small facility on the property so teachers can bring the kids out and give them some classroom time. They can look at the habitat – the animals and plants – *and* with a fellow with the reputation and knowledge of Freeman Patterson. So that's a good example. We'll manage it overall, but a lot of the management will be Freeman Patterson and the school board, so from the conservancy standpoint, it will be relatively inexpensive.

F.M. There seem to be many ways to transfer land to the protection of the Conservancy.

G.G. That's right. We've got some pretty creative accountants and tax advisers, and it's all very legal and above-board – we wouldn't do it otherwise – and there's a lot of latitude as to how we can negotiate it and over what length of time. Maybe the donation won't occur right away, but just the knowledge that it's going to come is important, and we can start managing it as a conservation area fairly early.

There's another area that we're just getting into. Tax legislation in the U.S. allows an American citizen to make a donation of a Canadian property to the U.S. Conservancy and get a full tax write-off. Brier Island was a case in point. We're working on one right now in Ontario that has a value of one million dollars plus. The American owners can make the donation and get a total tax write-off, and the U.S. Conservancy can then transfer it to us and we incur no cost other than land transfer taxes and legal expenses. So it's possible to get prime habitat that's owned by Americans back into Canadian hands at virtually no cost.

F.M. Oh, I like that.

G.G. We're really chasing it. The U.S. Conservancy's working very, very closely with us. There are some places we are looking at that we may end up selling, but we would sell to

Canadians who would agree to leave it in a relatively undisturbed state. In fact, one involves a group of thirteen American-owned islands in Georgian Bay. I thought it would be neat to put an easement in place on the islands so people couldn't develop them but could own them under something like an adopt-an-island programme.

F.M. Repatriating Canada!

G.G. That's it exactly. We are starting to repatriate Canadian lands. I think that's got some appeal.

F.M. What has the Conservancy accomplished as of now?

G.G. We've protected about eighty thousand acres and the cost to the Conservancy has been about $14 million in the dollars of the day – these aren't adjusted dollars – representing over $30 million worth of land.

F.M. What are the guarantees if I give a large piece of property to the Conservancy that if you in turn give it to somebody else to manage or look after, it's going to be protected and not eventually end up in private hands again?

G.G. We guarantee to protect it – we haven't always done this – but now we will do exactly that – we will put a caveat on title or an easement on it, which will require that certain conditions be met, or, as I mentioned, we'll retain ownership of it. We are very aware that if we developed the reputation of just flipping land, we wouldn't stay in operation very long. We take our mandate very seriously, so if we guarantee it will be protected, it will be protected, even though it may not always be owned by the Conservancy.

F.M. When you accept an offer of land, do you tell the giftor exactly what's going to happen to it, so there's no doubt in his or her mind?

G.G. If we are not one hundred per cent sure it's going to be held for ever for conservation purposes, then we'll say so. We will guarantee that either the land or the money received from that land goes into habitat conservation. It won't go into paying my salary or something like that – it will go right back into land. We've got two separate funds – a natural-area fund, none of which goes to administration, and a general fund for administration. A land donation goes to the natural-area fund.

F.M. How do you decide what land should be kept and what should be sold to buy more valuable habitat?

G.G. Not easily! You may think your property is just the best damned piece of habitat in Canada, but it may not be.

F.M. Or you may have a hundred like it.

G.G. The U.S. Conservancy, some fifteen years ago, developed a land inventory system which has been a real runaway success. It takes into consideration important parameters like resident endangered species, the size of the area, the diversity of the flora and fauna, the threat by developers or whatever, and it allows you to relate that piece of land and its location to properties elsewhere. The system now covers forty-seven U.S. states and eight Latin American countries and we are trying to bring Canada into it. It has also developed a tremendous reputation with developers and with industry as a way of getting very good data for environmental impact assessment work. If a developer – a utility is a good example – wants to run a transmission line, the data can do a tremendous job of routing it to avoid critical habitat. If the developer tries to ignore the data, at least he's been forewarned – and the conservation community has been forearmed! The system can be used for a sort of tit-for-tat trade-off too. A development may not have the choice of relocation, but if, for instance, they are going to take a wetland out of natural production they may be required to ensure that an equivalent wetland somewhere else is protected. The inventory can identify an equivalent wetland and *we* can even go and buy it on the developer's behalf and with his money. I think, with all the talk about sustainable development and linking environment and the economy and this sort of thing, that the day has arrived when we should be sharing a common data base.

F.M. In effect, this data bank will be a registration of all the more important ecological sites in Canada?

G.G. It's a registry of sites and information about sites that may not be protected yet, but, you're right, the sites will become known through this system. It will tell us that perhaps your piece of property is really important, and if so I'd be here asking if I could buy it rather than waiting for you to come and offer it to me. That's the type of thing it will do for us.

F.M. What *about* funding? Everybody's interested in that. They want to know how conservationists get their money.

G.G. We make a lot of appeals to corporations. We try to approach them through a director or something.

F.M. What's in it for a corporation?

G.G. I think a lot is in it – if they want publicity about how they are spending their corporate donations dollar. Xerox is a prime example. They gave us $25,000 a year for ten years for land acquisition. They haven't publicized it as part of their general advertising but they quietly go about saying, "This is one of the things we've done," and they can take people out and show them the property. It must give them a good feeling.

F.M. I'm somewhat cynical about the good feelings of corporations.

G.G. I am too. Most Canadian corporations are stingy, no question. They are very stingy compared to American corporations. We probably get one proposal accepted for every ten rejections. It's a tough sell.

Then there are philanthropic individuals – there are very few of them, but those we have are very generous. A few wealthy individuals, most of whom like to remain anonymous, give us very large sums of money – it can be $50,000, $75,000, $100,000 at a time.

We also get a little money from governments from time to time, but generally to match money we raise, and their money doesn't come directly to us. It will go directly into the project.

F.M. Some of the areas you preserve are going to go on being used as hunting grounds; most are not?

G.G. That's right. We're not anti-hunting, but we're not pro-hunting. If there's a good reason to not have hunting, there will be no hunting. There are some areas where there are really no game species at all but there's a tremendous plant-wild-flower display that's worth protecting. Or the odd time a place just may happen to be very beautiful. That's worth protecting too. We bought one of the small Gulf islands just off Vancouver Island. We had approached Wildlife Habitat Canada for help in funding for that, but they turned it down because although it has a virgin stand of trees and a fantastic wild-flower display there is very little wildlife to interest hunters.

F.M. Can donors of land stipulate that the land *not* be used for hunting?

G.G. Yes. The project in Alberta I spoke about – the donor hasn't stipulated there be no hunting but he said his preference is there be no hunting. There's a large elk population, and elk do not respect fences so they are not going to stay in that property, and if we allow the population to get out of control, we are going to have a problem with the neighbours because it is surrounded by acreages owned by some pretty wealthy and influential people. We would have a problem, so we have to control it. There are ways to control it. There is a Sarcee Indian Reserve close by, and I've been thinking maybe we could have the natives go in and cull the herd, and they can use the food.

F.M. That makes sense. Another solution might be to import a few wolves.

G.G. That's right. And we can talk to *you* about that.

F.M. I think I can arrange it, but the neighbours might complain even more strongly than they would about the elk.

What is the prime appeal of the Nature Conservancy to Canadians in general?

G.G. I think we offer an opportunity to do something very tangible. It's no secret that there's just a tremendous amount of land being lost to "development," and somebody's got to be protecting what's left. We can't rely on governments to do it. In fact, they may protect it for a while, then let it go again.

F.M. Governments change.

G.G. Governments change and politicians change, and they can be influenced. Our problem is getting the public to be aware of us. We find that once people find out about us, if they are interested in conservation, they join us and the retention rate is incredible. Once someone starts donating to the Conservancy, he or she usually stays in the fold.

F.M. Perhaps because you are a trust, holding land in trust for the future. If you're a member of the organization, you can say we just added ten acres here; we recently got a thousand there, twenty acres here, whatever; it's always growing. It's *real* growth, not entrepreneurial destruction masquerading as growth.

G.G. If the current generation doesn't have a guilty conscience, they should in terms of how they have mismanaged the environment. What are we leaving for all those kids we've produced? We find that there is an increasing number of people – grandparents, for example – who will donate money in the names of their grandchildren. It sends a pretty strong message that this is a way of giving something to our kids. On the other side of the environmental movement, which is the advocacy side, they certainly support what we do; we are not at odds with them at all; in fact, we need them to raise issues so we can be part of the solution. And that's what we really are all about – part of the solution to the problem of preserving this planet.

Nature Lovers on the March:

Paul Griss and the Canadian Nature Federation

Paul Griss is very much one of the new environmental executive types. Young, clean-cut, impeccably dressed, he knows how to get things done in the world of power politics and economics. He is a pragmatist who might conceivably consent to sit down and have a chat with the devil if, by so doing, he could advance those aspects of the environmental movement espoused by the Canadian Nature Federation, which employs Griss as its chief executive officer.

The Canadian Nature Federation is a loose affiliation of over a hundred naturalists' clubs representing "non-consumptive users" of nature. They include among their members the growing legions of bird watchers, wild-flower aficionados, nature photographers and those others who simply like to look at nature and feel themselves a part of it. In the past the CNF has not displayed much muscle in the ongoing battle to preserve what is left of the natural world, but under the leadership of their new CEO, that is changing.

F.M. Where did *your* interest in nature begin?
P.G. Ever since my childhood in England I've had an interest in animals, wilderness, wildlife. All kids are fascinated by nature. Children readily identify with other animals. That's how it was with me. But there was never any dramatic revelation that changed my life in favour of working with animals over people. I like people *and* animals.

There's nothing unconventional about me. Despite my interest in nature I didn't specialize past the undergraduate degree, because most people I saw who did specialize in zoology ended up counting moose shit in the bush for some game department, and that wasn't what I wanted to do for a living.

When the position of general manager of the Winnipeg Humane Society opened up, although I didn't have any formal managerial training, I did have some natural attributes for management, plus the interest in animals, and I saw a great opportunity to combine them. I was twenty-two then and am twenty-nine now.

I ran the Winnipeg Humane Society for five years, then the opportunity to manage the Canadian Nature Federation came up. I very much believe in building strong organizations dealing with the public, and working with an organization like the Humane Society was an excellent opportunity to translate my personal concerns into mobilizing seven to ten thousand people and making them more aware of the issues. I have an even greater opportunity at the Canadian Nature Federation.

I feel very comfortable philosophically with the positions the Canadian Nature Federation supports. I'm very much a naturalist. One of the key principles of our organization is that man is a part of and not external to natural ecosystems, and therefore human existence must be guided by ecological principles. My long-term objective would be to see us regulating our existence on this planet in a way not detrimental to other species or ecosystems. That doesn't mean we can't hunt or trap or have hydroelectric power; it's more how those things are carried out and regulated.

F.M. What you are really talking about is reducing the level of damage caused by man.

P.G. Yes. Ideally it should be at zero level in the long term. But the simplistic view of nature as a wonderful world in balance is a crock. Over a millennium, maybe it is, but in the short term it's a very dynamic flux, and I think the one advantage we have over other species is being able to assess and regulate the impact we are having on the world around us. This imposes a great responsibility on humans, and is why I feel there have to be much stronger efforts to educate people as to exactly how to minimize their impact on the world around them. There's virtually no aspect of modern human existence that does not, in some way, shape or form, have a negative impact on the environment. But I don't go to the extremes of some of the more leftist members of the animal movement, who want to leave everything alone. There is no way humans can remove themselves from the natural environment; we are a part of it and that imposes a role upon us. If the whole of Canada should switch to vegetarianism, we'd have just as many problems as we do because of the meat industry right now, because we'd have to clear so much more of the natural habitat to make enough agricultural land to satisfy the population's needs.

F.M. The vegetarians would say that production of meat is extraordinarily wasteful of land compared to production of vegetable foods. They say we would need much *less* agricultural land if we grew only cereal crops.

P.G. Whenever we are talking about long-term views, there are so many easily defensible and easily arguable points put forward, but I like to see us moving in the direction where, as a species ourselves, we are responsible for our actions and doing whatever we can to avoid undue deterioration of the environment. There is a very strong need for a radical change in the way we live.

F.M. So you *do* accept environmental radicalism?

P.G. Yes, but there has to be some rationalization if we are ever to achieve our long-term objectives. Probably the most prominent person on this issue is David Suzuki. In one of his columns in *The Globe and Mail* he talked about zero growth, and there were tons of letters that said in effect: "We had zero growth while Trudeau was in power; do we want to go back to those days?" – totally misinterpreting what Suzuki was trying to say. When people stand up and say we've got to change the way society works, everybody gets scared because they are still thinking back to the environmental movement of the sixties, and figure everyone has to become vegetarians and live in communes. Conservationists are still fighting that image.

Opinion polls say that Canadians are willing to spend more through taxes or whatever, if it means the environment is going to be protected to a greater extent. That is a typical Canadian attitude – we expect the government to do it for us. But the environmentally sound lifestyle has to start at home, with us, looking at everything we are doing, what we buy, what we eat and so on.

F.M. As a self-professed naturalist, how do you feel in general about killing other animals?

P.G. That's not a word you hear much any more in connection with animals. If you are a farmer, you slaughter them; if you are a scientific researcher, you sacrifice them; if you are a wildlife manager, you cull them; if you are a sportsman, you harvest them; if you are an animal shelter worker, you euthanize them; and if you are a veterinarian, you put them to sleep. A lot of people seem to think no animal should be killed at the hands of humans. I just don't buy that. You *can* stop eating meat; you *can* not wear leather; you *can* not take drugs that have been tested on animals; you *can* not wear cosmetics that have been tested on animals. But everything we do impacts on and kills animals, whether it is clearing your yard to put in a lawn, or whether you use electricity from the area flooded by a dam. These result in the death of animals by the destruction of habitat. The very fact that humans are here means that they are going to be killing animals.

F.M. But surely it makes sense to reduce the killing as much as possible. Take sport hunting, for example. If it was eliminated, there would be one less destructive element in the lives of non-human animals.

P.G. The traditional wildlife management response is that if we don't kill game animals, they are going to overpopulate, starve and die; so sportsmen are killing them for their own good. It's like the trapper who says he's concerned with the long-term health of a population of beavers; therefore he's going to kill some of them for the beavers' own good. I get tired of this argument, but it's partially correct. If you remove hunting pressure on some populations, then those species will overpopulate to a certain extent.

F.M. Assuming that natural controls are absent.

P.G. That's what I am coming to. If we are not going to be predators ourselves, then we have to be prepared to allow other predators in, but the one thing we have done very efficiently is to wipe out the predator competition. You can't have wilderness or a natural environment if you don't have large predators at the top of the line. We humans have extirpated these over most of their former ranges. So if you are going to eliminate hunting and trapping in certain areas, you have got to be prepared to allow the predators to come back. I think that a healthy system is to allow both human and animal predators.

F.M. Would you restrict human predation to need, as opposed to sport?

P.G. That's a moral question, and also it's very difficult to define need. The anti-trapping movement is saying to the natives, "You can hunt or trap animals for your subsistence if you are going to eat the meat and use the skins yourself, but you can't trap the animal and sell the skin so you can buy gas for your snowmobile because that's not considered subsistence." It's a thorny question. And you can even say that a sport hunter has a need as an outlet for his aggression to go out and shoot animals. I don't really have any strong problems with hunting, although I should say one of the most awful things I've ever seen was when my wife and I went down to northern Minnesota for a quiet weekend, and it happened to be the first weekend of hunting season. I have never seen anything like it in my life. Every hundred yards there was a truck turned off into the bush and a guy with a blaze orange vest and a shotgun or rifle. The deer just didn't have a chance. I can't argue in favour of that type of activity. I also can't argue in favour of trophy hunting or anything like that, but I don't see anything wrong with a regulated and well-managed sport hunt if the animal population can bear it.

F.M. One major argument against that is that it's not selective. It's an unnatural type of predation that takes out the physically best adapted animals in the population – unlike natural predation, which tends to weed out the unfit animals.

P.G. Certainly you don't improve the health of the wildlife population if you are taking the prime breeding specimens every time. But, realistically, some hunting has to be allowed. I don't think we can get away from it. There are going to be areas, particularly close to urban centres, where, due to favourable conditions, there are going to be large populations of deer. We aren't going to allow large predators that close to human habitation, so there is a role for hunting there. I think it has to be very carefully managed.

F.M. Is this the position of the Canadian Nature Federation?

P.G. What I have just explained is pretty much in line with the CNF's position. We are not an anti-hunting organization. We are very much in favour of maintaining the integrity of ecosystems, and we would consider the existence of predators like wolves, grizzlies and cougars to be an integral part of those ecosystems. We would come out opposed to hunting, if the pressure on the game species was so heavy that all human activities affecting it should be curtailed. We are not against hunting *per se*; it's more how it's carried out. It's the same with trapping. We're not against trapping, but are concerned how it's done. The argument I put forward is that we are not an animal welfare organization; we are not going to get too involved in the state of the individual animal; we will look at the populations of animals; we will strongly support activities minimizing the pain or suffering of individual animals; but that's not what we are about. We are here to promote conservation by protecting ecosystems and the integrity of those ecosystems and their wildlife components.

F.M. What's your stand on game ranching?

P.G. We're opposed to the privatization of wildlife. In Canada, wildlife is under public stewardship. It's owned by the government of Canada. I am having a real running fight with the Game Growers Association right now because I say right to their faces that we are opposed to game ranching. They are saying, "We've been domesticating species for hundreds of years; why shouldn't we just domesticate another one or two?" Well, soon as you start domesticating a species you might as well wrap up any hope of protecting it in the wilderness. Once an elk becomes second generation behind a fence, it's not wildlife any more.

F.M. A parallel might be that having domesticated horses, we have lost interest in preservation of wild ones. Maybe the same thing would happen to elk. But what about the argument in favour of game ranching as a way to cut down on poaching?

P.G. That's a moot point. Some say it will; some say it won't. Right now the sale of wild meat is illegal in most of Canada. You can't get it at a restaurant except in special circumstances and you can't buy it in a grocery store. If it becomes legal, if game ranching creates a market for it, and if the supply of ranched animals isn't enough to meet the demand, then there will be commercial poaching. It is a very controversial issue.

Ranching a species results in fencing off large tracts of habitat. For disease-control reasons, ranchers will do whatever they can to prevent wild species from coming into contact with domesticated or semi-domesticated species. They are going to do everything they can for predator control. Then they are going to get into genetic manipulation, like they do with other livestock, to try and maximize their production. Some of the new forms will inevitably escape and mix genetically with the wild stock. I think game ranching leads to expanded dominance of humans over the environment for no good reason except money making.

F.M. How do you feel about hunter-based conservation groups such as Ducks Unlimited?

P.G. I don't care *why* someone saves the wetlands as long as they *save* wetlands. Ducks Unlimited is saving it for ducks, but saving the habitat benefits everything else that lives in that habitat. If they are going to shoot the ducks that are produced from there, that's not a high price to pay to have the habitat saved.

F.M. It might be a high price to pay if the hunting pressure on the ducks exceeds their reproductive capacity.

P.G. Yes, but I think you've got to give some credit to the hunters. Quotas have been restricted on game birds for the last few years out on the prairies because of the decline in populations.

F.M. That's after the fact, though.

P.G. Even the Ontario Trappers Association voluntarily put a moratorium on trapping lynx when the population was at a low level. I don't see it in black and white. Everyone has their own motives for why they are doing it and I'm going to take advantage of it.

F.M. Pragmatism?

P.G. Yes. That's the best way to get results, as far as I am concerned. The Canadian Nature Federation is not moralistic or adversarial and controversial. There are no barriers to whom we will work with to promote our philosophy. I think, to a certain extent, that at this juncture in conservation the end justifies the means quite well. I'm not averse to making that statement because the situation is critical at the moment. If we had the luxury of time, we could afford to be less pragmatic. We can sit here and argue until the cows come home about whether people should hunt or trap, but hunting and trapping aren't the most serious pressures on wildlife and the environment right now.

F.M. The real problem is to preserve the habitat?

P.G. That's right. I'm more concerned with that than I am about reducing the amount of hunting or trapping.

F.M. But surely if people reject exploitive activities like hunting and trapping, they will be contributing to the preservation of the ecosystem.

P.G. To a certain extent I guess you are right.

F.M. Wouldn't the rejection of the idea of killing animals for sport, or for fashion or other trivial reasons strengthen our protective attitudes towards non-human forms of life?

P.G. I suppose so.

F.M. If the great arbiter up in the sky said, "There will be no more hunting on earth," wouldn't you accept that?

P.G. Providing we could change the way we lived so that the loss of hunting would not result in greater problems.

F.M. It would certainly result in some problems, but surely we'd be intelligent enough to find solutions.

P.G. The nice thing about being on the middle ground on these issues is that I can argue all around it. This year I will be going to the Federal-Provincial Wildlife Conference which brings together all the directors of provincial Game and Wildlife Departments. These are the government people most involved with hunting and fishing. They decided to open the conference up as a public forum this year. I'm on the programme committee. We selected as a topic "Is the current direction of wildlife management in Canada outdated? Are we doing what the public wants?" It's an outgrowth of the fact that all the public opinion surveys show that less than ten per cent of Canadians hunt, while the vast majority are only interested in non-consumptive activities such as bird-watching, hiking, canoeing and so on.

The whole conference is designed to be an evaluation of how the financial pie should be sliced, because most provincial wildlife management agencies are now spending over ninety per cent of their budgets to enhance game species and to support hunting and fishing, yet you've got ninety per cent of Canadians who don't participate in those activities. And the wildlife itself is the property, through the Crown, of *all* Canadians, not just the ten per cent who hunt and fish.

The wildlife managers are not the broadest-thinking guys in the world. A quote from David Suzuki: "The greatest thinkers don't go into forestry," really makes you realize what you are dealing with. Most of these directors, together with the federal government's Canadian Wildlife Service, want *more* money for *their* kind of conservation. In an editorial in the last issue of our magazine, *Canadian Nature*, I asked why the majority of Canadians should contribute more tax money. It's not going to benefit them when ninety per cent of the public funds are spent on game management.

If the wildlife managers really expect more support, then they have got to start developing and spending money on programmes of interest to the ninety per cent. I will get as close to anti-hunting as I am going to get in saying I am opposed to the way the pie is sliced up because you've got the vast majority of public funds being spent on the support of hunting and fishing and trapping in direct opposition to the interests of the majority of Canadians who appreciate nature for its own sake.

All across this country there's a declining interest in hunting. In Manitoba one of the senior guys in the wildlife branch wants a bigger budget so he can start campaigns in the schools to try and teach children the benefits of going out hunting. That's just missing the boat. If people aren't interested in hunting, they're interested in doing something else. So let the guys who want to hunt go and hunt, but stop making all of your wildlife management programmes cater to a very small percentage of society. Start looking at wildlife in the broad sense rather than only as game species.

The younger guys in the wildlife agencies are more sensitive to the naturalist point of view than those who have been entrenched there for thirty years or so. I think there's a big change coming. If there is a benefit to the activities of the animal rights groups, it's that they do get the government guys a little bit aware of public concern, and get them a little defensive so they are anxious to deal with groups like us who will offer them solutions.

There is another example where I will go up against the hunters. We as naturalists should have access to wildlife and wilderness areas without conflict with hunters. I feel very strongly about that. You can't put the two of them together. There's nothing to detract from a wilderness experience like hearing a rifle shot. If the CNF is going to take any stand pertaining to hunting, that's the area we'll be doing it in.

It's not just the short-sightedness of the wildlife managers; it's also the politicians who govern these departments. Revenue is generated through hunting, fishing and trapping licences. You can't issue a bird-watcher's licence, but there are creative ways of quantifying non-consumptive uses of nature.

F.M. Bird-watching brings over $2 million in income to the immediate region of Point Pelee every year. If money is the key to changing government attitudes, this is big money.

As a naturalist, how do you feel about the Committee on the Status of Endangered Wildlife in Canada?

P.G. This year the Committee will add about thirty more species to its list, for a total of 165–170 species considered rare, threatened or endangered throughout this country. But there is no co-ordinated national effort to get any of those species *off* that list. The federal/provincial governments and NGOs [non-governmental organizations] set up this classification system, but they never set up a programme for funding to do anything about it. Recovery efforts are left up to individual provincial governments, the federal government and some NGOs. But there is no real co-ordinated effort. World Wildlife Fund and Canada Life got the white pelican off the endangered species list. The white pelican was fortunate enough to be Canada Life's corporate logo. The animals that get attention tend to be those that are either cute or really dynamic like the peregrine falcon. If they are not going to capture the public interest, the only animals left on this planet twenty years from now will be the ones *we* like. That's one of the problems of management for gain. What most people are concerned about is retaining stocks of animals which have some use to us either because we like the looks of them or because we want to go out and hunt them and trap them. If any others survive, that's great. If we lose the others, tough luck. That's the attitude the naturalists are fighting.

We say, "Start looking at *all* the components of the ecosystem, not just a few."

There *is* a federal/provincial proposal for a recovery plan for national endangered wildlife up for approval, but it's only going to deal with terrestrial vertebrates. There's such phenomenal public support for endangered species I'm just amazed it's taken this long for the feds and provinces to put aside their parochial differences and say let's make a concerted effort to clean up the problem.

We are always fighting against this perception that we have to give preference to those species that have some human use or provide some revenue, and all others are secondary. A typical fiasco in terms of management for gain is in forest management, where they would have you believe that a healthy population of moose means you are doing good wildlife management in the forests. That is so biologically unsound it does not make any sense at all, but it's a benchmark they've been using up to now. In order to get lots of moose, you lose a lot of other species. The hunters are happy, but they are only a small part of the population and up until now they've had a much-too-favoured part in wildlife management. It's about time we started looking at the whole ecosystem and working to preserve and protect each and every species for its own sake, not for any usefulness it might have to humans.

That is a cornerstone of CNF philosophy – that all species have a right to exist, regardless of their usefulness to mankind. If you want to interpret that literally, you could call us an animal rights group.

The causes we are advancing will set us up in opposition to hunters and trappers on some issues, but in the long run I don't think it prevents us from working together. For example, the Ontario Federation of Anglers and Hunters is pressing for hunting in provincial parks. Unfortunately that has divided the two biggest conservation organizations – ourselves and the Canadian Wildlife Federation, of which the OFAH is an affiliate. But I don't see any reason why we can't disagree on specific issues but continue to work together on the long-term goals.

F.M. Tell me about the origins of the CNF.

P.G. The roots of the organization reach back to 1939 when a gentleman named Mr. Arthur Reginald Whittemore founded a magazine called *Canadian Nature* in memory of his wife, who had been a very devout naturalist. This was a children's magazine primarily designed to raise awareness of the natural world among young people. Not long after the magazine was started, a chapter of the Audubon Society was formed here in Canada and it took over the magazine.

In 1961 the chapter became independent of the National Audubon Society and set itself up as the Canadian Audubon Society. It was a small organization and primarily based in southern Ontario. It existed as such until 1971, when the various provincial federations of naturalists across the country decided to change the Canadian Audubon Society into a federation of provincial naturalist societies which then became known as the Canadian Nature Federation, and our magazine became *Nature Canada*. The first executive director was Ted Mosquin and he really went after growth. The budget went from almost nothing to about $1 million in five years, and from hardly any membership, up to eighteen thousand. But when Mosquin left, the board of directors promoted his office manager and took a very conservative approach to financial management for the next seven years. The timing couldn't have been worse because Ken Brynaert took over the Canadian Wildlife Federation right around that time, and promoted it like crazy.*

People make a big deal about the size of the Canadian Wildlife Federation now, but the one thing everybody overlooks is that CWF developed to its present size in the lack of any competition. If you take a very popular product like wildlife conservation into a very receptive market and nobody else is doing that, you are going to succeed. The Canadian Wildlife Federation has been able to develop by capitalizing on the public's concern. My biggest regret is that the Canadian Nature Federation wasn't out there going head-to-head with them at that time, because now I am having to start from quite a way back and catch up. I have to come from behind,

---

*The Canadian Wildlife Federation is the umbrella organization for nine provincial and two territorial wildlife associations, which themselves comprise most of the fishing and hunting clubs within their respective regions.

In trying to sort out who is who in the Canadian environmental movement, it is worth remembering that with the partial exception of the World Wildlife Fund *all* conservation organizations and most governmental departments which bear the word "wildlife" in their names represent the interests of the hunting, fishing and trapping fraternities.

but I'd rather be behind looking ahead than in front looking over my shoulder.

CNF brought me in in November 1986. I've spent much time since then reorganizing. I want a good structure in place. I don't mind taking calculated risks. You have to spend money to make money. But I want to be spending as much of my total budget as possible on *real* conservation programmes. I don't want to become a market-driven machine. You look at some of the organizations out there who are spending a fortune to maintain their volume, but the percentage of that money channelled into real conservation programmes is minimal.

Animal welfare organizations and conservation groups *do* appeal to the vast majority of Canadians. Probably ninety per cent of people would contribute to or support that type of cause. But the programmes have to be there. Everybody wants to contribute to a winner and you have to be *seen* as being a winner. The Canadian Wildlife Federation proved that – they raised a fortune without providing much to their members. You get a subscription to *International Wildlife*, which is an American magazine with four pages of Canadian content, and that's about it. They've also got a big merchandising programme. Most of the stuff they sell is trinkets. It doesn't do anything to advance the understanding of the membership as far as conservation is concerned.

I impose a handicap on myself. I won't fund-raise without trying to educate. I want people to know exactly what they are going to get in return. It's important to the CNF not just to raise money but to change individual awareness. The thing that bothers me about groups like the Canadian Wildlife Federation is that they've got supposedly great access, and claim to represent five hundred and fifty thousand people, members and supporters, and yet instead of using that to further the conservation message, they're channelling very little back to those people. The result is that the support for the Canadian Wildlife Federation is a mile wide and an inch thick.

CNF, however, is built on a solid core. This organization could stop doing any publicity and we'd still have about sixteen thousand core members who would contribute regularly. In addition we would still have a hundred-odd affiliated organizations that would keep us going because they are solidly behind this organization. We have a membership that's fairly highly educated, many of them with post-graduate degrees, and they're very aware people. Most of our people are very committed. I want to increase that support base of committed people. I don't just want to collect five hundred thousand names on a list.

We produce *Nature Canada*, which is *our* publication entirely, and deals almost entirely with Canadian issues. We make a point of telling our members just exactly how we are spending their money. Through our merchandising service we provide material the majority of which serves to enhance the purchaser's awareness or enjoyment of nature. Our conservation programmes are always reported in detail to the members. CWF's fund-raising pieces are very general – "Help us to continue helping wildlife." Ours go out with a detailed list of all the campaigns we are involved in, and exactly what we are doing. The CWF has very few on-the-ground resources. We've got a network across this country that's incredible in terms of being able to plug into issues, find out what's going on and get people to work on things for us.

We are structured differently from the Canadian Wildlife Federation. CWF is set up so that the only way you are a voting member is if you belong to a fish and game club; then you can vote through your provincial wildlife federation to put representatives on the national board. If you subscribe to *International Wildlife*, buy something from their merchandising section, or send them a donation, you automatically become an associate member. But you don't get a vote. You have no say in how the organization is governed.

The Canadian Nature Federation is completely different. Everybody who joins the CNF, whether as an organization or as an individual – everyone who sends in a $25 membership – is a full voting member. We have our annual meetings around the country, and all members in attendance vote. And we *listen* to those people. That's where our programmes, issues and ideas all come from. People send in suggestions and complaints and we take them very seriously. As I keep saying in my fund-raising literature, "You *are* the Canadian Nature Federation. It's not some ivory-tower Ottawa group you are supporting. CNF achieves its objectives through people like you, writing letters, raising your awareness of nature."

F.M. What's your budget and what do you do with it?

P.G. Right now we have just over seventeen thousand individual members and affiliates representing about two hundred thousand Canadians. The annual budget is about $1,500,000. We have something like seventy-odd national conservation and environmental issues we are addressing right now. The bulk of those are in areas where there is no strong local group to address them, because that's the most effective use of our resources. We are spending a lot of time in the north where there are no local conservation groups. We spend a lot of time in western Canada, because that's where most of the wilderness issues are.

F.M. Do you co-ordinate your efforts with other major organizations?

P.G. It depends on the issue. For instance, not too long ago Wildlife Habitat Canada organized a special day before the House of Commons Committee on Environment and Forestry to talk about wildlife and forestry interactions. The four groups that went there were Ducks Unlimited, Wildlife Habitat Canada, the Canadian Wildlife Federation and us – the first three all being sportsmen oriented. We all said slightly different things and I purposely took our presentation out a bit to the left of the other groups, but we ended up making roughly the same recommendations for what the committee should do to improve conditions for wildlife in areas utilized for the forest industries.

While we may have had different reasons for what we did and different needs in the long run, in the short term the important thing was that the committee made some of the right decisions.

About the same time, the CNF signed on to campaign with Pollution Probe. We work with Friends of the Earth, with anybody – as long as the name and image of the Canadian Nature Federation isn't compromised. We work with World Wildlife Fund more than anyone else. They don't have a constituency of their own. They don't have a philosophical position to defend. They are there to facilitate getting things done, and our major area of interaction with them is on the education front where we are partners in their Lifeline Education Programme, which is a children's programme designed to raise awareness of nature and the environment through endangered species.

I don't let philosophical differences get in the way of getting work done. The threat to wildlife and the environment is so great we can't bother about nickel and diming it over relatively small-scale differences.

Suzuki estimates there are thirty years of wilderness left in Canada. We can't afford to tinker if we've only got thirty years left. We've got to start now and make some pretty substantial decisions or in thirty years the whole debate will be semantic.

The problem is incremental. The average Canadian sitting in his living room watching television at night is not aware of the extent to which the destruction is progressing. There is no shortage of people who can stand up and recite a litany of problems, but there are very few advancing pragmatic and practical solutions. That's a role I see our organization getting more and more involved in – educating people in how they can make a difference towards restoring a natural balance.

It may get me in a lot of trouble by saying it, but the fact is we don't have a single good *all-round* conservation organization in Canada. They are all good at certain things – at doing projects, or acquiring land or raising money, but we don't have one that provides the service that the public is demanding.

F.M. Does the public know yet what it should be demanding?

P.G. The environment is a major matter of public concern, but I think the individual is largely ignorant of what he can do to address the problem. I think there is a screaming need for an organization to provide the information that's going to enable people to make the right choices and seek the right direction. The two philosophies closest to what we have to achieve on this planet are the naturalist philosophy and the traditional native spiritual philosophy. More and more people are starting to realize that living in harmony and in balance with nature is the way to go if we are to sustain ourselves over the long term. Somebody just has to show them how to do it.

F.M. Are you going to do that?

P.G. I'm going to try. I am not going to be the Jimmy Swaggart of conservation but we are going to do our best. I think it's a matter of offering practical advice and solutions, getting people involved, getting them to voice their concerns on issues, getting government and government agencies and industry to act. Robert Bateman says it well: "I don't give a damn which organization you join, just join one of them; it doesn't matter what their objectives are, just join because they are all going in roughly the same direction and they need that public support." Bateman would rather they join the CNF, but he's out there trying to get people motivated.

An expression that's used a lot now is "Think globally and act locally." It's vitally important for individuals to make changes. Whether that's using unleaded gas in the car, or buying certain types of fabric rather than others, or buying certain types of household cleaning products instead of others; every little bit helps. If you and twenty-five million others are doing these things, that becomes a pretty significant movement and that will make a big difference.

The public has got to demand of industry that if the technology is available, even if it costs a little more, we've got to pay the price to protect ourselves and our environment. According to opinion polls, Canadians are willing to pay the price. I see that as a major focus of the CNF over the next little while.

F.M. You are professionally optimistic; you have to be. But are you personally optimistic? Do you think we can do it?

P.G. I have to think we can do it. I'd go crazy if I didn't. We are already doing better. But *individuals* must do more. For example, how much is drinking coffee worth to you? How much is eating bananas worth to you? Because many of the conservation problems in the third world are because they are clearing forests to cater to a North American demand for those two products.

F.M. Plus beef from Brazil for our hamburgers.

P.G. Yes. It's ironic to have people sending money down south to save chunks of rain forest when it's their very own life style which is contributing to the demise of that entire ecosystem.

I think we can do something but it's going to take a massive effort, and I think Canada, more than any country in the world, has the opportunity to show what should be done and how to do it.

F.M. We in this "mediocre country" have actually been foremost in terms of ecological awareness and action. Greenpeace came out of this country. The International Fund for Animal Welfare came out of this country, as did Paul Watson and many others I could mention. There's been more ecological leadership coming out of Canada than there has been from any other comparable nation.

P.G. The problem is we are seen, rather incorrectly, in an international perspective as simply a raper and pillager of the environment.

F.M. Which we certainly have been, and still are.

P.G. To a certain extent, though, we are not as bad as some other countries. We are good at saying and doing great things here, but as soon as we get overseas, our officials make us look like ecological idiots. Not long ago there was a conference in Geneva to talk about nitrous oxide emissions in connection with the acid rain problem. The Americans were asking if they could base their future emissions on any level prior to 1985. Canada supported this request. It was quietly pointed out to our officials that if the Americans chose 1978 as their base year, it would result in tripling the amount of nitrous oxide spewing out of smoke stacks in the States. Two-thirds of that would fall on Canada. Here we are trying to get an effective acid rain treaty with the States, and our negotiators are over in Switzerland supporting a motion which would allow the United States to increase its emissions.

F.M. Isn't that the way it always goes in Ottawa when the U.S. wants something? But I wasn't talking about government when I suggested we are very progressive ecologically. The things our governments, provincial and federal, do are often unbelievably stupid. The federal government is currently trying to reinstate the seal hunt. The kill was up to about seventy thousand – mostly pups – in 1989. In addition, there was a massive slaughter of grey seals by fishermen with the full cognizance of the Department of Fisheries and Oceans. Thousands of grey seal pups washed ashore on Cape Breton Island, along with many adults. Nothing had been taken from them except the sex organs of the males, for the Oriental trade in aphrodisiacs. The government people responsible must be out of their minds. If they deliberately start up the seal controversy again, it will be even more destructive to our image abroad, because our government assured the world we weren't going to butcher baby seals any more.

P.G. I see a growing awareness on the part of the public. The environmental movement is only twenty years old in Canada. It's taken a long time to gain legitimacy. I think that concern is vested in the majority of people, rather than in government bureaucracies. What is needed are organizations to start taking advantage of that public concern and changing the way we operate as a society – to make some major modifications to the way we do business, to our expectations – so as to enable us to continue to exist on this planet in a healthy and diverse environment. That's the key. Do we have a healthy planet if we don't have wolves or grizzly bears or seals or any of the other major species that epitomize wilderness? We need them.

Biological systems and all natural systems go towards maximum entropy. We have been trying to take it the other direction. The more we try to control the natural world, the more futile are our efforts. We can't continue to go against the natural laws of the universe. We have to define the point at which we cease to exercise control and start to allow nature to regain her supremacy. That way we may have a chance.

John Muir's Followers:

Ron Burchell and the Sierra Club

Ron Burchell is another of the many immigrants who have helped fuel the environmental movement in Canada. During the first decade after his arrival here, this soft-spoken Englishman found himself becoming increasingly distressed by Canadians' lack of concern for what was happening to the natural world around them. No crusading activist, Burchell sought for some peaceable way to help change Canadian attitudes. He discovered what he wanted in the Sierra Club, the oldest conservation society in North America, which was then trying to establish a chapter in Toronto. The Club became Burchell's consuming passion, and for the past several years he has been its titular leader in eastern Canada.

Although the Sierra Club was cast from an establishment mould, this was not the modern one. Its origins are essentially patrician and altruistic, whereas the modern establishment is essentially commercial and self-serving. Perhaps something of an anachronism in today's world, the Sierra Club is certainly unique. It is also singularly effective in its dogmatically democratic and low-keyed way.

R.B. I came from England to live in Toronto in 1960. I had belonged to hiking groups in England where I was a surveyor. I saw a lot of the derelict industrial land of the Midlands of England. And the lack of wildlife. I was very concerned that we in Europe had destroyed so much of our habitat, our wildlife and our wild land. When I came to Canada, I thought it was – it sounds very holy – my duty to see that if I had anything to do with it, Canada would not go the same way much of Europe had gone. So in 1970 I joined the Sierra Club in Toronto. Our chapter is called the Sierra Club of Ontario but extends east from the Manitoba border to include the Atlantic provinces. There is another chapter in the west operating from Victoria. It is a little older and larger.

Initially the Sierra Club was a rather elitist group. To join, one had to be sponsored by an existing member, and that situation existed until about twenty years ago. Until then the club was very small and was basically still in the western United States. It had been started in 1892 by John Muir, a Scottish immigrant who lived briefly in Ontario during which time he hiked what is now part of the Bruce Trail.

The Club seems to be the oldest environmental group in North America. It's almost a hundred and is now one of the largest. It has something like four hundred and fifty thousand members, and is still growing strongly. There was a long period at the beginning of this century when the Club was still expanding very slowly, mainly in the west, and concentrating largely on wilderness activities, but as the effects of industrialization became more apparent, more people became concerned with environmental matters. More chapters were formed. The movement spread to eastern North America and then into Canada.

The major Canadian Sierra Club issue today is in British Columbia, and is concerned with old-growth forest preservation and preventing non-conforming uses in parks – things like hunting, mining and lumbering. They have real problems with logging in places like Strathcona, which is one of the oldest parks in British Columbia. It is also being attacked by the mining industry. Park borders are being changed to suit the demands of lumber and mining industries.

F.M. Vander Zalm changes the map.

R.B. Absolutely. There's also a good deal of Sierra activity related to the generation of hydroelectric power for export.

B.C. has plenty of power for its own use, but there is a big move to flood many more mountain valleys to generate power for sale to California. Interestingly, Sierra Club chapters in Oregon and Washington State are trying to get an injunction to stop the transmission of power through their states in order to help try and save the valleys in B.C. There's a good deal of north-south co-operation among the chapters along the western seaboard, though perhaps not too much connection yet between British Columbia and the prairies.

F.M. What is the Club representation in the prairies?

R.B. There is one group in Regina, one in Calgary and not a very active one in Winnipeg, all part of the British Columbia chapter.

F.M. Who makes the decisions?

R.B. The chapters make their own decisions within the overall policy of the Club. Providing we, as a chapter, do things which are environmentally sound, there is no restriction. When you have an organization that is continental in scope, obviously there are different priorities in different areas. Acid rain is not a big issue in the west but is in the east. If we make decisions to work on acid rain-related issues, that is our business.

F.M. What support do you get from the American organization?

R.B. Part of our dues is sent to San Francisco, but that is basically to pay for the Sierra magazine which comes to our members every two months. Twice a year the magazine includes a list of wilderness outings, Canadian, American and world-wide. All Sierra Club members can go on these. If one wants to climb the Himalayas with the Sierra Club, one has to be a member because they have more applications than they have spaces. However, at chapter level and group level anybody can go on our trips; we lead weekend canoeing trips, hiking, wild-flower walks; and one can bring friends along. Hopefully they will become members.

We also get a grant of $10,000 a year to help arrange meetings between the two Canadian chapters so that ultimately we can form the Sierra Club of Canada. We get back-up support too. When we put on a major forestry conference in Toronto two years ago, we financed it with an interest-free loan from Club headquarters in San Francisco. But we are not a branch plant of the U.S. organization. The Sierra Club is divided into twelve regions. There is one for Canada, one for Alaska, one for Hawaii, and the others are grouping of chapters in the south-east, north-east, mid-west U.S.A. It's a very democratic organization.

Members are free to get involved at any level they wish. It's not an organization run by an inner circle where the membership pays the money and has nothing to say.

F.M. What are the opportunities for involvement?

R.B. In our chapter, we have about eight different committees. Some are service committees dealing with public education. We have a parks and forestry committee (which takes up issues like preventing hunting in public parks and game preserves). There's a wildlife committee and an outing committee. If there was something that appealed to a person in any of these areas, or in waste management, or air quality, or whatever, one could join the appropriate committee and, if one wanted to get really involved, stand for the board. We have open elections every year for board members. One can also vote by mail for the board of directors in San Francisco. In our newsletter, which comes out four or five times a year, we advise our members that there will be vacancies, and people can nominate themselves or others for the board. Then, six weeks before the election, there will be a description of all the candidates in another newsletter, together with a mail-in ballot.

F.M. That must put an enormous load on your administration.

R.B. It does. But we think it's important that our members be involved. Very few decisions are made at the top. The decisions are made by the membership. The membership also decides on the priorities of the Club, on the ballot, which will have a list of maybe ten priorities. These could be something like "Should the Sierra Club concentrate on national forests, wildlife, water quality, air quality, outings?" The members then decide where their money is going to be spent.

The national office in San Francisco has a budget in excess of $28 million. They have a permanent office in Washington for continuous lobbying. Lobbying is where most of the money goes, although a lot seems to be spent keeping the membership informed.

F.M. I had no idea you were now such a grass-roots outfit. The Club seems to have gone from being very exclusive to the opposite extreme.

R.B. Yes. It may have been exclusive initially, and some people still think of it as being such, because many ethnic minorities aren't well represented. We do have quite a few Chinese and Japanese members, but you don't see many black members, or south Europeans or native people. It doesn't seem to appeal to them. I don't know why, whether it's our policies or priorities. It's particularly obvious in Toronto where there are fifty or sixty different ethnic groups but our membership remains predominantly Anglo-Saxon.

F.M. I suspect that's true of all conservation and environmental groups, but you are the first I've ever heard raise that issue.

R.B. People who have come from a third-world country or a poorer country perhaps have other priorities. Maybe their children will become involved with environmental issues.

F.M. Do you do mass mailings in pursuit of an expanded membership?

R.B. Until 1988 in our chapter we had not done any kind of mailing for new members. Members have joined because they have seen ads, they've come to meetings, they have friends who are members or they have perhaps bought a Sierra Club calendar. However, at the end of 1988 we did our first direct-mail campaign to increase our membership. The types of mailing lists we use include the Eddie Bauer catalogue, *Equinox*, *Scientific American* and *Harrowsmith*, which are not perhaps the types of magazine that appeal to a new immigrant from Costa Rica. Expanding the ethnic representation is a problem that I think urgently needs to be faced.

F.M. Do you think the nature of the issues might change if there was a different ethnic mix?

R.B. If you are talking about clean air, clean water, that sort of thing, these affect all kinds of people. Surely a poor black family is just as interested in having clean drinking water as some rich white family.

F.M. What are you doing to bring native Canadians into the Club?

R.B. We have had some contact. In September 1987 our chapter held a major conference at a lodge in Temagami. And the second chief of the local Indian band – Rita O'Sullivan (I don't know how she got a name like that) – came to our meeting. Following that she came to our annual meeting in November and was the chief speaker.

We are usually on the side of the natives. The native people had no problem with logging in Temagami as it was carried out until about twenty years ago. It used to be done in the winter – a horse went in with a couple of men; they cut a tree down and dragged it out. But now the massive machinery in use destroys more forest than is harvested, and the native people are beginning to see they have to join with other groups to be able to defend the wilderness. They don't have the financial resources to proceed on their own; there are not enough of them; traditionally they haven't been listened to. I think in the future that natives and the rest of us will work more closely together, although there has been some suspicion in the past about the motives of either side.

F.M. You were very involved with the struggle to save South Moresby in the Queen Charlotte Islands, and with the ongoing defence of the new national park there.

R.B. The issue came up again in May of 1988. I went to San Francisco for the annual Sierra Council meetings. The guest speaker at the banquet was our then-Minister of the Environment, Tom McMillan, who had been invited because the Americans were very impressed with him when they heard him at a conference in Colorado. He was given an award – the first foreign "statesman" to be recognized by the Sierra Club – for his work in preserving South Moresby. He let us in on a few insights into the mining claims which still existed there. Several mining companies were trying to pressure the federal government into buying them out. These claims had never been used, but I guess the mining operators thought this was a way to make a quick buck. The federal government had forked out $106 million to British Columbia to buy out the logging rights, and now the miners were having a go at it.

F.M. I don't see how any government could permit that sort of hold-up to happen twice. The original payment was blackmail extracted by B.C., and Ottawa knuckled under. We saved South Moresby, but Ottawa set a horrendous precedent. The next time we try to save a significant piece of habitat – publicly *owned* habitat, mark you – the feds will be *expected* to cough up millions and millions in pay-offs to provincial and private interests.

R.B. I am sure that had South Moresby been required for defence purposes or something like that, the federal government could and would have taken it over without cost. I know the provinces have jurisdiction over natural resources, but surely there must be times when the national interest overrides provincial interests. My chapter of Sierra got involved with Moresby because it *was* a national issue.

F.M. When you become a national organization, what will change?

R.B. Hopefully, we will then have a paid lobbyist in Ottawa who will pursue all sorts of national issues on behalf of the Sierra Club.

F.M. There now seems to be a general belief amongst environmental groups that they've got to be very professional, and that means hiring the best-qualified people they can get, even if they are expensive. Do you agree?

R.B. Not necessarily. When I became chairman of the Sierra Club eight years ago I had no special qualifications but I found I could more or less cope with issues that arose. I managed to obtain and maintain fairly good access to the provincial government. I have been holed up for a couple of days at a time with Alan Pope, when he was Ontario Minister of Natural Resources, to discuss what the bottom line was on new parks in the province. The ministers are amateurs, rather like I am an amateur, so we seem to be able to work very well together. The Sierra Club is very reasonable. It's not a radical group. We don't attempt to embarrass governments. We do not sit on flagpoles and engage in confrontations but tend to participate with governments on good conservation projects. We've recently been instrumental, acting in that way, in getting the removal of non-conforming uses from Ontario parks. We scored a really big victory there.

F.M. Tell me about it.

R.B. During Alan Pope's days as minister, he promised 270-odd new parks. That was whittled down to about 170, but eventually over 100 were established. These included 6 major new wilderness parks, but these were all what we consider second-class parks. They were still going to be open to mining exploration and hunting. So we threw all our weight behind persuading the government to give them the same status as first-class wilderness parks such as Polar Bear, Quetico and Killarney. The present government has now agreed to remove the non-conforming uses and to exclude mining and hunting (except for native hunting and trapping). It will probably phase out duck hunting in other parks; it may phase out lodge operations. We don't know all the details yet, but I am sure there won't be an edict to the present users: "You will be out next week." However, when these operations expire, they won't be renewed. We have been lobbying for this for a long time, and feel we have scored a good victory there.

F.M. Was the Sierra Club the major lobbyist?

R.B. We were on an equal footing with the Federation of Ontario Naturalists and the National Provincial Parks Association.

F.M. How do you feel you get along with the rod and gun fraternity?

R.B. A little while ago there was a proposal to establish a wilderness park in a couple of townships near Parry Sound, and the Ontario Federation of Anglers and Hunters and the Sierra Club formed a coalition to support the proposal, and in this case we agreed not to exclude hunting. We were prepared to compromise. Neither organization wanted to see these two townships divided up into cottage lots, which was the almost certain alternative.

F.M. You take the long view. Once an area is declared a park, there's always the possibility of changing the ground rules in the future.

R.B. There's no point in trying to save something after it's been destroyed, so if we can save a region with its trees and wilderness character intact we'll worry about the future when we have to. The Sierra Club is not opposed to the hunting of plentiful game, for food, on crown or private land. We *are* opposed to trophy hunting. If you get some pleasure from shooting a deer and you are going to eat it, I don't see anything particularly wrong with that. We *are*, however, opposed to any kind of hunting in any kind of park. This is where we differ markedly from the anglers and hunters who would like to be able to hunt wherever they please, in your backyard or mine. They want the right to hunt in parks, whether there are people camping or canoeing there or not. And while we do not oppose the hunting for *plentiful* game, as species become endangered we feel hunting must stop, even as far as native hunters are concerned. If we are running out of walrus, or seal, or beluga, then the natives must also eat hamburger like the rest of us. I think we are fairly pragmatic in these views.

F.M. I gather that you are primarily a lobbying organization.

R.B. Sierra Club in the United States is very much a lobbying organization. It is difficult for us to lobby at the same level in Canada because we are small and have very little money. So most of our work is done by letter writing; by submitting briefs, invited and otherwise; by arranging meetings with ministers and by increasing the public awareness of vital issues. At the moment, we are very concerned about the environmental impact of Free Trade. In my opinion it will confirm the old adage that Canadians are hewers of wood and suppliers of water to the Americans.

F.M. This is the first time I've heard concern about this matter expressed by any environmental group. I think it's a primary concern. I see it as a calculated attempt to integrate us with the United States – economically first, politically later.

It is going to have an enormous environmental effect upon this country. Where we as a sovereign people might be able to defend an area against, say, construction of a hydroelectric dam, once the production of electricity becomes continentally integrated, our chances of successfully opposing it are practically zero. Nobody's talking about that. But *you* are prepared to talk about that and make it an issue?

R.B. Yes. And we don't think it's too late. Although the bill has been passed, it's something that's to be phased in over ten years. I don't think it's too late to make changes to a bad bill.

F.M. One of the greatest threats to the preservation of Canada's natural environment is the U.S.A.'s growing and insatiable need for fresh water. American government and business interests expect to gain unlimited access to Canadian water, and the Free Trade deal will ease the way. What's the Sierra Club's stand on that?

R.B. The U.S. Sierra Club is very supportive of our view on Free Trade. They are against it – from an environmental point of view. The Club has a Great Lakes Committee which has been working with the International Joint Commission over a number of years on a variety of water problems. Acidic deposition onto the Great Lakes is becoming a serious problem. We are concerned about the effects of winter navigation. Americans periodically come up with the idea of keeping the whole system of the Great Lakes and St. Lawrence Seaway open all year, but there are serious environmental problems with that, mainly concerning habitat around the shores. We are extremely concerned with water sales and water diversions. I don't know what we are going to do about Lake Michigan, over which Canada has no control. The IJC is supposed to take that kind of thing into consideration, but it is only an advisory body and has no regulatory control whatsoever. We are concerned that the Americans may simply "tap into" Lake Michigan for as much water as they want, with disastrous effects to the lower lakes. Beyond that we see an attempt to divert northern Canadian rivers into a great canal to water the U.S. south-west. The Sierra Club is opposed to any major engineering projects which radically change the environment, either locally, nationally or continentally.

F.M. What are some of the other major issues with which the Club is concerned?

R.B. Priority number one is, without doubt, acid rain, or should we say clean air. A clean-air bill is something the U.S. Club is lobbying for heavily in Washington.

The Arctic Wildlife Refuge, which takes in huge parts of adjacent regions of Alaska and the Yukon Territory, is also a big issue. Great pressures are being exerted on Alaska to open up the wilderness reserves to hunting and to mining, and oil and gas exploration. We in Canada are working closely with the U.S. Club on this one too.

The Club is concerned with road construction in forest reserves. It seems to be difficult for provincial governments to realize that for every public dollar spent on forest access roads there is a financial return of about nineteen cents on timber sales. It makes no sense at all. Yet they continue to build roads into areas further and further away from the mills, at greater and greater cost.

The Club is also concerned about offshore activities such as oil and mineral extraction. The U.S.A. has never signed the international Law of the Sea Treaty, but Canada has, so our chapters funnel the U.S. Sierra Club's messages through to the U.N.

It's difficult to put a priority on these things, but forest preservation is a big issue. There is further concern about the loss of agricultural lands from erosion, mainly due to growing the wrong crops. Draining of swamps is more of a local issue than a national one, but most chapters have some horror story to tell about yet another swamp or marsh being destroyed.

F.M. Would you say that the essential drive of the Sierra Club is habitat preservation?

R.B. Yes.

F.M. You are not much concerned with the preservation of individual species?

R.B. No, that's too specialized. I think the World Wildlife Fund, at least in Canada, takes a very narrow but appropriate view on species. I think perhaps the Sierra Club has a more holistic view on the environment. If we save the habitat then we save mankind as well as animals. Like many other groups concerned with environmental problems we are severely hampered by lack of funds. The Club's annual budget may be $28 million overall but what can you do for an entire continent with that? You could perhaps build a new police station or something with that amount.
F.M. Or buy a lifeboat for one of Canada's proposed nuclear subs.
R.B. In terms of what is spent on *destruction* of the environment it's nothing. You have to try to get to the political people, such enlightened people as Norway's Mrs. Brundtland, for example, and work through them.
F.M. We need to get Prime Minister Brundtland cloned. Replace Maggie Thatcher with Mrs. Brundtland II; Brian Mulroney with Mrs. Brundtland III, and so on.

What are your personal feelings about where we stand in the battle to preserve the environment?
R.B. I doubt if we can reverse the degradation process. I think we can only hope to slow it down. I am rather pessimistic about the long-term future. It's all related to population growth. I know this sounds brutal, but at times I wince when I hear that the infant mortality rate in such-and-such a country has been reduced. That's bad news to me. Why are we trying to save people in Ethiopia who should not in any case be living there because there is nothing there to live on?
F.M. We don't seem to have developed enough socially to recognize the obvious, that the more of us there are, the worse the situation will be for all. There are already far too many of us. We make a big thing about "managing" other species to keep their populations under control – but do little or nothing to exercise restraint on ourselves.
R.B. Destruction of the environment in "newly emerging" countries with exploding populations is particularly bad. They are destroying forests at such a rate that while the

population is rapidly going up, their resources are coming down at an equally rapid rate. I don't know how they can continue very much longer in places like Africa where the desert is expanding very fast, or in places like India where there are just two or three small forested areas left. I am pleased that I am fifty-seven because I think there will be enough food to keep me alive for the next twenty years, or whatever my life span is, but I really don't see very much available for future generations. They certainly won't be enjoying the standard of living we are enjoying.

F.M. All local environmental problems eventually become global problems. Is the Sierra Club not being somewhat parochial in its concern with North America?

R.B. Not entirely. We are concerned with rain forests, and our chapter has been involved with trying to preserve rain forests in Costa Rica. Many of our members each bought an acre to add to a national park in Costa Rica, though that's a drop in the bucket I suppose. The Sierra Club has had some influence on the World Bank, persuading them not to fund projects which are environmentally unsound. I think the World Bank is taking a somewhat different view of things now. It used to like to fund mega projects because these looked good. However it's had a lot of negative press, not just from the Sierra Club but from many other organizations.

We are doing the same sort of thing closer to home. The Sierra Club of Ontario is fighting the current method of evaluating crown land timber reserves. The assessment at the moment considers only the potential production of timber on crown land. We are trying to get this changed to embrace all aspects, including the proper inventory of native needs, the needs of hunters, trappers, wildlife habitat, recreationalists. We are working with the Federation of Ontario Naturalists and three other organizations, including the Canadian Environmental Law Association. It's going to cost at least $300,000 to pressure the government to have the assessment changed. The government gave us $130,000 in intervener funding because they recognized that our coalition is a responsible group of environmental organizations that plans to bring qualified counsel to the hearings in the way of professional foresters, loggers, lawyers, biologists.

This is not the first time we've had government funding. Some years ago we received a grant of $35,000 to counteract Ontario Hydro's proposal to increase its generating capacity in Ontario, based on its calculation of approximately seven per cent annual growth. We produced figures to prove that it would be more like two to three per cent annual growth. I think we've established a responsible record with the provincial government.

F.M. Much of your effort seems to be in Ontario.

R.B. That's because this is where the eastern chapter was formed and where most of our membership at the moment still lives.

F.M. What are you doing in Quebec and the Maritimes?

R.B. In Quebec, very little. In the Maritimes, we've been involved in questioning military training over-flights in Labrador, which affect migrating caribou herds and the native people. Through our members in Newfoundland, we have been lobbying the Dutch government, who have recently signed an agreement with the Canadian government to carry out NATO training flights in Labrador. We haven't got anywhere, but we haven't given up. The Dutch over-flights are going ahead. It seems to be very difficult to get through to the military. The military seems to override everything.

F.M. Always.

R.B. Unfortunately we don't have a lot of organization east of Ontario.

F.M. Shouldn't you be setting up groups in the Maritimes?

R.B. We would very much like to see a group formed in Halifax.

F.M. I think it's vital. Almost none of the major environmental organizations are well represented in the Maritimes – except, of course, when the sealing season is on. That is a very large region of Canada and a very threatened region. Terrible ecological disasters are happening there, and nobody seems to be co-ordinating any major effort to do anything about it. I think there's an enormous opportunity for some organization that really puts its money where its ideas are to do something in the Maritimes. It might be difficult because Maritimers are convinced nobody in the centre of the country is ever going to listen to them anyway. Nevertheless, *because* they are convinced of that, they are probably ripe for a regional organization.

R.B. I feel very badly about the members that we do have scattered around in the east now. There's very little we can do for them. They receive the Sierra magazine from San Francisco; they receive our chapter newsletter which largely is dealing with Ontario issues, outings in Ontario, but very seldom anything in the east. We must, and will, do more in the east.

F.M. You could be a big and rich organization in this country, could you not, just playing on the Sierra Club name and doing the revolving-door kind of direct mailings that some conservation outfits employ? If you were to invest $100,000 in computer fund-raising, you could probably be a multi-million-dollar organization in short order.

R.B. We do get a lot of clout from our name. It is well respected in North America. But to simply capitalize on it to become rich has never been part of the Sierra Club philosophy. Most truly dedicated environmental organizations are rather poor. The Sierra Club in the States never has any spare money. It has some investments and it has a foundation that raises money for it. We also, in Ontario, have our own foundation which is able to give tax receipts for money donated. Governments place a stringent limitation on the use of that money. It has to be used purely for educational purposes, which includes some lobbying.

When I became the chairman, our chapter membership was six hundred and something. The previous administration I would not say discouraged membership growth, but they certainly did nothing to attract new members.

F.M. That sounds very Canadian.

R.B. We are trying to expand the membership. I do feel there is both the need for and the possibility of growth – if we had the same percentage of population in Canada that they have in the States, we would have forty thousand members. We have a mandate to spend every penny we can get our hands on on environmental issues. The more money we have, the more we will spend, so we won't become rich.

The Sierra Club should remain a grass-roots organization. We must continue to involve our members in all aspects of environmental work – socially, outings, issues – and encourage people to get involved at whatever level they feel competent. The Club takes a holistic view of the environment. We do not have a narrow, partisan view of wildlife, habitat, clean air. We think they are all inter-related. When we are better known, I feel we will be able to contribute much more, both provincially and nationally, to the restoration and protection of the environment.

II
A New Morality

The Guru of Animal Liberation:

Peter Singer

I talked to Peter Singer at his summer house on the outskirts of Melbourne, Australia, where he is the Director of Human Bioethics at Monash University. He seemed perfectly cast in the role of the mild-mannered professor of philosophy: small, neat, soft-spoken and somewhat given to pontificating in academic style. It was difficult to realize that he was the guru of the revolutionary animal liberation movement which has had an explosive effect upon modern western culture. His book - *Animal Liberation* - is the bible of those who accept the radical concept (radical in the west, at least) that *all* living things are of one blood and so deserve as much consideration as we human beings pretend for one another.

Although Singer is not a Canadian, he has close Canadian connections, and his influence has been of enormous importance in Canada. Animal Liberation, Animal Rights and Animal Welfare - the left, centre and right wings of the ethos which he represents - have among them fired an ethical and moral explosion which has energized the environmental movement, especially the new wave thereof, and given it new direction and determination.

Never again, or so one hopes, will human beings be able to justify our savage behaviour towards non-human beings on the grounds that they and we are essentially different creations and therefore subject to different ethical consideration and treatment. Thanks to the work of people like Singer, we can no longer justify or excuse our heinous behaviour towards other animals by claiming that they are no more than insensate lumps of matter.

P.S. I was born in Melbourne. My parents had come to Australia from Austria before the war; they were concerned to bring me up in the best possible way to fit in with Australian society, so they sent me to a reasonably good private school. Then I went to the University of Melbourne to study law but decided to study philosophy, and particularly the social-political-ethical side of philosophy. Had I not done that, I no doubt would be some sort of lawyer.

F.M. Well, you might have been defending animals in the courts.

P.S. I think it unlikely because I had no particular interest in animals at that stage. In my home background we never thought anything more about animals than most people do. We had a cat for a few years and then it ran away, or died or got run over. After it had gone, we didn't feel any great need to replace it, because we weren't particularly keen on pets. We all ate meat and regarded that as a normal, unquestioned thing to do. I suppose I was aware that there were societies like the Royal Society for the Prevention of Cruelty to Animals which did useful things in making sure that people didn't go round beating up their cats and dogs and horses, but beyond that I had never really thought about the animal issue at all.

F.M. You weren't a naturalist?

P.S. No. I don't think I had any great interest in nature. I did enjoy going for walks, something my father had introduced me to. He used to like to get outdoors, and would quite often spend a Saturday or Sunday going for a walk somewhere in the bush, which gave me some feeling for nature.

F.M. But did you feel any sort of empathy with the natural world? Or were you, like so many of us, growing up in an artificial world without really realizing there was another world beyond?

P.S. I always knew that there was another world. We would go for a few days, at Easter perhaps, to a place called Mount Buffalo, which is a national park, and certainly I always had the feeling of enjoyment of being away from cities. The peace and quiet of the mountains was something that I enjoyed. But I really didn't have any great feeling that the preservation of nature was vitally important.

I believed that humans were special, and I accepted all the standard myths about our superiority and the idea that animals simply didn't count in the same way as we do. I saw no reason to be concerned for non-human animals. What eventually changed in my understanding was a belated comprehension of the moral significance of animal suffering and what we are doing to animals and, for that matter, to the non-human environment in general.

F.M. What brought you around to this new way of thinking?

P.S. When I was twenty-three I was awarded a scholarship to study at Oxford. That was '69, so we are now talking about the period in which there was a lot of student radicalism. I had already been politically radicalized by the war in Vietnam. I was involved in a student movement against that war and in particular against conscription. Australia sent conscripts to Vietnam and that gave every twenty-year-old a personal reason to get involved. I was deputy editor of the student newspaper, and environmental issues were starting to crop up then. Once you are against the military/industrial complex in general, well, it doesn't take much to see its effect on the environment and the rest of the world.

The specific event that roused my interest in animals occurred after I had been in Oxford six months. I was attending lectures in philosophy and I started talking to Richard Keshen, a Canadian from Toronto now living on Cape Breton Island. We decided to have lunch together. When the food was served – it was spaghetti with some kind of sauce – he asked if the sauce had meat in it and when told that it did, said he didn't want any. So naturally enough I asked him why, and that really led to the whole thing because he had ethical objections to eating animals, and I was interested in what they were. And he said, "Look, if you are interested in this, you should come and meet Stanley and Roslin Godlovitch – who were also Canadians – and we can all talk about it." So I went around to the Godlovitchs' place where we discussed it, and I guess it was the first time that I had ever been confronted with the idea that there was a serious ethical basis to vegetarianism.

I had always thought of people being vegetarians either for their health or as cranks who thought that it was always wrong to kill, like absolute pacifists. But I wasn't an absolutist of any sort. I had a lot of sympathy with the pacifist view, but I didn't think you could defend an absolutist position on pacifism and, similarly, I didn't think that you could say it was always wrong to kill. But this discussion wasn't really revolving around killing or, indeed, any absolutist beliefs but rather was about the way animals were being treated, particularly in intensive farms, which at that stage I knew nothing at all about. So I borrowed a book by Ruth Harrison called *Animal Machines*, which was the first detailed description of factory farms, and it seemed to me really that there was a major ethical issue here that had been neglected. It wasn't, as I had assumed, a sort of sentimental attachment to animals that was the only basis for vegetarianism or for the kinds of changes that these people were advocating, but there really was a sound ethical basis for it.

At that time I was doing ethics and political philosophy, and was interested in the principle of equality and why we say all humans are equal when manifestly they differ in so many capacities. So the question was, Why do we believe that all humans are somehow morally equal, and yet non-humans are not? Non-humans are in a quite separate sort of category, and that's the way that I started to think about that issue after having been confronted with it. Had I not met Richard Keshen, I might never have seen the issue as essentially an ethical one that transcends species.

F.M. The issue is clear to you but it's unclear to most. How did you come to comprehend it?

P.S. I think you could say there was a combination of factors. In the late sixties, early seventies, there was an openness to new ideas. It did seem to be a time when there were a lot of new concepts around – there had been black liberation, women's liberation, there was the peace movement, there was the growing environmental awareness. All of these were new and exciting. Then there was the philosophical training I had had, learning to think through arguments as carefully as possible. There was definitely the influence of friends who had already come a long way down the path, and I give them great credit for it. I think I clarified, systematized and, perhaps most effectively, popularized what they had already thought.

F.M. Was there a subjective aspect in what happened to you?

P.S. I really don't think that hypothesis works very well in my case. I am not saying I am the kind of person who is always motivated by objective reason. If you are looking for subjective things, maybe there was a subjective attraction in the idea of taking up a new cause. It's as if you opened a door and here was not some trivial peripheral thing but something tremendously important that affects virtually everyone's daily life all the time. I suppose you could say there was a certain excitement and readiness to tackle our ethical obligations to other animals because it was such a neglected field in philosophy and, for that matter, in just about every other area of scholarship.

I think, and a number of people have said this about my book, that compared to what other people have written about, say particularly animal experimentation, it's detached, it's non-hysterical.

F.M. But it *is* impassioned.

P.S. Yes, it is impassioned but it doesn't start with the assumption that the reader is outraged and concerned by cruelty, or whatever, or even cares a lot about animals. It starts with the assumption that an ordinary decent human being who objects to things like slavery can and should extend his or her moral convictions, carry them further.

F.M. What effect have your ethical explorations had on you? Have you developed a new set of attitudes in thinking of yourself in relation to the rest of life?

P.S. Oh, very much. I am sure I am a totally different person now from what I would have been. On one simple level, shortly after my wife and I became vegetarians, I decided to start growing vegetables. We were living in a rented house outside Oxford and there was a neglected bit of land at the back, so I dug it over and planted vegetables, which is something that I had never done. As a child we lived in a house with a garden, but everything was ornamental. It was almost as if plants that produced food were banished.

Now I discovered that just the idea of digging up the soil and planting things and watching them grow and tending them, and the rhythm of the seasons, really does do something to you. I think it produces a certain rhythm in your life, there is a feeling of natural harmony.

I think, too, it's changed my general perspective so that I see all creatures as beings that have lives of value and whose lives mean something of significance. I guess you could say I have moved some way from being a shallow sort of environmentalist who would have said, "Oh yes, it's important to preserve the environment because otherwise I can't enjoy it, and my children won't be able to enjoy it," to being the sort of person who says, "It's important to preserve it because there are other beings who live there who are of value independently of human beings."

F.M. Have you moved beyond that? Have you moved towards a conception of the unity of life? I ask that question because it has to do with my own history. When I came back from the Second World War, I was so appalled by the behaviour of modern man that I fled to the Arctic to escape him. I hoped to become involved with natural human beings – the Eskimos – but I also became involved with the caribou and the wolves, and discovered that here was a whole world, very complicated and full of rewarding relationships, of which I'd had no previous conception. I was drawn towards trying to enter into the world of those "other" – the non-human creatures. And I began to realize that even if man had become a degenerate and dangerous species it was probably rather irrelevant, because the rest of life was continuing to function regardless of what we were doing. The world of non-human life became for me a sanctuary. Has something like that happened to you?

P.S. I don't think that really has happened to me. You see, when people say, as you did, that all is one, my philosophical instincts come out and I want to start making distinctions. I want to start saying well, sure there is some sense in which I can see that all life is unified and interdependent, and the divisions are vastly less significant than others have thought. And yet there are other senses in which we are not all one, in which there can be conflicts of our interests with theirs, or in which one can draw certain distinctions whereby we can produce an environment that is radically different from what they produce. The distinctions are certainly not all, by any means, to the credit of the human species. I think there are some that are, and there are more, perhaps, that aren't, but I still can see distinctions and, for that matter, I think that rather than saying that all is one, I would see life as a continuum moving outwards from the individual self.

F.M. But don't all the parts make a whole?

P.S. Yes. I think I can certainly see that and feel that, but it doesn't bring me the assurance of security you referred to because it seems to me that there is a real danger that the human part of that whole is getting out of balance with the rest. We do have the capacity to really destroy the whole. And that certainly worries me because the sanctuary you referred to is really not a sanctuary any more. For instance, things which we bring about thousands of miles from the Arctic can destroy the caribou, as happened after Chernobyl.

F.M. I am concerned about the vital importance of restoring the linkage between mankind and the rest of animate creation, and I think you are giving us direction. I see you as a navigator – technically skilled – charting a course which we must follow if life on this planet is going to survive. Is that too grandiose?

P.S. I think perhaps it is. I see my contribution mainly as asserting the status and importance of the non-human, sentient parts of creation, and the moral significance of their well-being, and their suffering and so on. My book is more about how we treat them and their goods and their lives than about the survival of the planet. You couldn't really look through my writings and find much in the way of arguments against some very damaging actions, like damming rivers, clear-felling forests, or whatever. I suppose what people do to rats in laboratories in terms of trivial experiments – such as how fast they can run through mazes and whether giving them electric shocks increases the speed at which they run – whether those experiments continue or are stopped has relatively little to do with saving the planet, but it has a lot to do with how much those rats suffer.

People could say, "All right, I agree we ought to stop giving rats electric shocks in labs," and yet their attitude to nature might not change that dramatically. They might continue to think it's okay to dam the rivers, though they might have some regrets about the animals that are trapped in the flood waters. They might still say, "You have convinced me that the suffering of the rat is wrong, but you haven't convinced me that the destruction of the natural world in itself is wrong."

F.M. But if we inflict pain, or otherwise maltreat any animal, are we not damaging the whole, no matter in what minute degree?

P.S. I think that puts the cause of unity more strongly than I would want to see it. I do want to say that the individual animal is a being whom we should regard as having a welfare or a moral significance that is similar, not necessarily the same but similar, to that of ours.

F.M. So we must be consciously and ethically aware of the individual animal, just as we ought to be of the human individual?

P.S. Oh, absolutely. Certainly.

F.M. If we accept that kind of consciousness, it's going to put considerable restraints upon what we do to, and with, other animals.

P.S. There ought to be very definite constraints on what we do, whether it's in the laboratory, in the factory farm, or in the natural world. We should apply constraints derived from the basic moral principles which govern our relationships with each other. The same moral principles that we accept or hold to in terms of dealing with other human beings are not, in their nature, limited to the human species, but apply beyond the human species.

F.M. If we become more aware of what we are doing to non-human beings, might that not also sharpen our awareness of what we are doing to ourselves, to each other?

P.S. I think that's true.

F.M. One of the criticisms made of your work – particularly the emphasis on vegetarianism – is that what you are saying is not biologically or historically applicable to man. Early man was a meat eater; he killed when he could do so, in order to eat. Doesn't this throw some doubt upon your ethical concept?

P.S. I agree that it's not applicable to early human beings. I see early human beings as on a par with wild predators today. If someone asks me, "Do your principles apply to wolves," I say, "The wolf is not a creature that has options, for a start, and it is not a creature that has our capacity for rational reflection in the light of broader principles." Not that I would deny all rational capacities to wolves, by a long shot, but the particular kind of ethical reflection we are talking about I don't believe wolves go in for.

F.M. Perhaps they don't need it because natural environmental constraints prevent the wolf from getting out of hand. Perhaps we need it because we have escaped the bonds of natural control.

P.S. Yes, I would be happy to put it that way. I think you could say there were evolutionary mechanisms that prevented things getting out of control and we have actually been able to negate many of them. Therefore, we need something else to put in its place. Of course you could argue about whether it's better or worse to do it the way we are doing it, as opposed to doing it the evolutionary way, but it's a fairly pointless discussion since we don't have a lot of choice now.

Early man may have inflicted a lot of unnecessary suffering too. I think that still happens among tribal peoples. I find it a cause for regret.

F.M. By eliminating the seal hunt, by making it unacceptable in our society, we deprive the Inuit of Labrador and Greenland of a market for seal skins, so they can't earn enough money to buy gasoline, and ammunition to shoot more seals. But they are not now living in the aboriginal state; they are living as modern man, therefore they must conform to the restraints that are vital for the survival of all of us. Is that valid?

P.S. I think so, where, as you say, they are wanting to sell the seal skins to buy modern products, but that may not always be the case. Take the remaining Australian aborigines who are still living in a tribal state. People who have gone and lived with them complain that there is appalling cruelty; that they will on occasion hunt an animal and deliberately not kill it, although it's injured, and they will then carry it back and keep it around for a long time in a clearly suffering state. We would say, by white standards, that that's shocking cruelty. Now, are you going to go out there and try to tell them that they should knock it on the head as soon as they can?

F.M. And put it in the refrigerator.

P.S. Well, exactly. If it's a matter of their survival, you could say that's one thing. But maybe they could survive through eating yams and berries, and the kangaroo or emu they have killed is just intended for a celebration feast which they could manage without. Those questions are very difficult, and I don't think I have any answer except to say that when we civilized people have put our own house in order, maybe that's the time to start worrying about what tribal people do. I think we are a long way from that.

F.M. What do you think about people who take your ideas and run with them into outright extremism such as breaking into medical laboratories, freeing the animals, smashing the equipment – that sort of thing?

P.S. I think you have to look at each case individually. In the case you have described, would it have been a medical experiment?

F.M. Call it a cosmetic experiment.

P.S. Right. I think that makes a difference. If animals are being systematically abused, for example, by having various solutions dripped into their eyes while they are immobilized with only their heads protruding from a little box, and then are left there for twenty-four or forty-eight hours until the technician comes back and checks whether the eye is blistered or ulcerated or liquified or whatever, then I would have a lot of sympathy for anyone who would take my ideas and say this is an outrageous thing to be doing, and act on it. I think one could say there were legitimate circumstances in which to break into those laboratories and remove the rabbits.

Having said that, there are forms of extremism that I would deplore. If, instead of releasing the rabbits (or even as well as releasing them), they went and found the technicians and beat them up, I would regard that as quite wrong. I think that the approach has to be non-violent in terms of harm to *any* animals, human or non-human.

I think the animal liberation movement has to be seen as serious and responsible. Though some people may over-react to the ideas, the great majority reacts in a sensible and responsible way and works to bring about change on all sorts of different levels, some extremely conventional, some less so but still well within the bounds of the law.

There has really been remarkably little in the way of mindless fanaticism. It did worry me at one stage several years ago when some letter bombs were sent through the mail by an alleged animal rights militia in England. None of us knew this group or who was in it, and it's been suggested it was not a legitimate group at all but an *agent provocateur* sort of thing. I don't know what the truth was because since it sent those letter bombs it has never surfaced again. But I was worried at the time that the movement was getting into an escalating cycle of violence, and animal experimenters were going to be physically attacked. I don't think any have been, although the homes of some have been daubed with graffiti, and cars damaged and so on.

F.M. What overall influence has your teaching had, do you think?

P.S. Not as much as I would have liked, by a long shot. Things are changing very slowly, very incrementally. They are changing in terms of the treatment of animals in laboratories. Some institutions are setting up procedures to stop the very worst abuses in laboratories, though goodness knows there are still plenty that are going on. In Britain, the confinement of veal calves in those tiny crates that I described in my book is being prohibited. Sweden announced only a year ago that it was going to really get rid of all the major abuses in factory farming – a very enlightened announcement. It will take some years to come to fruition, but they seem quite determined to carry it through.

But is it going to continue incrementally and, if so, how many years is it going to take? Or will it come up against a brick wall in areas like the use of animals in farming? Perhaps we'll get rid of cosmetic experiments, but what about the other experiments which are more medical in their nature? In the wildlife area we have got rid of some of the silliest and most unnecessary slaughters, but will we still permit the enormous, unnecessary carnage of sport hunting to continue?

The movement has had a successful initial period of making some change, and now I think there is a bit of a period of uncertainty about exactly where to go and how far to push.

Animal liberation hasn't reached the point of really becoming a major movement in the political sense. It's achieved some successes through being a radical minority, but how much further is it going to go that way? There has been a considerable focus on direct action, militant activities, but I don't see them as really the vehicle for major change. They will keep the issues on the boil, they will gain media attention, but more mass support is needed. However, we are in a period of economic uncertainty and so I don't necessarily see enormous progress in the next ten years unfortunately. I think it's going to be a longer term thing than that – a hundred years perhaps.

F.M. Do you think we've got that much time?

P.S. I don't know. I think the major threat really is the nuclear issue, and after that there are all the global pollution and climate changes that are being caused by us. My guess is that if we can really avert a major nuclear war, then in the next one hundred years we'll do a lot of other environmental damage but perhaps not bring about a complete ecological catastrophe. Perhaps there will still be something left to preserve. I should have mentioned the human population issue too. Maybe some progress will be made on that particular problem in twenty or thirty years, rather than a hundred.

F.M. What are you going to do now?

P.S. I'm not sure. I have been – and I still am – fairly active with the Australian movement. I am the president of the Victorian branch of animal liberation, which is a national movement here, and we are involved in a number of campaigns. That's a frustrating process. You try and work through government and through committees and it takes an awfully long time, but you do get some things done.

I'll probably do a revised edition of *Animal Liberation*, because even though I wouldn't want to change the underlying ideas very much, I think it would be useful to update it. The impact of reading a book which describes experiments carried out in 1972 is less than if we put in experiments done in 1989.

I have moved a bit towards looking at issues in medical ethics and biological sciences such as genetic engineering, new developments in reproduction, and ethical decisions about when to turn off life support machines and so on.

F.M. How *is* the animal liberation movement?

P.S. Well, it's not really organized. There are a number of different groups in many countries and they operate fairly independently.

F.M. There's no unified structure?

P.S. No. There is a unified structure in more conservative animal welfare groups, such as the World Society for the Protection of Animals. In Australia the animal liberation groups plus many humane societies plus some groups like Greenpeace are loosely linked in the Australian and New Zealand Federation of Animal Societies, of which I am vice-president. So in Australia we have a bit of a federation.

There is, of course, a certain potential for disagreement between animal liberationists and conservationists, but I like to stress the much larger range in which they are in agreement. There are issues in Australia to do with the control of so-called feral animals – like rabbits. There are some conservationists who basically want to restore Australia to what it was before Europeans got here, and any way we can get rid of rabbits is good because rabbits weren't here originally.

Animal liberationists would not take that view. They would say that there are moral constraints even on how you get rid of rabbits. If something like myxomatosis, which is a major method of control here, is a slow killer which causes a lingering, agonizing death, it ought not to be used. I think most animal liberationists would accept that we have somehow to control rabbit numbers, but they would want to see, if possible, non-lethal methods. It always strikes me as amazing that with all our technology we cannot find some way of administering long-acting, long-term contraceptives to animals – rabbits and pigs and donkeys and all the other feral creatures we have in Australia. If indeed there is no such thing yet, it could be developed. Until we develop it, most animal liberationists would accept shooting where there is a demonstrated need to preserve the environment; where rabbits, for instance, are causing prevention of re-growth, leading to wind erosion of soil and total loss of the environment. But conservationists are sometimes so concerned about the preservation of the species, or of the habitat, as not to be sufficiently concerned about the individual animal. I think you have to have both – concern for the habitat, yes, but you can't ever give up your concern for the individual animal because that's really, in the long run, what it's all about.

F.M. If concern for the environment becomes purely a mechanical and technical procedure, then you have lost the moral high ground – you've lost sight of the welfare of individual animals.

P.S. Yes, and you have provided an excuse for all sorts of brutality. Just as Stalin could justify the slave labour camps by what was predicted to happen fifty years down the track. I think the attitude which has to be insisted upon is that when we take the long-term view and concentrate on the importance of preserving the environment, we may find that sometimes individual animals may have to be sacrificed, but always with the greatest possible reluctance, and by the most humane methods.

A Radical Way:

Vicki Miller, ARK II and the Toronto Humane Society

Green-eyed, restless, and exuding a burning sense of mission, Vicki Miller at thirty-six years of age has become a major figure in the animal rights movement in Canada. At the high point of her activist career she led a group which succeeded in taking over control of the staid, grey Toronto Humane Society, which had long been an integral part of not-so-humane Toronto society, and whose good works consisted chiefly of acting as an animal control agency for the metropolis. Miller and her cohorts changed all that, with the result that she has been viciously attacked by an old guard which has even resorted to court action in its attempt to subdue her. For the moment, the old guard has been foiled, but the war goes on.

F.M. I recently asked environmental writer Barry Kent MacKay what he felt is happening to the conservation movement. He's worried that it may be taking a new and disastrous direction. Here's what he said:

"There is something dangerous afoot in the conservation movement. It is the perception that the only way we can save the environment is to tack a monetary value onto its various components. The theory goes that we will then have an incentive to save things. But in the real world it doesn't work that way.

"Suppose you have a forest harbouring fur-bearing animals. Both are given a monetary value. But the value of the trees is the higher, so the forest gets cut down, and the animals go with it. Giving a monetary value doesn't encourage most people to save something – it encourages them to cash in on it.

"There is also a strong attack on preservation and protectionism of the environment building now, on the grounds that as soon as you give a species full protection you have removed the financial incentive to save it. There may be validity in that in some special cases but I think it's a short-term validity.

"There has to be a value that transcends the monetary if we are to have very much left for future generations."

That's what MacKay thinks. How about you?

V.M. I'm in complete agreement. The problem is that we measure everything according to human interests and values. Everything revolves around human society. We can't expand our horizons to see ourselves as part of the whole life community, as opposed to the merely human part. We won't accept that we are part of the web of life; that every living thing has inherent value in its own right. We've had this attitude for millennia; seeing ourselves as central to the universe.

F.M. Surely that's a relatively modern attitude that only appeared with the development of civilization. Primitive man – that is to say, natural man – seems to have been free of it.

V.M. Of course that's true, and there are still some isolated communities of native people who see themselves as an integral part of life on the planet.

F.M. Where do you see the impetus to place an economic valuation on the environment coming from?

V.M. Obviously from the people who benefit therefrom.

F.M. Does that include elements within the conservation movement itself?

V.M. The conservation movement is filled with people who have that attitude. I think they are trying to rationalize the obvious need to conserve, with the expanding human push to exploit every living thing on earth.

F.M. Don't you think that as intelligent and conscious beings we can develop the capacity to "manage" the environment as effectively as nature did?

V.M. No, I don't think we'll ever have that capacity. We'll never have the ability to organize the entire planet. I think we are deluded when we try to do that. I think we are failing miserably. I would say the majority of modern civilized humans is convinced that we *do* have the capacity – maybe not yet fully developed – to organize everything to the advantage of ourselves and of the world in which we live, but our track record is of one failure heaped on top of another.

I use factory farming as an example of our inability to manipulate and control the world around us for mutual good. We wanted cheap food; we wanted an endless supply of it, and a higher profit level, and so the agriculture business combined with the petro-chemical and other industries to create what could not exist in nature. What we have created, using various kinds of intrusive technology, are artificial beings that simply aren't viable forms of life any more. For example, you put six chickens into a cage that's about sixteen by twenty-four inches. All their behavioural needs are frustrated. They can't express their complex social order and, in their frustration, they peck each other; they end up cannibalizing and mutilating each other. Our typically mechanistic solution for that is not to look at the fundamental problem but to try and cure the symptom; so we cut off the chickens' beaks. We use more and more intrusive technology to fix the problems that technology created in the first place. It's not a sustainable system in the sense that natural systems are self-sustaining.

F.M. What brought you into the struggle, Vicki?

V.M. I guess I feel an obligation and responsibility to this earth, so I have to fight for her protection, and I suppose in a way I am fighting for myself at the same time.

F.M. When did you become active in the animal welfare movement?

V.M. In 1983. I had been a member of the Humane Society, then I heard about what seemed to be a more radical organization called Mobilization for Animals. However, when I started to evaluate their philosophy it seemed to me to be a lot of armchair moralizing – this is how it *ought* to be; this is how we *ought* to behave, and what we *ought* to be doing; we're thinking about it. But I wanted to do more than think about it; I wanted to do something to help change it. Early in 1984 a group of us split from Mobilization and formed ARK II, which is a fairly radical group.

F.M. What was ARK II going to do?

V.M. Change the world. It is a grass-roots organization. It has no real, formal structure. We have a board of directors only to satisfy the legal requirements. Aside from that, decision making is informally done by a consensus group which puts in the effort and makes the decisions. We try to avoid a hierarchical structure. Primarily we are involved in direct-action types of things. We do protests. We staged a thirty-day hunger strike over the baboon experiments at the University of Western Ontario. They were imprisoning these animals in horrific little plexiglass restraining chairs for a year and a half. It was pure torture of animals, and we had done everything we could think of to try and change it. The university authorities essentially told us to go to hell; they weren't interested in talking to us. We tried their funding agencies, but nobody was interested. We went to the press, with very little effect. We realized we needed to do something to arouse public attention so we staged a series of demonstrations, including a thirty-day hunger strike. That's the kind of thing we have done. We did fur-burning one year at Toronto City Hall to protest trapping, and enraged the mayor. He was jumping up and down on the second floor waving his fists at us as we burned fur coats down below.

F.M. You might have burned them in the air conditioning.

V.M. There's an idea . . . maybe this fall.

F.M. How did you get involved with the Toronto Humane Society?

V.M. Early in 1984 I went to the annual general meeting of the Humane Society with some other ARK II people who were already involved. Eventually I was elected to the Board. I didn't do too much at first because it was a matter of getting used to the working of a big, old institution. I listened and learned and I really didn't have any aspirations or premeditated plans to take over the Society. I just wanted to influence it.

F.M. I assume there was already a little rebel group in the Society?

V.M. There were three of us – Barry MacKay, Merlin Andrew and myself. I was working with a group that was called radical, but we saw ourselves as progressive. In the case of the restrained baboons, the president of the Ontario Humane Society had defended what was being done to the animals. We found it an outrage that an organization that purported to be an animal protectionist organization would stand up and act as an apologist for those who were exploiting and torturing animals.

I discovered that this was the case with many humane societies. When the press wants to know whether animals are being maltreated, who do they ask? They ask the nearest humane society. And all too often they are reassured that the animals in question – especially lab animals – are getting along just fine. So what kind of advocacy is that? How does parroting the rhetoric of scientific experimenters square with protecting animals? Humane societies collect money to protect animals. They tell people that's what they do.

The Toronto Humane Society was and is a very wealthy organization, and yet what had it been doing? It had been acting mainly as a pest control agency. Its main function had been sweeping up dogs and cats and feeding them into the crematorium chimney.

That seemed to me dishonest, fraudulent and wrong. If you are going to protect animals and collect money to do it, then protect them. As president of the Toronto Humane Society I saw my job as pulling us back towards our mandate to protect animals. It's taking a long time to make real progress in that direction, but I think we are really starting to do it.

F.M. Where does your work with the Humane Society fit into the overall pattern of what we have to do in order to save the world?

V.M. Organizations like the Toronto Humane Society are

tools. I see them as ultimately producing more compassion in people – and out of compassion comes understanding. Without understanding, it is obvious we aren't going to achieve a turnaround in the relationship between human beings and the rest of life. The Toronto Humane Society now not only directly serves the needs of other animals, it is a tool to change human attitudes and so, indirectly, serve *all* animals, including ourselves, in helping to establish a better-balanced world. Every ongoing campaign we initiate is a tool for changing attitudes. We can't take on the whole world, but we can prod individuals and groups in the right direction.

F.M. What have you learned about the institutional side of the environmental movement? What does it do to you?

V.M. What happens when you are drawn into an institution like the Toronto Humane Society is you find it has a life of its own. As you become drawn in deeper and deeper, you find yourself being absorbed in the self-perpetuation of the institution. You see people who came in originally full of hope and commitment and who end up making decisions that are in the best interests of the perpetuation of the organization and not necessarily the best interests of the animals. I have to say the Toronto Humane Society continues to do that. We are still an institution.

F.M. Is that an argument for those who say, "If we are going to change the world, we can't do it through institutional activities; we have to do it in small groups of activists or through independent action"?

V.M. That's an interesting thought, because ARK II had an experience in this connection. We began moving away from the grass roots. We started to grow. Even before I went to the Toronto Humane Society, ARK II was getting bigger; our mailing lists were getting bigger; we acquired an office; we were on our way to becoming a Canadian environmental institution. More and more of our energy was going towards that goal, and the work we were doing for animals lessened in direct proportion to the growing size of the institution.

Eventually the really committed people began to drift away and ARK II started to break down. In order to revive it we had to abandon the office and spread things out among volunteers. Within three months the action level was going up again. We were not sitting in the office trading mailing lists and processing coupons and doing all that stuff. We were doing direct action. So we decided we would abandon the bureaucracy entirely. We are not going to even attempt to become the biggest and best; we are just going to do what we can with the modest funding we have. It takes a huge support system to sustain growth and bigness, and sooner or later the support system will take over and the spirit starts to die.

F.M. You mentioned that Peter Singer had had a considerable effect upon your thinking. Has his point of view become old hat now?

V.M. I think it's still the underpinnings of certain animal rights groups; maybe less so for the animal liberationists, who go further. The animal rights movement has become relatively respectable, but they are concerned only with the suffering of individual sentient beings, and the definition of those beings is arbitrary. Animal rights people tend to identify with those species closest to us. But animal liberationists tend to be part of the broader struggle for bringing the earth out from under the yoke of human oppression.

I think that a major failure of the whole animal rights theory is that it does not deal with the fact that we live on a predatory planet. People may well be eating other animals, but they do so as part of the natural system. They are only exploiting the system in the same way the leopard exploits it or the rabbit or any other species.

F.M. Singer seems quite dogmatic in his refusal to accept that.

V.M. Philosophers tend to be dogmatic. That's unfortunate because I think philosophy must be a fluid process; otherwise it becomes entrenched instead of changing with the need and with an evolving consciousness. People are far more ecologically conscious now than they were five or ten years ago, and the old dogmas about man's relationship to nature are being deeply questioned.

F.M. Why do you think this has come about?

V.M. Sometimes I think it's as simple as the expression "There is nothing more powerful than an idea whose time has come." We are all connected to the earth. The earth is having trouble breathing now, and we can start to sense that, without having to tell each other.

I think there is a collective consciousness too, and we are becoming more aware of it because we are endangered. Our sensitivity has become much more heightened to it. People are *feeling* the problem now instead of just *thinking* about it. It's instinctive.

F.M. It seems to me that a collective biological consciousness must exist. All forms of life are inter-connected in physical ways; it makes no sense to deny a psychic connection. It's got to be there, otherwise the inconceivably intricate living system wouldn't work.

But what do you see in the future of the environmental movement?

V.M. I know what I want to see. Too much energy is being spent on conflict and competition within the environmental movement. Everybody trying to achieve social change seems to be hooked on a particular ideology, a particular vision of how it ought to be. We all spend too much energy defending our own personal perspective of what we think needs doing. We must resolve our own internal bickering. I also think we have to begin to take much, much more responsibility as individuals. Every person has deep responsibility for the health and welfare of this planet and all the creatures on it. Too often we put that health and welfare in the hands of others, some of whom are actively engaged in destroying the planet. I think we have to take back the responsibility individually, although it's so much easier to close your eyes and let somebody else do it, and just assume everything is going to be alright.

Another problem that has to be overcome is our paralyzing respect for man-made law. Law is something that has been invented by humankind solely for *human* purposes. It's a reflection of the institutions in place. It's a reflection of corporate interests. It's a reflection of everything that is oppressing and destroying this planet and all the living creatures on it. People have to begin to be able to distinguish between the laws of man, which are essentially there to protect property, and the laws of life. It's essential that we acknowledge that the earth has her own laws. Those are the laws I respect. The real criminals are the people who break *those* laws. *Those* are the people who should be prosecuted, not the people who are upholding the laws of earth. Human law so often upholds and protects what is wrong, and we too often, and mistakenly, perceive "legal" as being synonymous with "just," and that is not the case. It's not "just" to destroy the planet.

F.M. Are we going to have to act outside human law, or are we going to try and change that law?

V.M. You have to answer to your own conscience. You have to uphold the laws of the earth personally, and if these artificial, man-made laws get in the way, you have an obligation to break them.

F.M. What else should we be considering?

V.M. We can't maintain this mindless consumerism that fuels what we call the first world. There is no question that five billion people certainly can't live in the style to which we are accustomed. If we are going to persevere as a species, we have to come to grips with the vital necessity of reversing the consumerist trend, and yet we do nothing in that direction, and our governments lead us in the opposite direction. We have to completely revolutionize our whole way of organizing the system of thinking about how we build and grow.

But most conservation organizations, environmental organizations and even some animal rights organizations ignore all this.

So there are lots of problems. But I have to believe we can solve them all – if we have enough dedication, and enough guts to really try.

Fighting Man:

Michael O'Sullivan and the World Society for the Protection of Animals

The O'Sullivan brothers are both fighting men. Shawn is an Olympic medallist and professional boxer; but Michael O'Sullivan fights on a different battlefield. As Canadian representative for the World Society for the Protection of Animals, he will, at a moment's notice, go into the ring on behalf of any animal, wild or domestic, that is being brutalized by humankind.

Big, burly, of fearsome visage when aroused (but otherwise of a sunny disposition) this man is the antithesis of the polished professional conservation managers. Forthright to a fault, afflicted (as he says himself) with an enthusiasm that causes him to talk too much, he fearlessly plunges in where angels fear to tread. He takes risks. He calls a spade a spade (one of his favourite phrases). He is an activist's activist – though not a radical. "I work inside the law," he says stoutly. "I take it that when we kill animals with no good reason or make them suffer for *any* reason, we are going against moral and ethical law, and I won't stand for that."

M.O'S. My original interest in animals began while spending a couple of summers working on a farm in Ireland where my dad was born. Following that I worked with some veterinarians and then as a part-time helper with the Toronto Humane Society. Then I went to the University of Guelph and the University of Toronto and graduated with a BSc in Agriculture. It would have been the usual thing to go on into the

Masters programme but I figured I should take courses I wanted to take for knowledge's sake, rather than curriculum's sake. And there were a lot of good programmes dealing with wildlife. These gave me an opportunity to pick up on areas of my education which I thought were lacking. Eventually I went on to manage the Essex County Humane Society in Windsor, and then the Toronto Humane Society operation. Then I went to the World Society for the Protection of Animals.

I really like animals, and I guess the reason I'm so involved in what I do is that I don't like their maltreatment, whether it's at the hands of individuals or industries.

F.M. I'd like to know why you feel that way.

M.O'S. I haven't been to confession in almost sixteen years.

F.M. Well, it will do you good. Were there any personal experiences that inclined you towards taking up the cudgel on behalf of animals?

M.O'S. Yes. When I was about twelve years old I spent my first summer in Ireland on a farm with my uncle who was a hunter and tried to teach me to be one. My father hadn't hunted much at all. One day towards the end of the summer I lifted the rifle to my shoulder, aiming at a young rabbit, and I just looked at it and thought, What do I want to do this for? I don't like doing this. I shouldn't do it simply because my uncle tells me it's the right thing to do. At a very early age I decided I enjoyed working with animals; I had a way with them. That way with animals has improved, albeit leaving a fair number of scars. I guess working in a farm environment surrounded by a lot of wildlife opened up something which was there already and gave it a chance to bear fruit.

F.M. People often ask me how *I* feel about them. I say I too like animals; *all* animals, including the human kind. That sometimes stops them for a moment. Then they say, "But don't you make a basic distinction?" and I say, "No, I don't make a basic distinction. We are *all* animals, and my attitudes towards the human animal should mirror those towards other animals." How do you feel about that?

M.O'S. I think that it makes perfect sense. And non-human animals in the main will always be nice to you; they don't expect much from you and they don't threaten you very much.

F.M. But we're the top dog.

M.O'S. That's because we've got opposing digits and guns and unfortunately a little bit more grey matter, which we tend not to use very well. I've always felt disappointed with our failure to develop a more progressive outlook in dealing with animals or the environment. I felt, and still feel, that basic problems weren't being addressed. That frustrates me because I'm an impatient person. From a pragmatic standpoint I guess I understand that society's got a lot of other priorities that it wants to deal with and, unfortunately, animals and the environment fall well down the list.

I would see my role as trying to bump them up higher on the list for public attention because without public attention and support you are not going to get any kind of meaningful action out of either government or industry. It's just not going to happen.

F.M. Some people think that if we don't learn to be kindly to the rest of animate creation, we ourselves don't have much future.

M.O'S. Without question. There was a case in the United States in the 1800s dealing with cruelty to animals, and the judge said something like: Even if we don't care a great deal about animals we should be kind to them so that we learn to be kinder to each other.

Sometimes people who are interested in animal welfare, the living environment in general, are characterized as bleeding hearts, and the idea is put forward that there will always be pain and suffering. Well, I don't doubt that for a minute, but the pain and suffering that we *deliberately* inflict – in other words, that doesn't happen as a matter of necessity – that's a different matter. And if we condition ourselves to deal with animals that callously, we'll deal with people the same way.

F.M. Tell me about the study the WSPA did of criminality in connection with cruelty to animals.

M.O'S. All of our staff has had extensive experience in

presenting cases of cruelty to animals before the court. Typically, at the end of the case the defence counsel will say, "Sure, my client did this to an animal but he's been embarrassed publicly; his kids are made fun of at school; hasn't he suffered enough; couldn't we have an absolute discharge, your Honour?" In other words, the matter isn't all that serious. And we are hard-pressed to counteract that attitude, except by showing that cruelty to animals usually reflects cruelty towards people, and vice versa.

For example, there was a woman we had to investigate who was keeping virtually every kind of livestock you could imagine crowded into a room filled with excrement and dirt. There were guinea pigs, chickens, rabbits, goats; they had broken limbs, open wounds or sores. She was reported to us and we carried out a seizure. I felt a little sorry for her at first because she claimed none of this was her fault. But then a worker with the Children's Aid Society told me the woman used to keep her own children locked in wire cages in the attic. It turned out she was a sadist through and through. The WSPA has all kinds of incidents like that on record, but unless we can qualify as expert witnesses, they have no legal weight.

So what the WSPA did was sponsor studies in the United States at Danbury Penitentiary and Leavenworth in Kansas. They examined violent and non-violent criminals. What they found was that people who were classed as violent criminals almost always had a history of abuse towards animals. Those studies have now been circulated around the world. We are making them available to the public, to legislators and educators and social workers, to make them aware that if a youngster is substantially abusing an animal, attention should be paid to the problem because that's an indication of a troubled child now and possibly a much more troubled future.

We once charged a juvenile (he was a former policeman's son, which caused us some difficulties) who used a snowmobile to run down a Great Dane after he had blown one of its legs off with a shotgun for no other reason than that the dog was on his property. The prosecutor said we were being too harsh, charging a juvenile. I said, "If you don't worry about that youngster's behaviour – blowing one of the dog's back legs off, then chasing a three-legged dog for over a quarter-mile on a snowmobile – if you don't do something about that, you are probably going to be dealing with that kid a few years down the road from now on a more serious charge."

F.M. Just what *is* the WSPA?

M.O'S. The World Society for the Protection of Animals was born in 1981 as a result of the merger of two other organizations – the World Federation for the Protection of Animals, founded in Zurich in 1950, and the International Society for the Protection of Animals, founded in Boston and London in 1959. The first organization did a lot of scientific examinations and investigations into animal welfare and environmental problems. The International Society was more involved in carrying out direct fieldwork to see that animals got a better deal. They were the two premier international organizations, and over the years they just got closer and closer until finally the merger took place.

WSPA is headquartered in London. We have offices in Rome, New Zealand, Costa Rica, Colombia, Boston, Montreal and Toronto, and in addition we've got more than 360 member societies and thousands of individual members in over sixty countries. We are the only organization of its kind that's affiliated with and has official consultative status with the United Nations, but virtually all of our funding comes from private contributions. We don't accept government funding of any description.

F.M. What are the objectives?

M.O'S. The objectives are to engender a world-wide attitude of decent treatment towards animals, and of leaving the environment in no worse shape than we found it. We have broad policy guidelines on the treatment of domestic animals, wildlife, laboratory animals and pets, and these have to be applied on a situation-by-situation basis. We are a very pragmatic organization. We do a fair amount of work in the developing nations, the theory being that we can assist with expertise and equipment. But basically our role in those countries is to try and apply a certain level of pressure for positive change, and, perhaps even more importantly, to teach our counterparts in the developing nations the kind of skills and knowledge they are going to need to mobilize public support within their own countries. It's not our role to go into anybody else's country and try and *impose* our viewpoints – that just doesn't work. We had a piece of legislation for animal protection, for example, going through the Senate in Colombia, but we had to exclude the prohibition of bull fighting and cock fighting from it, even though in other countries we have been successful in outlawing these atrocities. If we had insisted on those particular sections, the entire bill would have been dropped.

F.M. So WSPA works for animal welfare – but how does that relate to the environmental movement?

M.O'S. We have the same concerns as other environmentalists about maintaining a healthy habitat for both people and animals. We have the same concerns about populations of wild animals, but most conservation organizations normally stop there. We go a bit further. We are perturbed about the damage that human killing may do to the entire animal population, but we are also concerned over the *individual* suffering to an animal caused by humans. Most conservation organizations don't seem to be much worried with that. Then, finally, we look at whether the animal should be killed at *all*. We are not foolish enough to believe that animals aren't killed in nature, but many conservation groups don't seem to be overly distressed about the additive or synergistic effect that killing by people has. Nature has its own way of keeping populations down or adjusting the numbers, but the added effect that people have, not only through such activities as hunting or trapping but through environmental damage – you put all those together and they don't necessarily add up to one time, or two or three times as much damage; they sometimes combine and make ten times as much damage. We don't think that most conservationist organizations look at that.

F.M. I would like to get it into sharper perspective. Let's talk about a single aspect – the problem posed by fur-trapping.

M.O'S. Let me tell you how we differ from most other conservation or environmental organizations. There are about four million wild animals killed every year for the fur trade in Canada, about half of them being essentially wild fur-bearers raised in cages. Canada is the third largest killer of fur-bearing animals in the world yet *we don't have any kind of federal endangered-species legislation to protect any of our wildlife.* The fur trade now, as it has in the past, is imposing terrible reductions on populations of wild animals in Canada. It's right now directly responsible for drastic declines in populations of lynx and wolverine and prairie long-tailed weasels, as it has been for many other species in the past. The only so-called control mechanism that exists in Canada is COSEWIC, the Committee on the Status of Endangered Wildlife in Canada. But it is toothless. It has virtually no regulatory function at all. Its recommendations are routinely ignored. By and large, protection of Canadian wildlife is left to the provinces and territories. The existence of COSEWIC actually misleads the public into thinking that something positive is being done about endangered species in Canada.

F.M. It's misled me then. I assumed that COSEWIC advised the federal and provincial governments as to what was required to protect endangered animals and plants, and that the authorities then took the requisite action.

M.O'S. No. I can say safely that the level of protection for threatened species in Canada falls far below that of some developing countries.

But to get back to the trapping issue, it's our position that you should have a pretty good reason to kill any wild animal. Killing it for a fur coat with which to show off your wealth isn't a very good one in our opinion. Then there's the question of how the killing is done. There is *no such thing as a humane trap*. From 1974 to 1981 the Federal-Provincial Committee on Humane Trapping funded research and development into traps. They generated sixteen traps which, they claimed, showed a potential for delivering a "humane" death – under laboratory conditions. The problem is that their definition of what constitutes a humane death is so all-encompassing that it actually *includes* a leg-hold trap that even their own researchers admit is cruel.

If you can believe it, the Fur Institute of Canada, which is the umbrella organization of the fur trade, has now assumed the role of developing a humane trap! However, we can't find out what they have accomplished. We've sent registered letters to the head of the Fur Institute of Canada, as well as the head of their research team, asking for full disclosure. They didn't respond to us. Now we are fighting for that information under the Access to Information Act, because it's a project which is about two-thirds funded by the federal government. We think the humane trap projects are really a long-term exercise in public relations and that there is very little real concern with reducing animal suffering.

The fur trade is expert at using smoke screens. As another example: the statistics used to assess populations to be killed for their fur are based largely on historical records and not on active field population surveys to see what's really out there. The provincial quotas are arrived at by methods that might satisfy a bookkeeper, but any responsible wildlife biologist should be really worried about what's going on. Lynx is one example. The pelt price for the last three or four years has doubled almost every year because of the increasing rarity of a species on the decline. Each province claims to have set safe quotas on lynx, yet they also admit that pelts are being smuggled from province to province, and Canada's lynx population continues to decline.

The authorities – and the fur industry – argue from a historic standpoint that natives have always hunted furs so it's okay to go on doing it and, besides, the culture of the native people depends on it. The fallacy of that is clear when you look at a 1980 Department of Indian and Northern Affairs study on living conditions of Indians dependent on the fur trade. The report chronicles a litany of social and economic despair for Canada's native people at a time when pelt prices were never better.

F.M. How large was the catch that year?

M.O'S. Better than average. The bottom line is that the various governments of Canada and the fur trade outfits have to take responsibility for over two hundred years of social catastrophe that the fur trade, *introduced and invented* by Europeans, has visited on native culture. Natives have consistently been kept at the extractive end, where they make the least amount of money. There is only token native involvement in the manufacturing and retail phases of the industry. Nor are the natives involved in what constitutes over half of Canada's fur industry, which is cage-rearing of wildlife.

F.M. Yet, for all that, we are constantly told that the fur industry is vital to native survival.

M.O'S. Back in January 1987, we attended a two-day seminar called the Aboriginal Use of Wildlife, co-sponsored by the Canadian Arctic Resources Committee and the Fur Institute of Canada. Very few people from the animal welfare community would go, but we went even though not invited. We were told by the native spokesmen that historically they had a record of conserving rather than destroying wildlife, that it was their chief source of income, and that they could commercially kill wildlife by whatever means for whatever purpose, and it was not our business nor the business of the government of Canada to interfere.

I won't accept that attitude from anyone else, and I won't accept it from leaders of native groups, the reason being – and the analogy I will use will be bullfighting – when you go to Spain, you find a substantial industry built up around bullfighting. Substantial. A lot of people are employed. It is argued that bullfighting is actually quite humane, and that it is an essential part of Spanish culture. I don't buy any of that. I look at the amount of cruelty involved in what, to all intents and purposes, constitutes a money-oriented blood spectacle.

I relate that to the killing of a wild animal for its fur coat for someone to wear to a fashion ball. That's a blood spectacle too, although the blood isn't shed publicly. And the people who buy those fur coats don't do so to help support anybody's culture. I think it's a real trap for us to be dissuaded from doing what is right because of cultural and traditional claims.

We have come to the conclusion that there's an extremely good reason why a lot of native groups have become involved in the campaign to support the fur trade. Virtually every single land claim that's been filed and claimed by them is based on traditional land uses such as hunting, fishing and trapping. But those same land claims, if granted, will allow native control of minerals, gas and property rights. The land settlement reached in Quebec for seventeen thousand native people has to date provided them with over a billion dollars from such resources, and everyone is looking for those kinds of deals. I can't blame them. Native people have been badly served by the government of Canada. They have been badly served by the fur traders, and they are finally saying that they can make something out of past transgressions, and for that I don't blame them. However, from a standpoint of the mandate of our organization, which is to try and secure the most meaningful protection for wildlife, we are not afraid to take a stand against any segment of the fur trade, including native groups.

I won't say to someone, "This is how you have to lead your life." However, I think that I have a duty to say to a consumer who's thinking about buying a fur coat, "You've heard all the arguments on their side; now here's what I have to say. You make up your mind, because at the end of the day it's going to be your consumer dollar that continues the fur trade – or ends it."

F.M. The basic hypocrisy seems to be that until it became advantageous to the fur industry – including the sealing industry – to enlist the cause of native culture on their side, they did not give a damn about the survival of native culture. Now that the fur industry finds itself in jeopardy, both it and the federal and provincial governments, all of which support the fur industry, are making a great to-do about the importance of preserving the cultural heritage of the native peoples. Strange, isn't it?

M.O'S. I'll tell you an interesting story about the seminar I just mentioned. One of the top representatives of the Fur Council of Canada was on the podium and I stood up in the audience to ask questions. There were a couple of hundred people there supporting aboriginal rights to trap, and the atmosphere to conservationists was pretty hostile. I asked, "How do you feel about equal rights and opportunities for native peoples?" He said, "I think what *you* people are doing in that regard is terrible." "Really bad?" I asked. "Yes," he said. "Well then, tell me, how many natives have you got on your board of directors?" He said, "Well, we don't have any." I said, "I see your publications. Do you publish any of them in native languages?" He said, "No, we don't." I said, "But you represent the natives' interests?" "Yes," he replied. "Tell me," I asked, "is it fair to say that natives remain at the basic level of trapping and don't have any real contact with the manufacturing and retail phase, which is where most of the money is made?" He wouldn't answer the question, and the moderator, a representative of the Canadian Arctic Resources Committee said, "This isn't a court of inquiry, Mr. O'Sullivan." I thanked him and repeated my question. Finally the speaker replied, "There are only two companies [with native people involved in manufacturing and retailing] that I know of." And I asked, "Out of how many?" The moderator said, "Next question." But I said, "No, I'm not finished. Out of how many companies in Canada?" He said, "Oh, over four hundred."

The fact of the matter is pretty simple. When it pays us to make an issue of native culture, or whatever, we'll do it. If it isn't profitable to us, then let them whistle.

F.M. How do you feel about wild animals reared in cages for the fur trade?

M.O'S. An estimated one hundred million animals are killed world-wide every year for their fur. Approximately half are raised in cages and half are caught in the wild. The three primary producers of furs in the world are the Soviet Union, the United States and Canada, in that order. Cage-rearing was started in Canada around the turn of the century and we exported the idea to other countries. The primary species raised in captivity now are mink, fox, chinchilla and nutria – though there are plans to start rearing lynx and marten.

The animals are normally kept alive for an average of about six or seven months. They are born into captivity and die in captivity, but they are *not* domestic animals. They are wild animals raised in cages. Very often they are fed on *other* wild animals. In Newfoundland pilot whales were the primary feed for cage-reared mink until they ran out of pilot whales. The Soviets use whale meat for caged white and blue foxes. In Norway they use seal meat to feed mink, and there is a new scheme afoot in Canada's maritime provinces, with federal blessing, to use harp seals for feed. Most people don't realize that it takes one metric tonne of feed and about fifteen foxes to make one fur coat, and about three metric tonnes of feed and forty-five mink to make a coat.

It takes thousands of years to truly domesticate a species, and none of these species has been in captivity as much as a hundred years, so they display aberrational behaviour, including cannibalism, because they are wild animals subjected to grossly unnatural conditions. When you talk to an operator of one of these fur factories, as I call them, he will tell you that the animals are domesticated, and happy, and much better off than if they were out there struggling in the wild for existence. Well, let's call a spade a spade. He didn't stick that animal in a cage because he felt sorry for it not getting three square meals a day in the wild. He put it there because he wants the pelt off its back. So let's be up front about that. Then, if you tell him that Statistics Canada reported thousands of mink and foxes escaped last year, and ask him if these domesticated animals are going to die of starvation out there, he will say, "Oh no, they do fine on their own." Which is our point exactly: they are still wild.

And they don't exactly die happily in captivity. They are killed by three or four primary methods. A fatal injection is one way. The drug usually chosen is not a recommended drug but it's cheap and it's not registered, so anybody can use it. Death by this method is a grim way to go. Another way is to use car exhaust which is supposed to be cooled and filtered but often isn't. Think about how that must feel. The other two methods are electrocution and neck breaking. Electrocution normally applies to foxes and is extremely bizarre. The animal is chased around its cage with a grasper. Then one guy picks it up by the neck and another holds it up by the tail. They put an electrode in its mouth and clamp it in place, then they take another electrode and shove it into the animal's anus and deliver an electric charge which kills it without any risk of damage to the pelt.

In Ontario there are about 258 registered fur factories and there is *one* government inspector for all of them! You can imagine how much inspection they get, and how much protection the animals have. These are a few of the reasons we are trying to put a halt to the fur trade.

F.M. Apart from not making any friends with the furriers, what else is the WSPA up to in Canada?

M.O'S. We've put together a study which for scientific reasons soundly condemns wolf/bear predator control programmes in British Columbia, the Yukon and Alberta.

F.M. Why do you condemn them?

M.O'S. We condemn them because it's illegal, as well as immoral, for anyone – game officer or not – to sit up in a helicopter to shoot wildlife. It's also a violation of civil aviation law for a pilot to fly at such low altitudes. We also question how scientifically valid is the so-called population research, when it sometimes consists of tranquilizing a wolf, putting a radio collar around its neck, then tracking its return to the pack so the gunships can fly in and kill them all. We worry that part of the wolf-control project in B.C. was funded by a raffle by the B.C. Wildlife Federation, where the first prize was a big-game safari in Africa. We are concerned that the studies and the so-called control actions are based more on political expediency and the vested interests of hunters and those who profit from hunting than on scientific data.

F.M. Have you documented this?

M.O'S. As far as possible. But when we asked British

Columbia for the scientific data to back up the wolf kill, we were told that the budget for photocopying had run out! When we offered to pay for the photocopying, we never heard from them again. That reminds me that when we went out to Vancouver to the annual meeting of the Canadian Federation of Humane Societies in the mid-'80s, some of the provincial wildlife biologists came on invitation and gave a presentation on predator control. But when we tried to ask questions, we were told that they had been permitted to speak only on the condition that no one would be allowed to ask them questions afterwards!

I guess the basic reason we condemn the predator control projects is we think that they fail to examine a lot of the other environmental factors and human factors, which can contribute to the decline in game species. "Game species," of course, is a human term which a wolf doesn't take much into consideration while it's trying to survive. We feel there was totally inadequate scientific justification for what was done and *is* being done.

Other projects – well, there is the east coast seal hunt. We are trying to make Canadians and Europeans realize the seal hunt is far from over; that all that has happened is there has been a temporary subsidence and that in fact Canada is actively seeking out new markets in the Orient for seal products, including seal testicles and penises for aphrodisiacs.

We are also working to circumvent the possibility that Canada may withdraw as an observer from the International Whaling Commission because of our government's dissatisfaction with the way the Commission has finally moved to really protect whales instead of, as formerly, justifying the killing of them. Our Department of Fisheries and Oceans' representatives met recently in Iceland with the Icelanders, Japanese and the few other nations still actively whaling to discuss, among other things, an alternative to the IWC. There is some concern that Canada might sponsor such an idea in order to allow a greater killing of marine mammals in the Canadian north.

We are also continuing to apply pressure on the government for better CITES* enforcement in Canada, to live up to our international obligations. The biggest problem with CITES enforcement in Canada is that, as I've said, with few exceptions the control of wildlife falls within the provincial and territorial jurisdictions. So you've got twelve agencies operating independently of each other. Canada has signed this international treaty to protect wildlife, flora and fauna – signed it with other countries in good faith, but the provinces and territories aren't co-operating and so it's not being enforced properly. The bottom line is it's about time we lived up to our national and international obligations.

Another project: the Law Reform Commission of Canada is currently examining all sections of the Criminal Code, including sections dealing with cruelty to animals. Now, our current code doesn't make a distinction, in all of its provisions, between wildlife and domestic animals. In other words, under criminal law they are afforded identical protection, which I think is very progressive. But some commercial industries dealing with animals are pretty upset when they actually see what it says, and they are making submissions to get those provisions of the Criminal Code amended. We are making strong representations to strengthen those provisions.

We are trying to educate people via the studies we have talked about to realize that aside from the morality of having an attitude of humane treatment towards animals, be they domestic or wild, there are good practical benefits to people.

We are making inroads in eliminating rodeo events. None of these represent accepted stock-handling practices today. So that's one of *our* "cultural" traditions we've got to let go of. Rodeo events actually started in the mid-western United States in the late 1800s because cowboys were bored. We've scored some good public relations victories against the Calgary stampede, and we have actually been able, through our close work with member societies, to have some local rodeos cancelled. But rodeo still flourishes. Canada is a key promoter. In some of the European countries, rodeos are now outlawed.

---

*The Convention on International Trade in Endangered Species of Wild Fauna and Flora

We do all we can to stop the "sport" of dog fighting. A lot of handlers want Canadian dogs because they feel that they are raised in a hardier climate and they are better fighting dogs. International dog fighting is a big event, both in this country and in Europe, and there are connections with organized crime.

F.M. Who are your member societies?

M.O'S. The Canadian Federation of Humane Societies for a beginning, then most of the larger individual humane societies. The Ontario Humane Society, the Toronto Humane Society, the British Columbia SPCA, the Alberta SPCA, the Calgary Humane Society are all members of WSPA. We are the international umbrella organization for humane societies. Our publication – *Animals International* – comes out in English, German, French and Spanish. We have a scientific advisory panel to examine animal welfare issues and a legal advisory panel that looks at legal implications because the laws and systems of justice are so varied in different countries. We rely on our member societies around the world when we don't have regional offices, but we try to get a regional office in as many countries as possible. The bottom line is we have a fairly extensive network of affiliates and contacts in over sixty countries.

F.M. How about policy? When you take an active stand against the fur trade, does that mean all of your affiliates will take the same stand?

M.O'S. They're not required to do that, though most of them have done so as a matter of course. Some haven't. If someone says to me, "Why isn't the Canadian Federation of Humane Societies against trapping like you are?" I reply, "If you read their resolution more closely, you will find they *are* against trapping in principle, but they feel that by working for trap research and development, and tighter regulations, they can effectively reduce the cruelty that exists right now."

I keep harping back to the fur trade. They realize they have an industry based on probably the least defensible use of animals. So what they do is not try to answer the charges of cruelty; instead they try to erode the credibility of the people who oppose them. They have tried to suggest that people in my line of work are either so foolish they don't have anything serious to say, so you shouldn't listen to them, or are actually trying to destabilize society with their talk about animal rights. The truth is that these issues have very, very little to do with animals rights. To say "animal rights" implies that animals have some kind of an active say in what goes on in this drama we call life. What it all boils down to has less to do with animal rights and more to do with restricting the assumed *human* right to do as we damn well please to other animals.

F.M. What percentage of your money goes into field work and how much into administration?

M.O'S. Our bench-mark for administration is about ten and a half per cent. Our one-room office in downtown Toronto with light, heat, janitorial service and access to the building twenty-four hours a day costs $500 a month.

F.M. The Canadian operation is just you and one secretary?

M.O'S. That's the paid staff, but we've got volunteers. At the moment, two people are working on the campaign against the fur industry and have given us literally thousands and thousands of dollars of free advice and services. We draw on assistance from our member societies for help with local problems. We also have WSPA international resources and scientific advice to draw on, so that we don't need the kind of enormous budgets and overhead and paid full-time staff that a lot of the other groups seem to require.

F.M. How do you personally manage to keep body and soul together?

M.O'S. Oh, it's not a job where you can make a great deal of money. I am earning less now than when I ran the Toronto Humane Society five years ago. Then I was earning about $37,000 per annum.

F.M. Is that why you are driving a Jaguar?

M.O'S. That's a four-year-old Renault you see out there. I need a shoehorn to get into it every morning, but the work gets done.

To Save the Seals:

Brian Davies and the International Fund for Animal Welfare

Now in his late fifties, with salt-and-pepper hair and a neat little beard, Brian Davies looks like an amiable sage – sunny, gentle and easy-going. The appearance is deceptive. It masks a quiet soldier who, through the past quarter century, has fought tenaciously to save the seals of Canada's eastern seaboard from annihilation at human hands. Brian Davies *began* the battle to save them, and has been their foremost champion ever since. Long before other environmentalists became involved, Davies was out on the ice (where I first observed him in action in 1966) attempting to put an end to one of the most senseless and horrendous slaughters in modern times. Over the years he has been arrested and imprisoned, has been treated as a public enemy by much of the Canadian media, has been publicly vilified by federal and provincial cabinet ministers, has been repudiated by major players in the conservation establishment, and has never faltered. In later years he and his International Fund for Animal Welfare have taken on animal welfare causes all over the world, but the ongoing struggle to save the seals remains Brian Davies' chief concern.

B.D. I was born in 1935 in South Wales to parents living in poverty in a mining village. When I was eleven, I moved to England to live with my mother, and left school when I was fourteen. I had a succession of jobs – nineteen in all – but I could never settle in anything. I got married when I was nineteen, and had a dream about Canada. I saw those magnificent green fields, forests and lakes. I was so impressed with this dream that six months later we were on our way to Canada.

I became a nursing orderly for eight or nine months, then joined the Canadian army. I had been impressed with the Canadian soldiers I'd seen during the war, as a young boy. I liked the life so I stayed in the army for six years at Gagetown in New Brunswick.

F.M. What led to your concern with animal welfare?

B.D. I simply don't know. My family didn't dote on animals, though they liked them and respected them. In my early years I lived in the mountains of Wales where there was a lot of wildlife. I just simply liked animals for no reason I could put a finger on. I spent much of my time in the woods, in the mountains, just enjoying the closeness with nature.

F.M. You became a nurse. Does this tell us anything about your emotional inclinations?

B.D. I enjoyed nursing very much, the whole business of helping sick people, so I suppose it does. And sick animals too. But it was just chance that led to my becoming involved in animal welfare. It was all triggered by one incident. A dog got hit by a car outside my house. If the man in the car had left home five seconds later he wouldn't have hit the dog. If he hadn't hit the dog, I probably would not have become involved in animal welfare. I was in the army and fully expected to stay there for twenty-five years. I was not looking for new opportunities.

F.M. What happened after you picked up the dog?

B.D. It was a little puppy. There was the usual squeal of brakes. Then a passer-by knocked on my door to ask if I owned the puppy. He didn't know what to do with it and neither did I. I phoned the local SPCA (Society for the Prevention of Cruelty to Animals), but they had no staff to deal with the problem. So I took the dog to the Fredericton Animal Hospital. It had to be put down as it was very badly injured. I called the SPCA the next day and said if that type of thing happened again, I would be glad to help.

F.M. Why did you do that?
B.D. I liked animals. It seemed a shame that animals could be injured and just left lying on the street.
F.M. And the SPCA needed help?
B.D. It clearly did. That incident led to a relationship over two or three years where I became, in my off-duty hours, a volunteer SPCA inspector. I was sworn in as a constable and would, in my spare time, go out and investigate cases of cruelty to animals. Sometimes I would take the animal away from the so-called owners. Sometimes we would prosecute people for cruelty. I got involved only as a volunteer. I didn't expect it to go anywhere. But then the people in charge of the New Brunswick SPCA decided they would try to resurrect the organization, which had started in the mid-1800s but had been almost moribund for the last thirty or forty years.

The chief mover was Senator McGrand, an old-time doctor from Fredericton Junction, who believed that teaching people to be kind to animals would incline them to be kind to people.

There's a lot of truth in that. I never met anyone who was genuinely kind to animals who also wasn't genuinely kind to people. Similarly, I never met anyone who was genuinely kind to people who wasn't also kind to animals.

I believed this, and Senator McGrand felt I believed it. So when he decided in 1961 to try and revive the New Brunswick SPCA, he asked me if I would take over its direction. It wasn't exactly a big deal. The SPCA was effectively broke. The senator agreed to guarantee me a salary of $80 a week, but it would be up to me to find operating funds. So, with my wife's encouragement, I gave up the security of an army career – and took the job.

I did a lot of work investigating cases of cruelty throughout the province, with particular emphasis on the use and abuse of woods horses. A man would buy a chain saw and a horse for a couple of hundred dollars, go into the woods and cut pulp, and work the horse to death, mostly because he had no idea of how to look after it.

I learned during that period how to use the media. I built

up a core of contacts in the press who became personal friends and I used them to tell my story about the horses, and other animals. I would have the press waiting when I went in to do something. I became something of a controversial public figure – if a minor one. It was an uncomfortable thing to espouse animal welfare aggressively in a province that was by no means ready for that. Anyway, I plugged away, but I could never break the financial dam and bring in enough funds to really make the SPCA function as it should.

Then, in 1964, the international outcry against the seal hunt began. Cruelty was the major issue then, and the Canadian government didn't know what to do to quiet things down. So they went to the Canadian Federation of Humane Societies and asked for three representatives to go to the next seal hunt, in 1965, and tell them how to regulate it. I was one of the people chosen, only because I lived in the Maritimes, not because I had any expertise on sealing.

We had a meeting in Moncton of the sealing industry and government officials, where regulations were discussed for the 1965 seal hunt. People were there representing the aircraft hunt, the big-ship hunt, and the small-boat and ice hunts. These people admitted that some of their practices were cruel. Around the Magdalen Islands and off the west coast of Newfoundland they were catching adult seals with baited hooks. They used shotguns and small-calibre rifles that wounded several times more seals than they killed. They netted seals and drowned them. They hooked seals, dragged them on board their boats. I listened and said almost nothing, but I prepared a report for the Canadian Federation of Humane Societies, which passed it on to the Canadian government. I submitted a long list of things I thought the government should do to make the hunt less cruel.

At that point I had no thought of crusading to abolish the hunt. I was then only twenty-six and I hadn't even seen the hunt, nor had I grasped the concept of how terribly these animals were being exploited. My level of awareness wasn't very high. But some professors from the University of New Brunswick – in particular Dr. Murray Kinloch – were thinking about the unjustified exploitation of animals and the environment generally. Kinloch had grasped the ethical nettle of whether the seals could be legitimately destroyed for luxury items, and had decided that they shouldn't. He planted the seed in my mind.

I first went to the seal hunt in 1965. The government had made arrangements for us to arrive on the scene on the second day of the hunt, and see it on the third day. But the whitecoat hunt on the ice of the Gulf of St. Lawrence was over in two and a half days that spring, and so we never saw it. The quota of fifty thousand seal pups had been taken in that short a time. However, I did see the hunting of adult seals and was deeply disturbed. The adult seals were in the leads between the ice floes. They were being shot in the water with rifles – mostly .22 calibre – and many seals that were hit were not recovered. I asked about the loss ratio and was told it was something like six out of ten lost. It may even have been five out of six. It was really high. You could walk along the floes, and the leads between were blood red. Because there was fat in it, the blood rose to the surface of the water and froze. There was a bloody red, frothy slush across the tops of all the leads where the animals were being hunted. We found one seal that had been hit with seventeen small-calibre bullets but had still escaped to die later.

Going out on the ice amongst those animals was a profoundly moving experience. I can't say there was a special moment when I looked around and said to myself that I had to stop the seal hunt and that's what I wanted to devote my life to. But I suppose, in a sense, I must have come away from the ice that spring with that in my soul somewhere, even though I hadn't articulated it. I was deeply, deeply moved. I fell completely in love with the ice and the animals. It was unlike anything I had seen before. It, indeed, was unlike anything I would ever see.

After I made my report, the Fredericton branch of the SPCA decided that the New Brunswick SPCA should fight to abolish the seal hunt, and I would be the standard bearer. I made the point that I had not the faintest idea how to stop the seal hunt, nor did I think, if there *was* a way to stop it, that I would have the qualities to do it. How do you stop a hunt that has been going on for three hundred years? The government was supporting an age-old industry with lots of public resources, and here we were with a $7,500 annual budget and one employee, young, not well-schooled. It seemed an impossible dream – but I accepted the charge.

I decided that confronting seal hunters on the ice wasn't the way to do it. That wasn't my nature anyway. But I believed that if I showed enough people what the seal hunt really was like, the overwhelming feeling of revulsion that would result would lead the Canadian government – being a democratic government – to weigh public opinion in the balance and stop the hunt. I naively thought the will of the majority would prevail. You see, there were relatively few people actually involved in the hunt. A handful of men – St. John's and Halifax merchants and the fur people in Norway – made millions. Below them, a few hundred men – buyers, ships' captains – made a few thousand dollars each; below them, a few thousand men who did the actual killing made a few hundred dollars. It's the way it is in that kind of industry. You take ill-educated people from Newfoundland and send them out to beat baby seals to death, and you are not going to pay them much. The money is going to be made by other people. I felt the Canadian government didn't have a particular brief to care about the people making the millions, or even the people making thousands, but probably did for the people who were making hundreds, even though there weren't very many of these – about three thousand all told.

My plan was simple – to get the media out to witness the hunt. I followed that plan consistently from 1966 until I was banned from the hunt in 1977. In ten years, we went from one rented Piper Super Cub which held one passenger, through a range of ever-increasing sophistication, until in 1977 we used six helicopters to deliver fifty-five members of the media from all over the world to the seal hunt off Newfoundland.

F.M. Flying people out to the ice is extraordinarily expensive, and you obviously couldn't raise that kind of money from the Fredericton SPCA. How did you do it?

B.D. In 1966, an article was published under my name in *Weekend Magazine*, called "The Cruel Seal Hunt." In fact, it was written by one of the staff writers. They put my name on it because the writer had two stories in that issue and it was against their policy for a writer to have more than one story under his own byline. He took my report and made a colourful, moving story out of it that generated something over five thousand letters (not postcards or pre-printed coupons) from coast to coast. It was clear that a great many Canadians were offended by the seal hunt, about which most of them had been absolutely unaware.

In 1966, before television supplanted the major magazines as the vehicle by which people got their information, *Weekend Magazine* was the biggest media item in Canada. The letters written to the magazine were sent to me, together with many that came directly to me. And these people wanted to contribute to the cause! The income of the New Brunswick SPCA went from $7,500 a year to $30,000 or $40,000 almost overnight, which in 1966 wasn't bad. I quickly began to understand about fund-raising. Whenever I worked on a media story thereafter, I always tried to get in an editorial appeal for funds to the New Brunswick SPCA. We would retain the names of contributors, and so we built up an in-house list of supporters.

Soon we were seeing stories in major newspapers and magazines all over North America, the United Kingdom, France and Holland, including *Time*, *Look* and *Life*. The seal hunt became an ongoing international story that peaked every March. It was a media event that was particularly attractive to television. The blood on ice, the dark-clothed men swinging clubs. It had all the elements of a continuing allegory of man against nature, of good and evil. The clubbing of the baby seals deeply offended most people. The hunt really had no friends on the international scene, and not many outside the Maritimes, in Canada. But what puzzled me is that it seemed to have friends in the media in Canada. I never really knew why. Some national media people seemed as committed to maintaining the seal hunt as I became to ending it. Perhaps they felt they were defenders of a way of life that could be depicted in rather romantic terms. Perhaps our press was demonstrating the inferiority complex which dominates so much of Canadian culture. Our media was, perhaps, angered by the accusations and condemnation of the seal hunt from other parts of the world. The government quickly realized this and understood that it could feed the Canadian media anything, and the media would uncritically defend the government's stance. There were exceptions, but that was generally what happened. In spite of that, they didn't convince Canadians to support the seal hunt.

F.M. What did the humane society people think about the concerted Canadian media attack on the anti-seal hunt protagonists? Were they beginning to get a little edgy?

B.D. Absolutely. You know the old-line animal welfare organizations as well as I do.

F.M. Most of them are very conservative.

B.D. Exactly. And the New Brunswick SPCA was no exception. There was conflict about the way the society was now going. I would say that the bulk of the membership, and the governing body of the organization, were deeply committed to ending the seal hunt, but there was a small but vocal and powerful group which didn't want to go in that direction. Senator McGrand was a Liberal senator. I believe a great deal of pressure was put on him in Ottawa to get the New Brunswick SPCA out of the "save the seals" business. The result was that in 1969 there was an annual meeting at which it was decided that the New Brunswick SPCA would stop its involvement in the anti-sealing campaign.

Fred Beairsto, a Fredericton businessman, was one of the directors of the New Brunswick SPCA, and had worked in our anti-sealing campaign for years. He and I now discussed the possibility of forming a new organization. Since it was an international campaign we were involved in, we thought,

Why not form an international organization? So in 1969 the New Brunswick SPCA Save the Seals Fund became the International Fund for Animal Welfare.

In creating IFAW, we deliberately decided not to have an open-ended structure. There would be four trustees and they would direct the organization. I was one. Fred Beairsto was another; Jean Kinloch and Margaret Owen were the other two. These were to be permanent directors. They wouldn't be voted in; they would be there for life. I had no intention of submitting the purpose of the organization to the divisive behaviour that goes on at annual meetings of most animal welfare organizations world-wide.

We didn't change that way of operating until the early eighties. We concentrated on exploiting the goodwill of the international media. In a few years we were generating audiences estimated in the order of four hundred million people world-wide at the time of each seal hunt. The rest of the year I would go on media tours all over the United States and Europe and keep the pressure on. We always kept the protest directed at Canada – at Canadian embassies abroad and the Canadian government at home. I still laboured under the delusion that if the Canadian *people* opposed to the hunt significantly outnumbered those who were for it, the government would stop the hunt. I believed that up until about 1977, when the federal authorities slung me in jail. I believed that Canada was a democracy and would behave like one. I was wrong, and consequently I wasted a lot of time.

On the ice, things didn't change between 1970 and 1977. In spite of all of the official claims of significant improvements that the government and sealing industry had made, you couldn't have told one hunt from the other. They were still the same bloody massacres and we were still taking the story to the world in words and pictures.

New regulations were passed to keep us and the media away from the hunt, but the Federal Department of Fisheries wasn't prepared at first to charge people with landing closer than a half nautical mile to a seal, as they could now do. They reasoned that the fallout from actually enforcing unjust regulations to keep the media away from the hunt would have been more politically embarrassing than the pressure they were getting from the sealing industry to enforce the new regulations.

Up to then we had been solely concerned with the seal hunt in the Gulf of St. Lawrence. Then in 1975, we went to the Front hunt, in the open Atlantic. Prior to that it had been thought to be too hazardous an undertaking. But I had learned to fly a helicopter by this time, and so I flew with one cameraman across the pack ice looking for the main seal herd about one hundred miles to the north-east of northern Newfoundland. You can imagine what it's like there in March. It's pretty hostile. But we found the seal hunt – the Norwegian-operated big-ship seal hunt – and got the pictures we needed and came back. We never saw an official of the Canadian Fisheries Department on that expedition. They had not been expecting us.

In 1976 we went to the Front again, this time with the media and a group of airline stewardesses – rather a tacky thing to do, I must admit. It was as close to bad taste as I've ever come but, amazingly, it worked and the international coverage had a stunning impact.

Meanwhile, the federal government, under increasing pressure from the province of Newfoundland as well as the Norwegian sealing industry, had decided to take off the gloves. Maybe they thought the Canadian media, at least, wouldn't be much concerned by an attempt at censorship. And maybe they were right. In any case, when we flew back in from the ice and landed at St. Anthony, Newfoundland, our helicopter was seized and we were charged with the offence of landing closer than half a mile to a seal. Of course, if you have to land half a mile away from every seal, you can't get near the seal hunt at all. You would be closer than a half mile to a seal if you put down almost anywhere on the ice within twenty miles of the hunt. Often stray seals come up onto the ice after you've landed, so when the Fisheries helicopters come around they can always find a seal closer than half a mile from you.

From now on it was clear that a very hard line was going to be taken to keep people away from the hunt. The charges against me wound their way through the courts and I was found guilty, but on appeal the charges were dismissed because Canada still had only a twelve-mile limit, and I had landed a hundred miles offshore in international waters, or on international ice, if you prefer.

In 1977 we again went with the media to northern Newfoundland. Brigitte Bardot was with us that year. Again the helicopter was seized and people were charged. This time I was sentenced to three weeks in jail and fined $50,000 as well. I served two of the three weeks, and got a week off for good behaviour! I wouldn't want to go to jail again for very long, but it was one of the most interesting two weeks of my life. The prisoners were mostly Newfoundland kids who were in for things like getting drunk, fighting with policemen, breaking into liquor stores. But the common denominator was lack of education; because of that, no opportunities to go anywhere in life. The Newfoundland courts were simply Draconian. The day I lost my appeal and was told I had to serve the sentence, a young man was being tried who had a wife and three young children and had been out of work most of his life. It was wintertime and cold. He had shoplifted a pair of gloves for one of his children and got caught. It was his second offence. He had stolen food the time before. So they put him in the penitentiary for five years! That's the kind of justice they were meting out in Newfoundland.

F.M. You have a remarkable ability to follow the scent of injustice. Why weren't you distracted from sealing to reforming the judicial system of Canada?

B.D. It wasn't the judicial system of Canada, it was Newfoundland. It was straight out of the Dickens era. It was vicious and cruel and designed to keep people in subjugation so that those who benefited from subjugating Newfoundlanders could carry on doing so.

F.M. Which brings you back to the seal hunt, because that is why the Newfoundland "aristocracy" made such an effort to keep the seal hunt going. It was an exploitive enterprise that benefited only a few of the many.

B.D. Beyond that, it was good politics in Newfoundland to be on the side of the seal hunt because the average Newfoundlander was filled with the kind of mythology of heroism on the ice that you wrote about in *Wake of the Great Sealers*.

F.M. Long tradition. And a sense of chauvinism, because Newfoundland has always felt hard done by. Now here were you mainland people trying to take away something of theirs, regardless of whether it was worth anything or not. One could understand their attitude. But the stone-wall confrontation in Newfoundland now forced you to change your tactics.

B.D. Yes. There I was with an organization which now had something like three hundred thousand supporters and a great deal of contact with the media in many parts of the world. I had spent eleven years trundling media people out to the seal hunt. Now, part of my sentence in 1977 was that I was forbidden to go to the seal hunt for three years. The regulations being enforced, not only at the Front but now in the Gulf, were going to make sure that *no one* the government didn't want to go to the hunt was going to go.

The only avenue open to us was to go to Europe and finally do the thing we should have done in the beginning – to locate and destroy the market for seal products. We didn't really know what the market was until we did a study in 1978, but it clearly identified Europe as the major market, and Germany as the major user of baby seal products. Had I gone to Europe to try to destroy the market in 1968, would we have stopped the hunt a decade earlier? Who knows?

F.M. It might well have been premature. Awareness of man's ecological responsibilities was only beginning to awaken then.

B.D. Yes. We might have shot our bolt and failed then, because the momentum and timing weren't right.

Anyway, we put a young researcher on finding where the seal product market was. He spent about nine months on the job. Meanwhile I also spent a great deal of time in Europe.

Since I couldn't go to the seal hunt, I used films and stills I already had to generate publicity, and we began trying to wipe out the market for seal skins country by country – England, France, Germany.

That was a strategic error because there weren't enough Brian Davies and lifetimes to do it that way. Finally I was given some good advice by the French Minister of the Environment, M. Crépeau. I was able to reach him through Brigitte Bardot who, by the way, in spite of what the Canadian media said, *did* in fact get out to the ice and *did* handle baby seals, and is an absolutely passionate animal lover who did what she did because she cared, not because she was an aging film star who wanted more media attention.

So in 1982 I went to M. Crépeau's office and told him what we were doing and why. He said we were going about it the wrong way. He said we could not do it country by country because Canada had threatened economic reprisals which individual countries were not prepared to deal with. He said, "We have a market for French wine and many other French products in Canada, and Canada is telling us if we ban the importation of baby seal skins, they will ban the importation of something that's important to France. We won't do it. What you have to do is get the European Economic Community as a whole to ban the importation of baby seal products. Canada can't fight the Community as a whole. There's a huge trade imbalance to Canada's benefit. There is nothing that Canada can do to the Community as a whole that can't be done ten times more destructively to her. Do that and you'll have the support of France."

Meanwhile, Stanley Johnson, a British member of the European Parliament, had got a letter from one of those much-ridiculed little old ladies in tennis shoes, one of the bleeding hearts who cared about the seal hunt. She wrote to him pleading that he do something about the killing of baby seals. Stanley, without giving much thought, said there wasn't much he could do but he could at least put a motion before the European Parliament to ban the import of baby seal skins. He could have said the import of *all* seal products and I think it probably would have flown. Eighty per cent of what was coming into Europe was baby seals, so who was going to fight very hard for the other twenty per cent? In any event he tabled his motion: "The European Community will ban the import of whitecoats and bluebacks [baby harp and hood seals], and products derived therefrom." He just put that motion in to the European Parliament and actually forgot about it.

Then the Canadian press got wind of the motion and started making a fuss about it in Canada, which spread to Europe. Up to that point, it was a no-go motion. No activist, including me, even knew about it. The European Parliament has thousands of such motions every year. Most of them never come out the other end. This would have been one of the no-goes, except that the Canadian media, fuelled by federal hand-outs, became so outraged about it. The fuss directed the attention of people like me to the motion. It directed the attention of the European media and other animal welfare organizations such as Greenpeace. It caught the attention of Stephen Best, who was working for me. I had seen the motion by then but I understood the European Economic Community so poorly that I didn't recognize the potential. I thought it didn't address the issue. Stephen recognized the potential and rapidly convinced me, for which I will always have the deepest gratitude towards him. We might have missed it otherwise.

I went over to Europe immediately and talked with Stanley. Clearly we had to make his motion a major issue, particularly in the United Kingdom since the Conservative members of the European Parliament from the U.K. could be expected to align the support of other Conservatives against it.

So IFAW committed substantial amounts of money to a public-relations campaign in the United Kingdom with full-page advertisements in major newspapers, mass mailings to the British people, and also outside the United Kingdom, to create a wave of public concern which would translate into letters to British members of the European Parliament asking them to support this motion.

It worked. We raised and spent about a million dollars in a very short period of time and members of the European Parliament, who were used to getting two or three letters from their constituencies a week, were getting hundreds a week. Politicians will respond to that. We were able to turn around almost all of the British members of the European Parliament to favouring the vote. They were responding to clearly expressed feelings by their constituencies which diffused whatever support Canada had in the more conservative groups in Parliament. The opposition never did have the support of the socialist members who, just by instinct, are against beating up helpless creatures with clubs, and don't see that the fact somebody makes money at it is a good enough reason for doing it.

The campaign in England turned the Conservatives around. When it came to the vote, only 6 people in the European Parliament voted against it. Over 130 were for it. The seal hunt for whitecoats collapsed instantly and has never really recovered.

Unfortunately, primarily because the British government fought against the resolution, it was passed for only a two-year period. So we had to go back in 1985 and re-do the campaign. At that time, because Denmark stood out bitterly against it on behalf of Greenland, we only got the ban renewed for four years. So we are going back to re-do the campaign again, and we hope this time it will be renewed on an indefinite basis.

The omens look good. The European Parliament has passed a resolution, by a huge majority, recommending a permanent ban. The European Economic Community has recommended to the Council of Ministers that it be permanent. Denmark seems about to drop its opposition, and so does the United Kingdom. It begins to look as if only Norway will oppose it, although Canada will lean heavily on everyone it can to prevent such a ban.*

---

*The ban has been renewed.

F.M. So the market for baby seal pelts in Europe has been virtually eliminated, and it is no longer profitable for the big ships, Canadian and Norwegian, that used to kill vast numbers of young seals to continue sealing. But the seal hunt still continues, even if much diminished. During the spring of 1988 Canadian shore-based and small-vessel sealers killed some seventy thousand, and the federal and Newfoundland governments are actively seeking new markets for seal products, particularly in the Far East. Have you won your fight, or not?

B.D. What we haven't knocked out is the small-vessel hunt off the east coast of Newfoundland and some hunting on the west coast of Newfoundland. This has averaged in the past about forty-two thousand seals a year. No doubt it will average that kind of number in the future unless they are successful in finding other markets. That is a possibility. We will watch that.

In the past I have been as much guilty of using rhetoric and overblown statements about the seal hunt as anyone else. There was a time for that, but the time now has come to stop it. I believe there is absolutely no possibility of getting the Canadian government or the Newfoundland government to tell those local men they can't go out and take seals. Absolutely none. I believe that if you confront those people, in Newfoundland in particular, you will generate within Newfoundland such a groundswell of public support that the government will react to it by subsidizing the seal hunt by those men and be damned to what the protest movement can do to the fishing industry or any other element of Canadian business in response. You will not get them on their knees in order to end that particular hunt. I believe attempts to do so can do more harm than good, but that's just one man's opinion. I respect the right of others who think differently. All of us in the protest movement represent the desire of the seals not to be killed by man. Period. That means *no* seal hunting at all, but I believe that's unobtainable in my lifetime and that it has the potential of doing more harm than good if pursued.

What I want to do with the rest of my life is the most good for the most amount of seals. I think I can do that by building up a tourism industry centred on seal watching in the Gulf to beat back whatever possibility there may be of the big ships ever coming back again. I believe that we can have a seal-tourism industry worth in the order of about $3 million in today's dollars, which is as much as the seal hunt ever brought to Canada. We are half-way there now.

F.M. How and when did you start the tourism concept?

B.D. I thought about it almost from the first day I was out there. It was such a fantastic, moving experience for me I thought it would be the same for other people. As far back as 1973 I convinced a small tour operator to come down and take a look at the seals to see if there was a tourist possibility. He was enthused and soon had tourists going to the Magdalen Islands – about fifty a year for two or three years. But seal watching and seal hunting in the same place are simply incompatible for a number of reasons. The seal watchers were badly harrassed by seal hunters on the Magdalen Islands. Then, too, tourists don't go out seal watching unless they love animals. Flying out across the blood-streaked shores and ice of the Magdalens and watching men dragging carcasses to land and seeing the ships in the ice disgorging hundreds of hunters to kill seals was a total turn-off. So the attempt died away and I didn't do much more about it, although it was always in my mind.

Then, about three years ago, we decided to make a real effort to build up seal watching as an alternative to resumption of the big-vessel hunt.

We wanted to ensure that enough people would make enough money from seal watching so that they would form a counter-balance to the people who would like to kill seals to make money. We wanted to demonstrate that live seals were worth more than dead seals. We were able to do that within two years. In 1988, six hundred people went out to see the seals and almost a million dollars were generated to the local communities, mostly in Prince Edward Island. In 1989 we had nearly nine hundred tourists. We had been asked by the federal government to send some to the Magdalen Islands. It seemed only fair that they got some of the money being generated by seal watching, so we sent four hundred plus out there. I was nervous that they might be harrassed and abused by seal hunters who don't want seal *watching* because it is the final nail in the coffin of any possibility of a resumption of the seal hunt but that didn't happen.

F.M. You have been able to replace lost income by using the seals instead of abusing them. But isn't it possible that the development of a big tourism industry might be detrimental to the seals?

B.D. Logic tells me that people out there taking pictures of seals are less intrusive and harmful to the seals' survival than ships, clubs and guns. Would the seals be better off with nobody looking at them? Probably the seals would prefer that; it's hard to say. But that isn't the way of the world. I believe that people will either kill those animals to exploit them, or they will exploit them by taking out people who love seals. Someone will exploit those animals one way or another. We would rather it was exploitation by people with cameras.

F.M. There's another factor to consider. Pressure from fishing interests which see seals as competitors may persuade the government to institute an annual "cull." This would mean that federal fisheries people with hired gunners would fly out to the herds to slaughter young harps and hoods, and maybe adults too, as they have systematically done with grey seals in Nova Scotia. Very few people would know about this. It could be done with a high degree of concealment. But if there are tourists on the ice watching seals, it cannot be done.

B.D. Yes. Seal watching opens up the herd to scrutiny. It prevents covert destruction by industry or governments.

F.M. Ending the killing of seals has always been at the core of the IFAW activities, but your organization doesn't stop there. What other projects are you involved in, and what do you see the IFAW doing in the future?

B.D. We generally have twenty to twenty-three different projects going on at any one time. Some are scientific research projects. Some are small, such as helping an Ontario organization build nesting boxes for bluebirds. But the seals will always be the issue to which we give whatever is needed in terms of energy and money. We now have two scientists full time and much consultancy work being done to challenge the premise that seals eat too many fish – that if you have fewer seals, you automatically have more fish. According to superficial logic that seems right, but the evidence is quite the reverse. Ninety-nine per cent of all fish die because they are eaten by other fish. That leaves not very much of a percentage the seals can do any harm to. They are operating in a very narrow spectrum in terms of fish eating. We don't know how many grey seals there are – the government says about seventy thousand but we've only ever been able to count something in the order of about thirty thousand. How many harbour seals are there? – very few. If you take the whole area down the coast of Labrador, down the east coast of Newfoundland, Nova Scotia, the Gulf of St. Lawrence, Davis Straits and count all the seals including harps and hoods, a low figure is about one million. A high figure would be about two or three million. That many seals can't possibly have a significant impact on the uncountable billions of fishes in those waters.

F.M. But the Canadian fishing industry replies that even if seals don't destroy vast numbers of fish, they do infect some fish with codworm – which the government now calls sealworm – therefore that is a sufficient justification for destroying them.

B.D. Harp seals are not a significant part of that problem. Not only that, you couldn't kill *all* the harp, harbour or grey seals if you tried. And just killing some is no solution. There is evidence to suggest that in killing part of the host population – seals – you stimulate the reproduction of codworms in what's left. No scientist I know at this time, and we've had meetings with the Canadian government on this, is suggesting that if you have a seal cull it is going to significantly reduce the incidence of codworm. We understand codworm. It's not harmful to human beings, merely unsightly. If the industry wants to take the time and effort, it is possible to design mechanisms for getting virtually all of the codworm out of fish fillets. Codworms are something that can be lived with. It seems to me that the fishing industry in Canada had simply better learn to live with them and not attempt to eradicate them. I have floated that one by the fishing industry, but it doesn't get anywhere.

F.M. Will IFAW extend its interest to other areas where animals appear to be in trouble?

B.D. We try not to over-extend ourselves. One of the weaknesses of the animal welfare movement has been that it attempts to fight all of the battles all of the time, and the end result is that very few of the battles are ever won. I guess the war against human rapacity may never be won, but we like to win some battles. We have won battles for the seals, but have not won the war. There will always be people who want to exploit them to destruction.

So we tend to limit our activity to a relatively small number of campaigns and hope to achieve success. One of these is a campaign in the Philippines. We had seen newspaper reports of dogs brutally ill-treated as part of a trade in pet flesh for the dinner tables of well-to-do Filipinos. Dogs with their front legs tied behind their backs and dislocated in the process; the jaws wired together, with the wire cutting through to the jawbone; the animal unable to pant and almost drowning in the fluids building up in its throat as it overheats in the market places under the brutally hot, humid Asian sun; no food or water for days before they are slaughtered. We went there and investigated the trade, just because I am a dog lover. It seems about seven hundred and fifty thousand animals were caught up in this trade in the Philippines each year. It was even more brutal than we had read. The pictures we were able to get were even more shocking.

I remember going to one of the slaughter houses where these animals were killed and a nice Toyota drove up and a lovely young Filipina lady and her well-dressed young bridegroom-to-be got out and walked into the slaughter house, surrounded by the filth, stench and screaming animals. They wanted roast dog as part of the wedding feast. They looked in the cages and picked a little black and white mongrel. A man from the slaughter house pulled it out and slammed it down on top of the cage. He picked up a light club, tapped the animal on the head, stunning it somewhat but not rendering it unconscious, then took a knife and cut its throat. The animal was struggling and screaming on the top of the wire-mesh crate, with its blood spurting down all over the other animals. It was a long, unpleasant death. Then the animal was butchered right on top of the cage. Bits of bone and offal fell down onto the other animals. The victim was taken to a fire to have the hair burned off and the skin charred because they like to pick the skin off and eat it at the wedding feast, then the butchered parts were given to the young couple and off they went. That sort of thing was repeated hour after hour all day.

We campaigned strongly against this trade, again using the media lavishly. And the Manila media came out hard against it. Finally Metro Manila banned the transport of dogs for eating, which wiped out about eighty per cent of the traffic. Some still goes on. We maintain a full-time employee in the Philippines and have an active lobby at work in the Philippine parliament to improve animal welfare legislation.

F.M. IFAW doesn't seem to work within any set structure in terms of what it does. If something comes along, you or one of your directors get involved and you simply follow where it leads, doing the best you can to alleviate a bad situation, wherever, whenever.

B.D. We are totally committed to protection of seals. Other than that, we are opportunistic. If we see areas where it is possible to achieve something in the moderately near term, we will go in and do the best we can. We have had some success in the Philippines. We have had areas where we have had less success. A similar situation existed in South Korea and we have worked at it for about five years. I would say we have made precious little headway there. It's a long hard grind.

Another project is helping start a national park in Nepal. We funded fifty per cent of the costs of starting up a park that takes in part of Mount Everest and harbours a wide variety of unique animal species. It is expected to eventually include part of China and part of India. As it has grown, our participation in relative terms has become less.

F.M. You seem willing to operate in almost any of the areas of environmental concerns as well as animal rights.

B.D. Yes. You can't separate cruelty to wild animals from the preservation of the habitat. The worst cruelty you can do to an animal is destroy its habitat. Same as with people.

Another area we are involved with is ocean pollution. It seems that pollution of the ocean is the cause of many recent large-scale marine mammal deaths. One has to suppose a clean ocean environment is something that's good for marine mammals *and* people and that you can't afford to take the risk of waiting until we can prove that oceans are seriously polluted before doing something about it. I think it's reasonable to assume that polluted oceans are bad; let's clean them up; it's the right thing to do.

F.M. You don't have a membership in the usual sense?

B.D. We have an in-house list of supporters of six hundred thousand plus. I define a supporter as anyone who has given any money to the organization over the last couple of years.

F.M. How do people become supporters? How do they hear about it?

B.D. The initial list started with the *Weekend Magazine* article. Then we went through a phase of advertising the story of what we were doing, and eliciting a coupon response. That became prohibitively costly as the price of newspaper advertising went up and the response rate didn't go up commensurately. So we went from that to direct mailings. That took us from about three hundred thousand supporters to the six hundred thousand plus. We have reached something of a natural plateau at the moment. That list decays at the rate of about one hundred and twenty thousand plus per year. Regenerating that loss is getting increasingly difficult and increasingly expensive because direct mail costs are going up all the time.

As a matter of principle, I'd like to have a million supporters to ensure that the work continues. None of us lives forever, so I have set up a Brian Davies Foundation which now has $1.3 million in it. I want to build that up to $5 million over the next four or five years. It is to be used as a back-up if anything happens to me – a sum of money available after I'm dead and gone, available to another Brian Davies to go out and fight any resumption of the seal hunt that might take place.

As for me, when I go I want to be cremated. It would be nice to be spread over the ocean somewhere to become a physical part of what I've fought for all these years.

III

Mavericks and Activists

The Nature of Things:

David Suzuki

To a growing number of people David Suzuki *is* Mister Environment. Now in his mid-fifties, Suzuki began his career as a geneticist. However, over the years he became increasingly disillusioned with the way many scientists chose to distance themselves, their professions and discoveries from the ever-escalating destruction being wrought upon the living world. As the destruction mounted, so did Suzuki's concern. In the late 1970s he began to be seen and heard on radio and television and to be read in magazines and newspapers. By the mid-'80s his Oriental visage, framed in a corona of wiry black hair over a wispy beard, had become familiar to every Canadian who cared about what was happening to the natural world. He had also become *persona non grata* to many of his peers in the world of academe and, more importantly, to the denizens of the glossy boardrooms of business and politics who so largely control our world. Many powerful forces would like to see him hushed. But he continues to survive as a voice of passion and reason both, defending a world under siege. He remains at the leading edge of the crusade to save the world.

D.S. As a kid I was always a daydreamer. From as early as I can remember my greatest joy was to go out on a bicycle and dip in the creeks with nets for bluegills, sunfish and catfish. I discovered insects when I was around ten or eleven.

I was always a loner, an outsider. When we were in the

wartime detention camps, I was one of the few Japanese kids whose parents had been born in Canada; most of the other kids' parents were from Japan and they were bilingual. I only spoke English. There was no question Canada was my country. Most of the other kids were rooting for Japan. I used to get beaten up by them and I hated the Japanese part of me. I didn't fit in.

But I was not *alone*. I had a whole world of my own where I could spend hours just sitting in a field and watching a spider catch flies. I knew insects. I had an entrée to their world. So it's not surprising that I went on to study insects when I went to college.

F.M. That parallels my own experience. Birds gave me the entrée into the natural world. I undoubtedly would have become a biologist if it hadn't been for the interruption of the war, which took four years out of my life and changed my attitudes. When I came back from overseas I tried science but could no longer think like a scientist. What I *felt* for the animals around me was so intense that I couldn't see them simply as subject matter to be used to advance a career or to increase the body of scientific knowledge. The "other" animals had been transmuted for me by the war experience. I saw them as co-inhabitors of our planet. But you followed the scientific road.

D.S. I've always thought of myself as a very linear person. As an outsider at school the one thing I could do was excel as a student. My parents always taught me that the one way out of the trap of being a coloured person in Canada was to do well in school. I saw this as my way out. Science seemed to be a natural for me. I was good at math. I could memorize. When I discovered genetics I fell madly in love with it because it was so precise and mathematical. In those days we geneticists had nothing but contempt for ecologists – we thought they just went out to listen to birds. What they did seemed too subjective and non-quantitative.

My eventual questioning of science did not initially come from an interest in animal rights or from ecological awareness; it originated from my deep involvement with civil liberties. When I came out of the camps I was terrified of white people because I thought they all regarded me as the enemy. When I hit puberty I was afraid to ask girls out. Because of my Japanese hang-ups, I got involved with civil rights. I identified with minority groups – blacks especially. I became totally wrapped up with that in college and graduate school. I did a post-doc. in Oakridge, Tennessee, where the atomic bomb was built, and I was the only non-black member of the NAACP in Oakridge. I got so wrapped up with that movement that I became a reverse bigot, thinking every white person with a southern accent was a racist. So much rage would pour out of me that I used to get literally sick when I saw "whites only" signs. That's when I realized I couldn't stay in the United States, not because Canada was any better but it was smaller and I felt I might have a greater effect there.

I started teaching in university, and students started asking me about eugenics, which I'd never heard of. I read up on the subject and found that the eugenics movement had swept North America in the early 1920s, that the Carnegies and Rockefellers were saying whites were superior and the society ought to use the new genetic insights to get rid of all of the inferior types. It turns out that the very rationale leading to my incarceration as a Japanese Canadian was the rationale of the whole eugenics movement, namely, that there are inferior and superior races of people, that a trait for treachery in the Japanese was demonstrated by their behaviour at Pearl Harbour.

In this grotesque way, my interest in civil liberties resulted in my realization that genetics, which had become the great love of my life, had in a way been responsible for my incarceration and what was happening to the blacks. That's when I began to realize that science has incredible ramifications that ripple throughout society. Over the years as I began to reflect on science and its limitations and potential abuses, I realized how value-laden it is. I don't think it's an accident that science achieved its greatest power in Europe. It arose out of the Judeo-Christian tradition that we can and should use this great gift we call a brain to understand, control and manipulate everything around us in the name of progress.

I was struck by an idea of Ted Roszak, who wrote *Where the Wasteland Ends* and *The Making of a Counter-Culture*, that in eastern religions or cultures one of the most important symbols is a circle. In the west, scientific philosophers recognized the cyclic nature of the world, but chose to break the circle. In eastern and most native religions you start at a point, and you cycle back to the same point. What western science did was to introduce direction by creating a sine wave. The minute you introduce direction, rather than seeing life as a cycle, you have the idea you are going somewhere, and that's *progress*. That's the whole thrust of the scientific paradigm – that we use this very powerful way of knowing to *get* somewhere – that's our definition of progress.

F.M. But we haven't the least idea what direction we are going in. Progress is really only movement – change – for its own sake.

D.S. That's right. We westerners believe that if you are going *some*where you must be doing the right thing.

F.M. All of life before man and all life now, except human life, attempts to maintain stability. Changes take place, but they are usually small in scale, and are mostly internal. The essence is a closed system, equilibrium within the circle. Modern man, abetted by science, has abandoned that concept. How did the discovery of this affect you?

D.S. I first began to ask myself questions about the legitimacy of doing experiments with animals. There was a lot of self-interest in this, because I was using invertebrates – mostly fruit flies – in my genetics work. And also I was an avid fisherman. There was a question about the way we rank other life forms – are they on a level playing field with us or intrinsically inferior?

F.M. We invented the hierarchical concept of life.

D.S. We did that because we are rationalizers. We rationalize that the primates are the "highest" forms because they have the most complex neural structures; then underneath that you have the various mammals arrayed – all warm-blooded. And so on "down" the line. It was only when I began to apply for grants because I had discovered mutations in fruit flies that affected nerves – and found myself arguing that we study nerves in fruit flies because nerves in all organisms are essentially the same, and so by studying the nervous system of the fruit fly we learn something about humans – that I realized you can't have it both ways. You can't say we are distinct and different from all other animals when that suits your purpose, and then claim that we are really all of one family when *that* suits another purpose. It put me in a very great dilemma.

F.M. Weren't you also in a dilemma regarding your passion for fishing?

D.S. I do not sport-fish. I am astounded at the people who go out just for the fun of fishing. I am fishing for food, and I no longer go out to catch fish on light tackle so that they will play and jump. It's a very important part of my diet. I still feel that I am an omnivore. But I take no joy in torturing another animal either for sustenance or pleasure.

F.M. Isn't that a neat rationalization in itself?

D.S. It's a very difficult thing. I remember talking to John Livingston about this. I asked how he rationalized being a meat eater with his attitude about animals and animal rights. He said, "I'm not totally consistent. I'm not a perfect animal and I understand that there are going to be these paradoxes." He lives with that.

F.M. Why do you think you have become so dedicated to the defence of the non-human world?

D.S. I don't see any one epiphany, but I could cite a major event in my life in the late 1940s when we lived in Leamington after the war. My dad took me to the Detroit Zoo. That was regarded then as one of the great North American zoos. That was an epiphany for me; I was mind-boggled at the variety and abundance of life on the planet. But my sense of injustice at what human beings were *doing* to the living world didn't suddenly happen. It was a gradual understanding that science is fundamentally flawed because scientists focus on parts of nature and study these in isolation from the rest. For a long time people actually believed if you studied a chimpanzee in a zoo you knew everything there was to know about a chimpanzee. When Jane Goodall went and lived with wild chimps, that was a revolutionary approach. But even she was stuck with the paradox that by imposing herself on those animals while observing them, she affected them, they were no longer totally wild animals. It's the whole Heisenberg Uncertainty Principle – you can't observe nature without changing it, so you can never know nature as it really is. That's a fundamental flaw I came to appreciate.

F.M. Perhaps we can only know nature by becoming a part of it, which is what our ancient ancestors did, and what the survivors of the hunter-gatherer tribes still try to do.

D.S. But science doesn't recognize that kind of knowledge. I have come to appreciate the limitations of the scientific method and the arrogance that comes with it. It's an arrogance that comes from the intellectual insights we gain, which seem to give us such power but are actually restrictive. Extrapolating from little bits of knowledge to a whole ecosystem or to the whole planet seems to me to be fundamentally wrong.

The great insight that physicists claimed in this century was that you can learn all about nature at very simple levels. A physicist can describe oxygen and hydrogen in their most intimate details. He knows with absolute certainty that if he takes two atoms of hydrogen and combines them with one atom of oxygen he will get a molecule of water. But if he is asked, "On the basis of what you know about those individual parts, what will be the *property* of water?" he won't know. The reason is that those components interact synergistically. Which is just saying that the whole is greater than the sum of its parts. The biologist who takes predator and prey data out of an ecosystem and puts them in a computer, then looks at energy flow through the system and thinks he has now recreated a model of the ecosystem, doesn't know what he is talking about. When I hear foresters tell me they know enough to be able to clear-cut an old-growth watershed and then replace it with the likes of what they cut down, I think that is the absolute height of arrogance and stupidity. They know so little about the enormously complex interacting components in an ecosystem that they can't possibly reproduce it. It's the arrogance of modern man to think that we, viewing the world through our tiny windows of science, can control, dominate and direct the natural world.

I can remember vividly when I first started with "The Nature of Things" in 1974, arguing with producer Jim Murray that we *humans* give value to everything outside humanity. That was my very chauvinistic, human approach. I thought that because *we* valued whooping cranes it was our job to save them from extinction and that our struggle to save them somehow made human beings nobler beings. It took years of association with Jim and with John Livingston to force me to realize that we are just one species out of thirty million, and how dare we think that *we* give value to the rest of the ecosystem.

What sticks in my memory is John Livingston's assessment in our television series, "A Planet for the Taking," of the James Bay project and the vast area which was going to be flooded. "It's totally undeveloped in our view until we put a dam in, and yet to the millions of plants and animals that have lived there for millennia, it is fully developed and occupied." That could even be an epiphany. That simple phrase changed my perspective.

F.M. Of all the people I know in the environmental movement, you have probably come the farthest because you came out of the inner fastness of science and have had to make a huge leap to re-establish a subjective awareness and understanding of the living world.

D.S. I have essentially walked away from my scientific colleagues. That's been painful. But I had to do it. One of the most important experiences I had was about eight years ago when Jim Fulton, NDP MP from Skeena, called and said I had to do something about saving the Queen Charlottes, and Lyell Island in particular, from the logging industry. I didn't know anything about it, but I talked to Jim and we decided to do a piece on it for "The Nature of Things." I flew in, we filmed, and I interviewed a young Haida Indian. I said, "If they cut these trees down it's not going to kill you; you still have your jobs, your carving, welfare. What difference does it make to you if they cut these trees down?" He shrugged and said, "Well, I guess then we'll just be like everybody else and we won't be Haida any more."

That's the first time I comprehended a radically different relationship with nature. To the Haida, if you destroy the trees you destroy what makes the Haida unique. It's not only their culture and their history, it's their very identity. Last summer at the Stein Valley, Ruby Dunstan, the chief of the Lytton Indian Band, said, "If those people (the logging companies) put a road into the Stein Valley and cut those trees, they might as well line my people up and shoot them because they will have destroyed my people." That's what natives have shown me, that within our own country there is a radically different perspective on our relationship with the land, and that of course includes sky and water. Land is not a commodity; it is not property that you buy and sell, that you profit from; land unviolated is what makes it worthwhile being a human being on that particular piece of turf, and that's been a very profound lesson to me.

When I think of my grandparents who came here from Japan, I know they didn't care about this country or the land; they came as strangers who only wanted to make their fortune and go home. I think most recent immigrants in the past five hundred years have regarded the land in that way.

F.M. I think you can say practically everybody who has come to this country "from away," as the Newfoundlanders would put it, since the European history of the continent began, had the same attitude, and that attitude hasn't really changed. It has been smoothed over and given a new tone. The basic belief that this is not where we belong, psychically we belong somewhere else, and so we can do what we want here and get away with it, still remains unchallenged. Wreck it and leave it! What odds?

D.S. That's right. I split my time between Vancouver and

Toronto, where people are paying hundreds of thousands of dollars for a little piece of property. They don't care about it as a home, as a singular *place*; it's an investment, or an indication of their wealth or status. A friend of mine in Toronto owns four houses. Why? Not because he prizes those pieces of land or feels he belongs there, but because he can sell them and make a quick return on his investment. That attitude is totally contemptible. It seems to me the spiritual values associated with land are far more important than dollars and cents. Recently I got a letter from a real-estate agent in Vancouver who said, "Offshore money is pouring into Vancouver; property values are escalating; you ought to put your house on the market; you will make a lot of money which you can use to buy up more land somewhere else."

Jim Murray, my best friend, helped me fence that house, and he carved a handle for the gate. Every time I open the gate I think of Jim. We have an English garden because my in-laws live upstairs, and they are English. My father-in-law has built a beautiful flower garden and planted asparagus and raspberries because he knows I love them. When I harvest those fruits and vegetables and when I look at the flower garden, there's my father-in-law. In the kitchen my dad, who is a cabinet-maker, built our cabinets and everytime I use them, there's my dad. My wife is in every part of our house. In the backyard I built a tree-house for my kids in the dogwood tree. When they play in it, I remember the many happy hours I spent building that tree-house. They have an animal cemetery under the tree, where they have several snakes, a hamster, a chipmunk. Along the back fence is a clematis plant. When my mother died four years ago, we put her ashes on that plant, and when my sister's daughter died last year, we put her ashes there too. When that clematis plant blooms I know my mother and my niece are there. Those things make my piece of property priceless to me, but are absolutely worthless on the market. In the fifteen years I have lived there, that land has nurtured a history that makes it beyond price to me. So just think of what native people, who have lived on their land for thousands of years, must feel.

I wrote a piece about this for my *Globe and Mail* column and was astounded at the response. I got more letters and phone calls and personal comments over it than from any other article I have written. It touched something in people; they know there is something wrong with the way we are doing things. Maybe we are at the point where people are ready to make a shift in values.

F.M. Let's consider the problem of man's self-alienation from the rest of animate creation. How are we ever going to heal *that* rift? And heal it we must if either "they" or "we" are going to survive on this planet.

D.S. It's a paradox, but perhaps science is going to help undo some of the damage it's done. The Haida talk about their orca whale brothers and their raven sisters. I always used to think this was just a poetic way of talking, but then I began looking at new developments in my own area of genetics.

Geneticists are now finding that all life forms evolved from the same original cell, some three and a half billion years ago. Cells are made of the same six basic atoms; the macro molecules are all the same, and if you compare the genetic material of different organisms, you can measure the number of genes we share. The genetic difference between us and chimpanzees and gorillas is less than one per cent. Ninety-nine per cent of the genes in humans and gorillas are identical. What molecular biology is now telling us is that native people are describing what is literally, physically true. We are all brothers and sisters. I find that very exciting and encouraging.

F.M. But how do we go about restoring unity to the living family? How do we bring modern man back into the fold?

D.S. I don't know. When I look at what humans do to each *other* on the basis of the most superficial differences, like whether your skin is black, white or yellow, I wonder if we can ever learn to treat other animals as members of one family of which we are part. And yet when we can take the heart of a baboon and transplant it into a human baby, surely that's telling us that these animals are closely related to us. So how can we continue to treat them the way we do? Once you begin to realize that these animals are not much different from us and that there is a moral question about the way we treat them, that is the beginning of dissolving the line between "them" and "us." We have to make that leap.

I think we are going to confront it over AIDS. The scientific community is pushing like mad now to import more chimpanzees for research into AIDS. Chimpanzees numbered in the millions not long ago. Today there are only about forty thousand left and they are going fast. Now we want to catch and import many of these remaining few because they are so closely related to us they are ideal subjects for AIDS research. I say that we had better start confronting some hard realities here. What essential difference is there between a chimpanzee and a human being? If we are so concerned about AIDS, why don't we do the research on ourselves? We are the ones who stand to benefit if AIDS is beaten.

F.M. What can we do to bring us back to some semblance of sanity in our relationship with the rest of life?

D.S. I don't know of a strategy for how to do that. I think we are saddled with incredible blinders, which are historic. Ninety-nine point nine per cent of human existence has been spent as small numbers of hunter-gatherers or very primitive agriculturalists. Nature during that period was always vast and endlessly self-renewing. Then our numbers exploded. In 1830 we reached a billion people; in 150 years we have doubled twice to reach four billion; we are going to double again to reach eight billion in another 30 or 40 years. The explosive growth in numbers, combined with the acquisition of technology, has given us a power far beyond anything any organism has ever had in the history of life on earth. But we continue to use a mind that says, "We've got to cut those trees down; we've got to kill those animals; we've got to do all this for our own safety." We are attacking the environment as if we were still puny, but we've got all this incredible technological muscle power. Now, instead of bouncing back, natural structures are falling down under our attacks. Our mind-set just hasn't realized the overwhelming power of our species in terms of numbers and technological prowess.

F.M. We are still behaving as our early ancestors did, but we now exercise the powers of Jove.

D.S. Exactly. I was struck by this in the Queen Charlotte Islands. The Haida told me that two centuries ago it used to take them over a year to cut down one of their huge cedar trees. They only had stone implements. After they made contact with Europeans, two men with saws and axes could do it in about ten days. Today, one man and a chain saw can do it in minutes. I think it is almost built into us to believe that the natural world is limitless. We think: there're lots more where that came from. And we don't or won't realize that we are *part* of what we are destroying.

Jack Vallentyne at the Centre for Inland Waters in Burlington goes around with a globe on his back and calls himself Johnny Biosphere. He talks to young children. He says, "We've all been in this room for an hour. Do you know that in every one of you are atoms and molecules from me? That we've all exchanged these? Not only that, but you have atoms in your body that came from all the people on the planet. Not only that but from people who lived thousands of years ago. You may have atoms from Jesus Christ. And you are made up of atoms from trees and worms and birds and fish. Why? Because we all share land, air and water."

We share everything. In Tokyo children think that chicken is just this stuff you buy in a cellophane-wrapped package. They have no idea that they are eating the muscles of a bird, a once-living animal. *But nothing we eat wasn't once a living plant or animal.* Everything, because it is finite, must recycle, and so we are deeply imbedded in nature. That perception, if children can understand it, has got to change the way we act. There was an Indian chief called Seattle who said, "If you spit on the earth you spit on yourself." We don't live in a vacuum. We aren't above nature; we are still deeply embedded in it. Whatever we do is ultimately going to come back on us.

Usually there is a time lag – but that won't help us escape the inevitable consequences of what we do. It's incontrovertible that the greenhouse effect is real and whatever we may do now, the effect is still going to increase for the next twenty or thirty years. We have no idea what the long-term consequences are.

One pound of dioxin in the Great Lakes will sterilize it. There are now more than 1200 pounds of dioxin buried around the lakes and leaching into them. The whole planet is a ticking bomb waiting to go off. It's going to go off.

F.M. Why do you continue to fight if you are so sure our number is up?

D.S. Because I have young children. And I have two older children who are married and who may have their own children.

F.M. So the primal, biological drive impels you. Paul Watson, who leads the Sea Shepherd Society, has similar ideas about the future, yet continues to sink whaling ships. Is what he does, what everyone in the environmental crusade does, worth the effort?

D.S. I don't know. My emotional response is with Paul all the way. He has put his life on the line, yet he has never deliberately set out to endanger another life, human or otherwise. He's out there on the line right now fighting for whatever bits of nature he can sustain, not for any intellectual reason, but because he must.

F.M. Function is probably sufficient unto itself. And the prime biological function is to fight for survival, not just of the individual but of life itself. I don't think you or I or anybody else needs to analyze our chances of success in the struggle to preserve life in order to justify being on the side of the angels.

D.S. Right. What matters is what we *do*. It's the action that defines us. Whether we make it or not is really not that important. Those who say there is no point in trying to stop "progress" and just want to make their money and have a good time at the expense of the future of the planet are effectively non-functional.

I think I define what I am and who I am and what my values are by my actions. My father taught me when I was very young: you are what you do, not what you say. One of the problems with our species is that because we can write and speak, we get hung up in what people *say*. Watch what people *do*, don't listen to what they *say*, just watch what they do.

As to the question of what we can do individually – everybody has to decide on what level they are ready to do something. We are all at different places in terms of our sensitivity. For some people it may be supporting Paul Watson, for others it may be a radical activist group spiking trees, for others it may be stopping herbicide spraying of the local schoolground. The important thing is to act, because sitting back and saying there is nothing one can do is giving tacit approval of the way things are going. No matter how seemingly unimportant, individual actions are everything. You don't have to be pure or at the leading edge; you just have to act at a level you can live with.

F.M. What about group action? We are a group animal, a social animal, and we should function best in groups. What do you think of the multitude of conservation and environmental groups that now abound? Are they too diverse and diffuse? Is membership in them just providing some individuals with an excuse to shirk their personal responsibilities to nature?

D.S. The problem, I feel, is not that there are too many organizations, but we can delude ourselves if we think that by concentrating on a given issue we are somehow going to magically solve the environmental crisis. I can remember when we were very involved in Ban the Bomb in the sixties, and we really felt if we could make a breakthrough, then people would really come to grips with the dangers of technology. Now we have switched over and think if we could get a handle on acid rain, or PCBs, or the greenhouse effect, we are somehow going to come to a new level of awareness.

It seems to me we are stamping out brush fires. We *have* to deal with the PCBs, or the dioxins in the Great Lakes and from the pulp mills in British Columbia, but we delude ourselves if we think that in solving these problems, if we ever do, we will have come closer to a long-term solution. We expend a huge amount of energy and money on these specific issues and they exhaust us. But the cause of the conflagration is still pumping away. And the cause is our abiding belief that Earth really is a planet for the taking; that progress is to be measured by how fast our economies grow and how much profit we make.

That's the main problem we have to deal with. I think we need to look at root causes of the dilemma we are in now. We at "The Nature of Things" tried to do that in "A Planet for the Taking," which asks how we translate the insight or recognition of root causes into radical action which will change or deflect us from the path we are on.

I don't think there is really any organization doing that. We need a foundation that can engage that problem without diverting people from the issues of spraying in playgrounds or acid rain. There has to be one solid group that is looking at the environmental disaster in a much more global perspective.

With some others, I am now looking to native culture for inspiration. I am completely enamoured of the fact that in spite of all of the atrocities we've inflicted on native people, in many places they still retain a radically different sense of connection with the living world. That perspective is one of their greatest possessions. In spite of everything we have done to them they may, ultimately, give us the most precious gift you could imagine, which is a viable alternative world view. Native people are at the centre of everything that matters to me in terms of the environment. In British Columbia, for example, the major environmental battles all have to do with natives. They are saying, "Listen, you've destroyed or defiled most of the world. You aren't going to do that to the few remaining patches of healthy land still in our hands." Environmentalists who really care have got to throw their weight fully behind native land claims because their battle is ours in the end. Non-natives are very suspicious of natives; they believe that all the natives want is to get hold of that land so they can rape it themselves. Some bands may; 150 years of colonization has given them a lot of our bad habits. But the astounding thing is that there are still pockets of people who have kept that original sense of oneness with nature in spite of what we have done. That's what we have to treasure. They can't do any worse than we have done and, chances are, they'll do a lot better.

F.M. You are already an institution in your own right. How do you assess what you have accomplished?

D.S. When I started broadcasting in 1962, I had the conceit to believe that my work was going to be so fantastic that millions of people would say I was right and we would see the population lifted to a higher plane, which would result in the government changing its attitudes. I thought my programmes would be like diamonds glistening in a cesspool. What I found was that because most people tune in and out of television, at the end of five hours of watching, their brains are mush. They are just as apt to associate me with something they've seen or heard on the "Mary Tyler Moore Show." However, there are a few people who turn on the set because they know "The Nature of Things" is coming on, and they get something out of it and talk about it and are moved by it. They are a tiny minority. What television has done has astounded me – I never set out to seek this – it has made me a star. I can walk anywhere in Canada and there will be people who recognize me. But that has done nothing to raise awareness of what I am trying to *say*; it just means they recognize me in the way they recognize Peter Gzowski or Knowlton Nash.

F.M. Recognition means you are listened to. If you are listened to you get more recognition, and so it goes. But "listened to" doesn't necessarily mean being heard.

D.S. That's true. I began in television because I thought I could empower the lay public by educating them to do something. Instead, what they have done by watching my programmes and supporting them is to empower *me*. When I say something to a minister of the environment he doesn't listen to one person; he knows there are a million and a half people who watch my show. He can't just treat me lightly. It's exactly the opposite of what I wanted. I find it very difficult to handle that power, because I tend to speak out spontaneously and it gets me into a lot of trouble. It's very dangerous to have that kind of power and be an emotional person.

F.M. Why are you so leery of emotions?

D.S. It's not so much the emotions as the consequences of the emotions. Although I doubted my intellectual ability in the strictly rational requirements that academia has, deviating from that kind of behaviour is something that has always been a scary thing for me because it's the unknown.

F.M. Perhaps you feel uneasy with the subconscious man within you, the functional, feeling, subjective animal who is admired by native people. You too admire the concept, but you are afraid of where it might lead you personally.

D.S. There are very few discussions I have ever had where something has been raised that I've never even thought of before, and that's exactly what you have done now.

F.M. It suggests that you are still a captive and a victim of the intellectual concept of man, which is a concept that doesn't really exist in nature. We invented it.

D.S. Of course we invented it, but it has been made real by the whole process of academia. I have had it pounded into me. It makes it hard to recognize or accept one's true affinity with other animals. It's very deeply imbedded.

John Livingston says if you watch a child at play with a pet dog or cat, unaware that you are watching, you will see a profound demonstration of a genetic need to connect with another species. Not only are we social animals that need to be with others of our own type, but we need empathetic association with other species. If you take a dog or cat into a nursing home or hospital, people respond and get better faster. We have lost the connection, and we desperately need it. That's a very profound idea. If you look at a very young infant and show it a butterfly or flower or spider or snake or slug for the first time, you will not see revulsion or fear, you will always see instant fascination. I think that's genetic. It's a built-in interest in others . . .

F.M. . . . which fosters a sense of belonging.

D.S. It's almost as if infants have no sense of separation between man and other animals. But nowadays eighty per cent of Canadians live in cities, and most of the rest live on farms that are groomed in the urban image. If you take a six- or seven-year-old city child – I have seen this with friends of my children – and dip into an aquarium and pull out a salamander and offer it to him, you will see the child recoil in fear or disgust. I find it difficult to reconcile that reaction with the reaction of an infant. What's happened in the interim?

F.M. Conditioning has overmastered instinct.

D.S. Yes. They have been *taught* that nature is dirty, disgusting or dangerous; that nature is an enemy. If mummy or daddy find a cockroach in the kitchen sink, or a mosquito or ant or housefly or mouse in the house, or slugs in the garden, they march out with an arsenal of chemical weapons and do war with nature. The message is very clear – mummy and daddy hate nature. I think once you teach children that, then as adults they feel they should pound nature into submission and make it over the way they want it. By so doing you are getting rid of the horror or fear that was injected into you as a child. That's progress; that's what our society is all about.

F.M. Do you think we can turn that around?

D.S. I don't know. I think children respond very well. I am now telling teachers that we have to stop this insane idea that we have to concentrate on recruiting children for the market place by putting computers into elementary school and so conditioning children to be little robots. We have to put our *best* efforts into kindergarten and the first three or four years of primary school to reconnect those children to nature – not to our machines. At that stage, it's possible. When they get to high school it's too late. Give the children good hand-held magnifying glasses; give them stethoscopes; let them dig up the school ground; don't spray it and put in grass; let them grow weeds or flowers or vegetables; let them root around in nature and exercise their inherent curiosity about all forms of life. We have to reconnect our children, and when we do they will never forget it. We are losing our place in nature. And that means we no longer belong anywhere. We're losing our home, and we have to relocate our home, the place where we will feel comfortable.

Just today a teenager asked me what I feel about rockets to take us to another place in outer space? I said that that is the ultimate technological evasion. We have so polluted our home where we have lived for three and a half billion years that we may have to abandon it, and then we expect that we are going to find some place out there which will be the paradise we have destroyed. It won't work. This is our *only* home. "Progress" – high tech – may take us out there, but we'll be aliens for ever. This earth is where we belong. Lose it and we are lost.

Grass-Roots Crusader:

Elizabeth May and the Budworm Battle

Elizabeth May appears ageless – a sort of female Peter Pan. She has an air of beguiling innocence, talks a blue streak, and is as bouncy as the proverbial cat on a hot tin roof. Her manner is not an affectation – it is real enough – but it masks inner qualities comparable to those popularly attributed to such woman as Boadicea and Joan of Arc. Appearances to the contrary, Elizabeth May is a fighter – and one to reckon with, as a number of major international industries and Canadian governments have come to realize.

E.M. I'm thirty-five now and I was born in Hartford, Connecticut on a seven-acre hobby farm – we always had animals – ponies, sheep, dogs, cats. I was born with an environmental consciousness and I don't know why. I was much more interested in the natural environment – my mother says – when I was little, than in anything man-made. When I was about three I told her I didn't like airplanes because they scratched the sky. I can remember feeling very attached to teeny weeny little flowers that only I could see because I was close to the ground.

My mother had been working against nuclear weapons testing ever since I was small. When I got a toy phone, I mimicked my mum and I would be playing with it, calling ministers, priests and rabbis to get them to sign a " 'tition," because that's what she did all day long. When the test ban treaty happened, as far as I was concerned my mommy did that. When the U.S.S.R. was going to explode a one-hundred-megaton bomb in the atmosphere, my mother went on a six-day hunger strike on the sidewalks of New York in front of the Soviet Embassy. What I learned at my mother's knee was that one person can have tremendous influence. As she got more involved in the peace movement and against the Vietnam War, I also learned about grass-roots organizing. She organized; she'd go into a town where there wasn't a committee and call a meeting. By the time she was through, there was a committee.

F.M. Why did your family leave the U.S.A.?

E.M. My dad was, at that point, a vice-president of a big insurance company. We had been living in a very beautiful part of Connecticut. We had woods and nice places for our animals, so it wasn't a question of urban congestion that got to us. When Americans move to Canada people often assume they must have fled some sort of urban rat race. However, my father, being British, didn't have much love for the United States in the first place and certainly didn't feel patriotic about it. As the Vietnam War years rolled on, he became increasingly unhappy. He came home from work one day and asked, "What happened in America the Beautiful today?" and it just so happened that was the day the students were shot at Kent State University.

When I was eighteen, in 1972, we went to Cape Breton on vacation for two weeks and fell in love with it. My mother, on impulse, bought a one-hundred-acre abandoned farm and a house in Baddeck. We stayed there for two months that summer, and then my dad decided he would rather dig ditches in Cape Breton than be the president of a life insurance company in the U.S.A. My mum and I found a business for sale – a decrepit restaurant – in Margaree Harbour, so we bought it and the family moved north permanently. The restaurant needed a tremendous amount of work. We spent the winter living in a fool's paradise, running up huge bills. At the end of our first season we were $60,000 in debt. One of our waitresses, who had to go on welfare when we couldn't pay her, was bringing *us* soup.

Nevertheless, Daddy was happy we had moved, because he didn't have to go to the office. Mum was miserable because she felt she had bankrupted us and ruined my life and my plans to become an environmental lawyer. Instead of going back to university, I spent from 1974 through the summer of 1982 working in the restaurant with my brother and parents, and we gradually made it into a going concern.

F.M. But you never lost interest in environmental problems. Your mother tells me you read everything there was to read on the subject. You trained yourself, she says, like some medieval knight expecting a challenge. And then the challenge came. Exactly how did your involvement in the spruce budworm war come about?

E.M. That was the winter of 1975-76. We read in the local press that the Swedish-owned Nova Scotia Forest Industry pulp company wanted to spray much of Cape Breton to stop a budworm epidemic. The Nova Scotia minister of lands and forest of the time announced that he was not in favour of such a plan. There was general agreement that we had had budworm in Cape Breton before, and we would get it again, and there was no need to spray. But in February it was reported that the government had changed its mind under pressure from the pulp companies, and was going to spray a hundred thousand acres from the air with Fenitrothion. This is an organophosphate and an extremely toxic substance to all forms of animate life. I was very disturbed that they would do this, and soon afterwards an anti-spray petition was brought to me from a group in Inverness. The local priest had put it out using the mimeo machine in his basement. Unfortunately the petition didn't provide much information about the spray, so I saw a need to get a fact sheet together.

Because I had been concerned in the environmental movement since about 1970, I had collected quite a reference library. There was nothing in our local public libraries in Cape Breton on Fenitrothion, but I had Rachel Carson's

Silent Spring which had some good information on the dangers of organophosphates. There was also a chapter in Rachel's book on the budworm spray programme in New Brunwick, which demonstrated how insecticide spraying doesn't stop such epidemics; it simply perpetuates them so they never die out as they do when left alone. I also had some good material from the Science Institute for Public Information on analyses of different types of chemicals; how they work; what they are likely to do, and what the problems are going to be with their use. I put together a fact sheet and began to distribute it – and that's how I first got involved.

Within a very short time a wave of protest had coalesced, and we had formed a "sort-of" organization called Cape Breton Landowners Against the Spray. Then we heard a rumour that there was a medical connection between Fenitrothion spraying in New Brunswick and children dying there of Reye's Syndrome. We checked it out and after a reporter from the *Cape Breton Post* printed the story, there was an emergency meeting of the Nova Scotia Cabinet. We mustered at least a hundred people to call on the government to reverse its decision to allow spraying. We got everybody phoning until the lines were jammed into Halifax. The minister of health, Allan Sullivan, got the message and managed to convince the premier and the rest of the Cabinet there was no way they were going to spray a chemical where there was even a suspicion that it might cause the deaths of children. He was a Cape Bretoner, and was not very impressed by the spray programme to begin with.

So the spray programme was cancelled for that year. But every year thereafter for the next six years we had to fight the battle over again because the pulp companies pulled out all the stops to have it done. They were determined to spray, and just as determined not to pay for the spraying themselves; it was to be something done by the Nova Scotia government to help the industry. That's very much along the lines of the New Brunswick model, where Forest Protection Limited is a Crown corporation that sprays every year largely for the Irving pulp and paper interests.

F.M. Do you remember when spraying started in New Brunswick?

E.M. In 1952. Since then they have had a perpetual spruce budworm infestation, because it never peaks and collapses. They have created their own continuous plague of spruce budworms because of using spray.

The first year I think they sprayed two hundred thousand acres. It seemed to be a highly successful programme. All the reports said there were high budworm kill ratios and everything looked great. Next year they were quite surprised to find that the area of the epidemic had spread, so they made the spray programme four times as large. Eventually they were spraying virtually half the province. In 1968 they started to use phosphamidon and that resulted in the worst of the kills that devastated New Brunswick song-bird populations.

They started using Fenitrothion about 1972. In 1976 New Brunswick was about to get a ten-million-acre Fenitrothion spray programme, and we were trying to stop the pulp companies from spraying the whole of Cape Breton Island.

As far as most of the Nova Scotia media was concerned, our opposition was an emotional one based on the reports that Fenitrothion made children sick. But the opposition to spraying in Cape Breton was much more widely grounded. Much of it came from elderly people who had lived in the area a long time. Old men who had cut pulp in the woods as youngsters had a living memory of several previous spruce budworm outbreaks. They could remember exactly how bad it had been. Archie Walker talked about working in the woods as a young man in the early 1920s when they used horses, hand saws and axes. Two thousand men were employed in the Cape Breton Highlands then, many more than are now employed because the companies have mechanized the operation so much. He said they could remember when the budworm threads – the worms lower themselves from branch to branch by long, silky, sticky threads – would get so bad they had to clear the threads from the horses' eyes because the horses couldn't see their way through the forest hauling the logs out.

There was another outbreak in the early 1950s. Always the same pattern – the infestation would grow for a few years, peak, then disappear naturally. But the outbreaks were getting closer together. That was because of logging practices which favoured a monoculture of balsam fir, the budworms' favourite food. By deliberately changing the composition of the forests, the forest industry was shortening the interval between epidemics. Most Cape Bretoners could figure out for themselves what was happening. And they wanted to get back to a more natural forest. They knew we needed a good hardwood mix and more black and red spruce. Balsam fir happens to put its buds out perfectly synchronized to when the budworm larvae are ready to start chewing; so it's ideal for them.

By 1976 the Cape Breton Highlands were almost ninety per cent balsam fir and most of it quite over-aged. The foresters had themselves classified big chunks of it as "moribund." The budworm is a good silviculturalist, and was going to get rid of that stuff. So we had a very broad argument for not spraying.

F.M. Were the woodlot owners against spraying too?

E.M. Yes. In Cape Breton, and in Nova Scotia in general, most of the wood is still in private hands, which is quite the reverse of most provinces. Most privately held woodlots have been well managed, because you had generations of owners who had taken out just what they needed each year, and it grew back. They had good mixed-species, mixed-age forests. It was in the Cape Breton Highlands – Crown land leased to the pulp companies – that the even-age, balsam monoculture situation which invited budworm epidemics had developed. These lands were the pulp industry's private fiefdom, and they felt they had to control the budworm there at any cost, even if they had to use lethal sprays. In fact, Cape Breton as a whole could have provided all the wood they needed, but it would have had to come in greater and greater proportion from woodlots in private hands, which would mean the mills would be faced with the possibility of having to pay competitive prices for the logs.

We managed to get the Nova Scotia Forest Industries' mill manager on a local radio show to confirm that it actually cost the company *more* to do their own mechanized cutting on the highlands than to buy from private woodlot owners, but the mill owners wanted to maintain a virtual monopoly on the supply side so they would be able to pay the independent operators as low a price as possible. The truth is that the wars over spraying in Cape Breton were largely economic wars between people with private holdings and the companies.

So we had the support of the woodlot owners and operators. We had the support of beekeepers, sheep producers and those involved in marine farming – none of them wanted to see pesticides used here.

Now it just so happens – surprise, surprise – that the three big pulp and paper companies in Nova Scotia are all foreign-owned. N.S.F.I. by Stora Kopparberg of Sweden, Scott Paper by U.S. interests, and Bowater-Mersey in Britain. They had the very strong support of the Canadian Forest Service which was, at that point, a branch of the Federal Department of the Environment – if you can imagine such an outrageous conflict of interest! In Nova Scotia, the Department of Lands and Forests is the institutionalized bought-and-paid-for arm of the forest industry.

So we environmentalists were up against an alliance of forestry companies and chemical companies supported by just about every professional forester you could find in Canada.

F.M. Isn't that rather a universal situation? Isn't that the way most extractive industries operate – hand-in-glove with government and its agencies?

E.M. Yes, but there has been some evolution in at least the sophistication, if not the real motivations, of some major industries in an effort to appear less selfish and more environmentally aware. The leaders in this evolution are the big multi-national oil and gas guys, who are getting pretty savvy on environmental stuff at this point. Even the chemical industry is coming along. But one of the last hold-outs of the "we are unshakeably opposed to environmentalist interference" syndrome is the forest industry.

They are very intransigent and can be vicious. In 1976 Eric Sundblat, the president of Stora Kopparberg, flew over from Sweden and told the Nova Scotia government and the press, "If the budworm is allowed to continue it will destroy half the forests of Cape Breton; we will be forced to close down our existing operations within five years. This will put two thousand people out of work." He was talking about his employees together with those in direct spin-off. Then he said, "Nova Scotia is sick. It must take the medicine."

We had to counter this threat, which got very full media coverage, as quickly as we could. But the media wouldn't give us space in those days, so we began to put together a fact sheet we could mail to all householders in Cape Breton, since that was the only way we could reach them. We had to counter the gloom-laden prophecies of Nova Scotia Forest Industries, which a lot of people were inclined to believe and which made them, not unreasonably, afraid for their jobs.

N.S.F.I. had issued a hundred-page report to substantiate Sundblat's doom threats, and we got hold of a copy and had it analysed by professional accountants and statisticians headed by my father. It was amazing. We were able to prove, using their *own* statistics, that they weren't going to run out of wood for another forty years even if the budworm infestation was allowed to run its natural course. We publicized this for all we were worth, even buying newspaper space when the press wouldn't cover it as news. In the end, the Nova Scotian government continued, if reluctantly, to stand by its decision to deny permission for aerial spraying of pesticides.

By 1981 the budworm population had collapsed – naturally – and the infestation was over.

F.M. So the spruce budworm war was won.

E.M. Yes. And there were no casualties – human, animal or economic.

F.M. And you had set an example that will be difficult for pesticide sprayers to ignore in future. If you leave nature to solve problems such as this – she will do it.

E.M. The pro-sprayers have tried to turn that around. The dean of forestry at the University of New Brunswick took the line that the vast fir forests of Cape Breton had been uselessly sacrificed on a high altar of environmental purity. Industry and their propagandists produced some ghastly films showing the area of the worst infestations, and said this was the fault of the environmentalists. They didn't say that these were over-mature, monoculture stands of trees that had originated from, and been doomed by, bad forestry practices. They did have an effective visual point, though. It is always sad to see the remains of a forest, whether it has been destroyed by fire, budworm, or by the pulp and lumber industry.

F.M. It *is* sad, until you look at the ground after a natural disaster and see the living trees poking up again – the rise of a new generation.

E.M. But in Cape Breton and most other heavily harvested woods, the new forest won't be the self-sustaining one it once was. The pulp industry doesn't want the mixed stands of beech, maple, oak, birch, pine and many other species. They want balsam fir and, to a lesser extent, black spruce as the sole "crop." For them, silviculture equals monoculture. It is just like corn farming. You end up with rows and rows of one kind of tree, all of one age. To do that you have to first clear-cut all the natural tree growth, then use "site preparation" which entails "cultivating" the whole area using enormous machines. You end up with naked "fields." Then you plant the species you want, and to make sure that's all you get, you spray herbicides over it to kill everything that might grow naturally.

These people talk about managing a forest, but there is not even a rudimentary concern about other plant species, much less what's happening to insects, birds, mammals – all the things that make up a forest ecosystem. It also is not naturally sustainable because, when you finish that kind of rotation by clear-cutting the mature trees, the fields require artificial fertilizing – usually from the air – because clear-cutting and monoculture result in the loss of the natural nutrients in the soil.

F.M. What did you do after the budworm episode?

E.M. By 1980 the budworms were pretty well gone and I was studying law in Halifax – environmental law – while taking on the New Brunswick forestry interests, because their pesticide spray programme was continuing. It still *is*, although in 1988 they did agree to spray half of the area with the bacterial agent BT, instead of using lethal chemicals over the entire region.

Then a new issue began to surface in Nova Scotia. A French-owned company – Aquitaine – had discovered significant deposits of uranium, and pressure began building to start a uranium industry in the province. During the winter of 1980-81, I did a lot of speaking on the uranium issue which became the major environmental issue of the day since nobody was worrying about aerial spraying any more. Perhaps our budworm victory had made us smug and careless. In any case, the next attack on the environment caught us unprepared.

What happened was that the forest industry decided to begin massive aerial herbicide spraying to kill off competing forms of vegetation – trees, raspberries, bushes – anything and everything that might compete with the "crop" of pulpwood trees.

All three Nova Scotian political parties had supported Liberal Premier Gerald Regan against budworm spraying. When the Conservatives, led by John Buchanan, came to power, their official position was that they too were against chemical spraying. Now they began to try to weasel out of it by saying, "We were against insecticides, not herbicides. We never said we were against herbicide spraying." What happened was that the Conservatives, who really *are* the party of big business and big industry, thought they wouldn't have much of a fight on their hands because it looked like all the environmentalists were totally absorbed in the uranium issue.

I dropped out of the uranium scene when the press announced a herbicide spray programme in the middle of June. I was on the phone the next day to Halifax to find out what was going to be sprayed and with what mode of spraying. It took me two days and lots of long-distance calls to find out they were going to use a mixture of 2-4-D and 2-4-5-T – the infamous mix known as Agent Orange – over a lot of sites in *lowland* areas of Cape Breton and mainland Nova Scotia where healthy, mixed forests in private hands still existed. Spraying would be done by air – and would start within two weeks! All hardwood trees would be killed so that softwoods, largely spruce and balsam, could take over. All three pulp and paper companies operating in Nova Scotia already had their permits to go ahead.

I had never before felt more powerless. Here we had a new and major chemical pollution threat without any warning, and I was panicked. I wondered if I could organize a general strike of the whole province, but there was too little time to try that. What I did was to convert my home telephone into a toll-free line, and put out a press release advising any Nova Scotian who might live near an area due to be sprayed to call our Herbicide Hotline. This time the media picked it up, and the number got so well known that calls would start at seven in the morning and didn't stop until after midnight.

Within a week we had at least twelve different communities holding community meetings, and I had to speak to them all. There was no organization at that point. Cape Breton Landowners Against the [budworm] Spray had been inherently ad hoc, with no ongoing structure. There certainly was no bank account. But I am a firm believer that action is doomed if it begins by saying, "First we get our by-laws, then raise a lot of money, then we can do something." I believe that if your cause is good you don't need to worry about your finances; people will look after you. I have faith that the universe will provide. But this was the only time I've had to sell my car to pay a phone bill – one month it was $1200.

The public meetings multiplied. Concern for what might happen seemed everywhere. Company officials and government experts were invited to come and answer questions, but after one meeting at Big Pond, they almost never showed up again. That night there were representatives from Dow Chemical to defend 2-4-D, and from the Nova Scotia Department of the Environment, the Nova Scotia Department of Lands and Forests, and Nova Scotia Forest Industries to defend the spray programme. Father John Hector MacGregor opened the meeting. He welcomed everyone. "I was talking to my sister in New Waterford and she said, 'John Hector, you know you can't wear your clerical collar to that meeting.' I said, 'Why not?' and she said, 'Because you know you can't swear with it on.' " Then he undid his collar, took it off and put it down.

If the pro-spray men sitting there in their dark business suits in the front row had had any sense, they would have made for the door at that point. He said, "I welcome you to Big Pond, gentlemen, but I'm telling you right now it doesn't matter what you say, you won't be spraying in Big Pond. We will stop you if we have to go to court; we will stop you if we have to fight you with our bare hands; but you will NOT be spraying in Big Pond."

The whole hall erupted in applause, then these "experts" tried to answer questions. People were courteous, but these guys didn't have the answers. A nine-year-old girl stood up: "Isn't it true that this material was used in Viet Nam and isn't it true it used to be part of Agent Orange?" The Dow man replied, "This is a different version, but I'm not sure how different." She said, "I heard about someone who went blind from this stuff." He said, "Perhaps if you could give us the specifics and the information we could check that." Whenever they couldn't answer a question, they said, "Give us your name and address and we'll mail a reply."

My mother told them, "I drove all the way from Margaree Harbour because I wanted to see a representative of Dow Chemical. I've never *seen* one of you before. I know you've made Napalm and I've wondered about you and Agent Orange for years, and now here you are. I just have one question. Have you no concern for your immortal soul?" More cheering.

I spoke at most of the public meetings. I tried to be as fair as I could. I would state the company's position. "Their view is that the alders and blackberries and all the hardwoods are suppressing the softwood trees they need for pulp, so what they are doing is good silviculture. *Our* position is that they can send people into the woods to thin out 'weed species' mechanically, and do it cheaper, if it's so important. But what you *can't* do is spray, especially from the air, because these very toxic chemicals will drift over people and habitations, and foul the watersheds as well."

We now had quite a ground swell going, and it continued to build very fast. It even swept up the Micmac Indians, who had never before become involved in any of the white man's environmental wars. Finally it led to such popular pressure on the government that they bowed to it. Or seemed to. Greg Kerr, Nova Scotia's minister of environment, announced that there wouldn't be any spraying of herbicides that year, pending a report from a Royal Commission on Forestry.

There was jubilation. It looked like a quick, conclusive, one hundred per cent victory. The spraying had been announced on June 20th, and by July 8th it was reported in *Maclean's* that we had won. I went sailing for a while to celebrate. On August 3rd I caught a bus in Halifax for Cape Breton, and opened the day's newspaper. There on the first page of the second section was a notice of herbiciding: "Select areas in Inverness, Victoria and Antigonish Counties will receive a treatment of government-approved herbicide." It said spraying would commence August 11th.

I was shaking angry when I got home to Margaree. I managed to reach the minister of the environment by phone and said, "We are going to have a big public meeting tonight in Cape Breton and there is going to be a lawyer there. I'm begging you. I do not want to go to court. I'm in law school. I've been learning that basically people don't want to go to court. Let me bring to your office the expert witnesses that we would call *if* we went to court. I trust you to make the right decision. Please let us see you." He said, "I'm sorry. There has just been too much pressure ever since we decided not to allow the spraying. Your only choice if you want to stop it is to go to court."

At the meeting that night our lawyer laid out, in not very encouraging terms, what it would mean to go to court. As a group we would have only a proprietary interest, so what we needed were people living close to each spray block as plaintiffs. Those individuals would be financially responsible in the event we failed. Even if we did get an initial injunction to halt the spraying, and it was then overturned, each plaintiff would be on the hook for all costs and damages to the company. There wasn't time to really consider the risks we would be running. We had to work fast because the application for an injunction had to be in the court within the week if it was to work.

The first person to offer herself as a plaintiff was Vicky Palmer, who had chemical allergies and sensitivities and lived near Lochaber, in Antigonish County. We had another series of meetings. Over that week many more plaintiffs volunteered, even though I explained that they could lose everything they owned. People from all over Cape Breton and Antigonish County volunteered. The oldest plaintiff was Jack MacGilvray, who was an eighty-year-old, retired campus police officer from St. Francis Xavier University. He had a bad heart condition and his wife was terribly nervous. He was also quite deaf, but he insisted on being a plaintiff. I was also a plaintiff, but I was trying to sue all *three* pulp and paper companies so that we could stop the spraying all across the province.

We put the whole thing together between August 3rd and 10th. We got affidavits from expert witnesses including Nova Scotia physicians who were prepared to say they thought this was a dangerous thing. The judge gave us a temporary emergency injunction for Cape Breton, but said we would have to reconvene on August 19th, for further consideration.

While we were preparing for August 19th I got a call from a reporter who said the pulp companies had just sprayed one of the sites in Antigonish for which we didn't have a plaintiff. The reporter asked them where they were going next, and they said Cape Breton. She said she thought there was an injunction there. They said, not on the highland sites! Now we found out there were six thousand acres more of permits we hadn't been told about. We were in total shock. When we went back to court on the 19th we told Judge Burchell what we had learned. He wasn't very impressed with the companies. He said, "I thought at last week's hearing we were told those were all the sites in Cape Breton." The company representative replied, "We didn't feel we were under any obligation to enlighten the plaintiffs as to other possible sites." The judge looked down his half-glasses at them as if they were microscopic bugs. The injunction was thereupon extended to cover all the new sites.

That was the end of our August hearings. We had at that point seventeen plaintiffs covering thirteen sites. The case was then adjourned until such time as a full trial could be held. This meant we had won for that season; there would be no spraying by N.S.F.I. in north-eastern Nova Scotia for that year.

The pulp companies filed an appeal against Judge Burchell's decision. Now we had to prepare our case for the appeal. The costs were mounting furiously. Scott Paper, against whom I had withdrawn my own suit, was now claiming $23,000 in costs against me and the other plaintiffs. Our only source of funds was from volunteer givers. We were getting in deeper and deeper, but there was no way out short of withdrawing the injunction, and we were told that if we did that the paper companies would kill us with punitive claims for costs and damages. Anyway, we had no mind to quit.

We knew the case was going to be heard in May. At this point in my personal life everything was horrible because I was trying to finish third year law, while working flat out on our legal battle. To make it worse, I got a letter in February from Scott Paper's lawyer requiring payment of $15,000 by the end of the week. We simply didn't have the money. But then, without telling any of us, Mum sold the land we owned at Baddeck – for $15,000 – and paid Scott off.

It was a thirty-day trial; there were thirty expert witnesses. During it we lived in a horrible little place over a pizzaria in Sydney. It was like a guerilla war. We had no secretaries, office, anything. Friends from law school came for parts of the time. I missed my graduation because I was cross-examining witnesses. Before the trial started, we put an ad in the local paper: "Herbicide case starting in Sydney. Needed: furniture, desk, typewriters, volunteers, food." We would come home from the trial and there on the table would be lasagna from someone in East Bay, and so on. Sometimes there would be a wonderful bouquet of flowers from the Mary Rose Flower Shop.

Unfortunately this time we didn't have Judge Burchell, but a new man who had only been on the bench for nine months, and at the end of the trial he said he would reserve decision for further study.

On September 15th I had lunch with the leading lawyer of the firm I was articling with in Halifax. He was convinced we had won, because it would be irresponsible for any judge to wait this long to give a negative decision, since the delay, if the decision went against us, would have caused us to incur an additional year's costs and damages.

The next day the decision was announced. We had lost. In his decision the judge had written that this kind of case must be "discouraged in its infancy." People who come to court essentially seeking political aims should be encouraged to use other forums. To discourage this sort of thing, costs and damages will be assessed. We were told these would amount to as much as half a million dollars.

We were knocked for a loop but at once started raising money for an appeal. Ryan Googoo, Chief of the Micmacs of Whycocomagh and I went to Sweden to try to raise money there. Our travel expenses were paid by Swedish environmentalists. Stora – N.S.F.I.'s parent company – was saying in Sweden that the highest court in the land in Canada had just decreed that herbicides were safe, and so they should now be used again in Sweden, where they had been banned.

We took Sweden by storm. We were on the national news every night. Olof Palme endorsed us. Stora was being vilified in editorials all over the country. People were selling their shares of Stora stock. One of our witnesses in the herbicide case had been a Swedish epidemiologist so we had a connection built in. So many people supported us that we returned to Canada absolutely convinced that we would be able to raise whatever amount of money we needed for an appeal, and that Stora would never take our homes and farms; that they would be destroyed in Sweden if they did. We weren't feeling so vulnerable any more.

The pressure we created on Stora meant that they told N.S.F.I. to settle. But there was a catch. In return for not being assessed enormous costs and damages, which would have bankrupted most of the plaintiffs if we lost the appeal, we had to withdraw the appeal. That was one of the hardest things I've ever had to do but, in the end, we dropped it.

There is a strange epilogue. We lost our case in Canada, but won it in Sweden. The stockholders and board of Stora got so much flak that they decided to dispense with Eric Sundblat, who had been their chief executive since 1975. While driving to the meeting at which he was going to be ousted, he pulled his car to the side of the road and shot himself.

As for us – we went on with our lives. The attempt to stop the herbicide spraying had cost me and my family more than $30,000. But we *had* helped to prevent Nova Scotia from being sprayed with Agent Orange. Although the pulp companies started spraying herbicides the following year, they switched to a different and less lethal chemical. Nor is the fight over yet. It won't be over until the spraying stops.

Elizabeth May went from the war against herbicides in Nova Scotia to a broader stage. She was instrumental in organizing the Canadian Environmental Defence Fund which provides legal assistance to groups all over Canada fighting to protect and preserve the natural world. In August 1986, she was asked by Tom McMillan, minister of the environment in the federal government, to become his senior policy adviser on environmental matters. She held this enormously influential post until June 1988, when she resigned in protest against what she saw as a political deal between Saskatchewan and Ottawa whereby, in exchange for federal permission to proceed with two potentially disastrous dams, Saskatchewan agreed to translate its statutes into French and allow the federal government to go ahead with plans to establish a prairie grasslands national park.

Before her resignation, May had been instrumental in helping to implement plans for several new national parks, including South Moresby in the Queen Charlotte Island archipelago. She also worked on the Ozone Protocol, reforms to the federal Environmental Assessment Act, and obtained nearly a million dollars of government funds for the assistance of environmental groups all across Canada. In the autumn of 1988 she organized a nationwide publicity campaign in an attempt to force the three political parties in the federal election to give more than lip service to environmental problems. She is currently executive director of Cultural Survival (Canada), a non-profit organization involved in such issues as the preservation of rain forests, assistance for the indigenous people of the Amazon and Malaysia, as well as support for native people in Canada in their efforts to preserve their traditional lifestyles.

Effervescent, ebullient and optimistic as ever, Elizabeth May continues her crusade to keep us from despoiling the earth.

Let There Be Harmony:

Michael Bloomfield and the Harmony Foundation

All the prime movers in the conservation movement acknowledge the vital need for a massive educational effort to help slow the slide towards environmental disaster. However, few organizations have given education much of a priority, perhaps because it has little intrinsic glamour. Designing and attempting to implement an environmentally attuned school curriculum hardly offers the kind of kudos which accrues to a well-publicized attempt to save the panda from extinction. The leaders of the conservation establishment have, for the most part, been content to give lip-service to the educational option, perhaps in the hope that someone else will embrace this seemingly lack-lustre project.

They are fortunate that someone has indeed chosen to take up the challenge.

Hot-eyed, scraggily bearded and fervently vocal, Michael Bloomfield looks like a younger prophet emerging from the desert. His unvarnished message is that unless mankind radically alters its ways, it has no future on this planet.

A graduate biologist, Michael spent a decade in the employ of several government departments nominally devoted to conservation. Concluding that such bureaucracies were not only ineffective but sometimes downright harmful, he set out to try and change the world in his own way by establishing the Harmony Foundation – man in harmony with nature. Some old-guard environmentalists (and, yes, there *is* already an old guard) view him as an idealistic dreamer, but others have become convinced that his is the way to go.

M.B. I grew up in Ohio and Alberta. My family still is there in Alberta. I was always in the thick of things – curious about everything, even more so than most kids. Into everything that was going on. I was the stick that stirred the drink most of the time.

F.M. An agitator?

M.B. Yes. I still am. I've just become more subtle over time.

F.M. What awoke your interest in the natural world?

M.B. I'm not sure. Chris, my wife, teases me because I don't have a vivid memory of that part of my life, whereas she can tell you to the last detail of when she was four years old . . .

F.M. Like when she met her first frog, and he smiled at her and she's loved frogs ever since.

M.B. That's it. But my attitude to nature is a reflection of a whole lot of things. It was a gradual process through experiences such as investigating the woods adjacent to the school, where there were jack-in-the-pulpits and salamanders; or Japanese beetles on the roses in the garden. I wasn't a kid to catch things. I think very early on I wanted to be more of an observer than an intruder. I wasn't out there catching a baby rabbit to examine it, and then turning it loose only to find its mother had rejected it. Early on I recognized the way we treat animals in our society was rather one-sided, and there was a lot of pain and suffering they experienced at our hands for reasons I really couldn't understand or feel were justified.

I was the kind of kid who, when my dog went missing, would refuse to eat until she came home, and would phone the SPCA every hour, and put posters out on every streetlamp because I was determined she was going to be found.

In my teens I worked for the SPCA as a volunteer, and my concern about how animals were treated kept on developing; in agriculture, for instance; and in the issues of hunting, trapping and whale killing. When I went to university I was already a blossoming vegetarian. I enrolled in the faculty of animal science to challenge the parameters – my own and society's – to find out where the truth lay. I figured I would either find I was worrying about nothing, or they would train me to be a more compelling advocate for animals. So I studied biology and the mechanics of animal-based agriculture and natural-resource management. These studies convinced me that my moral and ethical concerns were valid. I had a better understanding of the nature and effect of such human activities as intensive agriculture and trapping. My empathy for animals was now grounded in some good knowledge and understanding of why I felt the way I did.

F.M. Did you find much conflict between the accepted attitudes taught in university and what you felt to be right or wrong?

M.B. Before going to university, I went for a while to a small community college. I remember a sheep-production class I took with farm kids who were fine-tuning their agricultural skills. One day they were all teasing me saying, "Bloomfield, we are doing sheep castrations today. You know how we castrate sheep? We bite their nuts off." I said, "You guys are just kidding me." That was the day the teacher decided I was going to be first. He demonstrated how to do it, but the demonstration wasn't clear. I couldn't get the testicles off this poor, ten-day-old lamb. I came up with blood all over my beard in front of thirty or forty other students, and had to say I couldn't do it.

It was a disgusting experience and it certainly made my concern for animals more compelling. At university I had a job cleaning up after some of the experiments on animals, and I didn't like what I saw. I got myself in hot water a few times by going to faculty and complaining that the animals were not getting good care. Of course they objected to that. I became determined to go toe-to-toe with these people and tell them, "If you want to throw me out because I'm concerned that this horse's fistula has become festered and pulled loose and you are ignoring it, then throw me out." A fistula is a hole cut into one of the stomach compartments of the living animal; a rubber plug is put in. You pull the plug to sample undigested stomach material.

I was learning more than the technology; I was learning that the humanitarian ethic was more of a myth than a reality, and I was awfully discouraged.

I also knew I was being very narrow if my concern was limited to animals used in agriculture or as domestic companions, and that wild animals were not doing any better at our hands. So I did my graduate work in wildlife biology. The first year I had some funny experiences. I gave my graduate seminar in the faculty of animal science on the obsolescence of animal agriculture. I made points about the need to recognize that agriculture has grave environmental implications, and that there were humanitarian issues that weren't being addressed. I timed it so there were only thirty seconds left for questions, then the bell went and there was chaos. A few of the older faculty went to the chairman's office and said, "This man is dangerous. What is he doing in our programme?"

F.M. What led you into wildlife biology as a profession?

M.B. By this time I was twenty-two and had a degree in animal nutrition, specializing in ruminant biology; was married and needed a job. There was a project available on caribou biology in central British Columbia. It was mid-winter, so I put on my down vest and flannel shirt and flew to Prince George. The B.C. Fish and Wildlife Service put me in a helicopter and threw me out in the middle of nowhere with snowshoes and cross-country skis, not realizing I had no experience on either, and said, "We'll see you in ten days with more food."

Sometimes I would find the caribou, and in an hour they would be gone. Then for days I wouldn't see any at all and I'd sit there and eat peanut butter and jelly, wondering what I was doing out there. I had a lot of time to think. I was living in snow caves mostly. In time I got the hang of the job. I studied the ecology of caribou in that area and the impact of human activities on their well-being. It was fascinating, but I soon found myself rubbing up against an establishment that really wanted me just to document a nice little natural history of these animals, whereas I was trying to develop recommendations for how industrial activity and human settlement in the area might be modified or, in some cases, stopped, so that this declining herd would stabilize or even, hopefully, recover. I was not prepared to cook my information so that it wouldn't look too bad for humans. There was little evidence of wolf predation. It was really overhunting, increased accessibility because of logging and coal mining, too-liberal seasons, and allowing both males and females to be shot that had hammered the population to a very small percentage of what it had historically been. And continued hunting was really preventing them from any recovery. I said all this in my reports.

F.M. You must have been as popular as a pole cat with the provincial bureaucrats.

M.B. I don't think I was popular, but when you tell the truth you are often not. All of a sudden I was starting to realize you put the best efforts and years of your life into something and no matter how compelling the tale, there is someone who is going to manipulate it to justify killing wolves, or ignore it because there was something else at stake.

F.M. You weren't prepared to be a biologist of the hired-gun variety?

M.B. No. I was going to do the best I could. If that sat well, I was happy. If it didn't? Well, I couldn't help that.

I was about twenty-eight at that point, and a job came up in Edson, Alberta, in the foothills of the Rockies. The region included the booming Pembina oil field, one of the biggest recreational hunting areas in Alberta, and which was also probably number one or two in logging activity. Together with coal mining, oil and gas exploration it was a pretty busy place. In February of 1978 unhappily the entire four-man Fish and Wildlife staff for the region had been killed in a plane crash.

I applied to be head of the replacement group. Normally an interviewee for a job with the Alberta Wildlife Service would be asked: "Do you hunt and fish?" and if the answer was no, you weren't getting the job, as if a non-hunter couldn't be a good biologist. But the guy who usually did the interviews was on holidays and hadn't sufficiently briefed the substitute, so they hired me and sent me to Edson.

Here's my first big job, a really high-powered situation with a lot of activity, and it was my *official* role to see to it that the wildlife and habitat of the Pembina region didn't get flushed down the drain. There wasn't a clue what to do, and there was no one to rely on for guidance. But I had two of the best people I've ever worked with – Kirby Smith, habitat biologist of the group, and Bernie Goski, wildlife technician. We flew by the seat of our pants, all with the same commitment to make sure all this heavy industrial activity had as little impact as possible. We were the Three Musketeers.

F.M. Would it be fair to say you formed a little cell inside the establishment that really *did* work for the well-being of wildlife, and not simply to the advantage of hunters and fishermen or industrialists?

M.B. Yes. Alberta Fish and Wildlife had a few more people like that, but they've nearly all since left or been purged. At first there was an assistant deputy minister who supported us, but he was replaced. We worked really hard to do a good job and that bothered some of the senior staff in Edmonton.

We were doing the right things on the wrong side of the fence. We would go out and find a company still drilling on a well site twenty days after their permit had expired, and by the time we got back to the office we already had a phone call from the deputy minister saying, "Stay off it." How did he know we had been out in the middle of nowhere talking to people at the well site? The drillers phoned company headquarters; headquarters phoned the deputy, who phoned us.

Industry was taking note of us by then. My brother's a dentist. One day he asked a patient in the chair how things were going, and the guy said, "Some son-of-a-bitch biologist up in Edson is giving us a hard time." The guy worked for a major oil company. My brother asked, "What's his name?" and the guy just turned pale because suddenly he realized the connection.

You really have to work inside government to realize just how weird it can be. For example, there was a unique, small population of mountain goats in our district, which long ago had broken away from the mountains and travelled eighty or a hundred miles into the foothills and was living on the cliffs in a river valley. Now one of the companies wanted in there to drill an exploratory well and we were concerned about the disturbance to the goats. "Not to worry," the deputy minister told us. "You just tranquilize them, take them out, move them to the Edmonton Zoo and keep them there until the well is finished." Once we were over being flabbergasted we said, "By the time the well is done these goats will be dead." He said, "I can guarantee you we'll give you the money to find more goats, take them and train them to go wild again."

That's the kind of thinking we were trying to contend with. This was the deputy who was responsible for Fish and Wildlife. There was going to be a collision sooner or later. We tried to learn how the process worked, and to be a little more subtle, but it was hard to anticipate such thinking.

By this time I had concluded that caribou in Alberta were in worse trouble than they were in B.C. The government decided to make me the provincial caribou management biologist, as well as the regional biologist at Edson. We started a five-year study, which never was funded, that soon proved conclusively the caribou were declining. I began to advocate the closure of the caribou hunting season throughout Alberta. I wasn't placing blame entirely on the hunters for the decline, but since we weren't going to be able to stop oil and gas exploration we had to cut out of the picture as many of the adverse factors as we could. Hunting was one. The government didn't want to do it because they were afraid the hunting lobby would blow its stack.

Now, ministers always want someone to write their letters for them, and I was told to write one of the usual fluff letters to the president of the Fish and Game Association of Alberta to smooth his feathers. So I did. But I also told him we had just committed to a comprehensive five-year study on the status and ecology of caribou in the province, and were going to close the season for a minimum of three years and perhaps indefinitely. I figured the minister's assistant would phone me up, as is typically the case, and say, "We've got to change this letter." But evidently nobody looked at it and it went through. That and a few other things probably sealed my fate as a provincial wildlife biologist. Those of us who were trying to do things were probably doomed anyway, but I was young and naive and really thought I was expected to protect wildlife, and I worked hard to succeed at that.

Some company executives and just average joes were building landing strips in the middle of nowhere, and they'd fly in, build a hunt camp, scout the animals from the air, maybe even shoot them from the air, butcher them, have a gay old time and come out. I decided to go to the Federal Department of Transportation and find out if these strips were legal. They said, "No, they are illegal and shouldn't be there." I said, "With your blessing, can we close them?" They said, "The law requires ninety days' notice." We posted the notices, then hired summer students and got volunteers and destroyed the landing sites in our region. We planted poles across the runways with post-hole augers. We did all sorts of things so they couldn't land aircraft there any more.

We weren't out there to make mischief. Far from it. We had a mandate and were young, energetic and committed to wildlife enough to go and do things that would be meaningful. We weren't sitting in an office saying no, you can't do this or that. We were out on trail bikes, stuck up to our hips in mud, out in the middle of winter getting frost bitten; we were doing a lot of things to try and prevent problems before they became really serious.

We were always willing to work with companies that would co-operate. We'd say, "You want to drill a well? If you will work with us, we'll work with you to try and minimize the impact." We were spending three or four hundred hours a winter in small aircraft doing surveys. There were other regions where the field staff was doing twelve hours. What really annoyed some people is we were collecting information that made them abide by their obligations.

When we started, our mandate was to save wildlife for wildlife's sake. If you can save caribou, save caribou; if you can protect the interests of moose on a pipeline, do it. There's development all over the map. You're not going to stop it but you try and minimize the impact. Then we got a new assistant deputy minister whose attitude was "Wildlife should be exploited for its human value as an economic development." The new wildlife policy was "to maximize recreational benefit for Albertans."

Soon they were trying to get me to poison wolves on the flimsiest circumstantial evidence. I wasn't prepared to do it. It wasn't my job to go and destroy wildlife because someone wanted to raise sheep on fringe land or hunters felt wolves were competing with them.

At the same time, I was trying to bring a more humanitarian ethic to wildlife biology. Most biologists capturing animals, including caribou, for research programmes such as tagging and fitting radio-collars use tranquilizer guns. These result in very high mortality – in some cases fifty to sixty per cent. It was, and is, disastrous. I said, "There's no way I'm going to kill any animal, let alone fifty or sixty per cent of them, to do studies to save the rest." So for caribou we came up with a combined technique of drift nets in the trees and a net shot from a helicopter over caribou in deep snow, so the animals' falls would be broken. I insisted that pursuit would be limited to three minutes in order to not overstress the animals. This was pretty frustrating for the guys working with me when we would follow animals' tracks for four hours, find them, and I would only let them pursue for three minutes, win or lose. We weren't about to harrass them to death. Nevertheless, in three winters we caught approximately thirty-five caribou, without causing one injury or death.

We did some good biology and gained the support of a lot of industry because they knew that we were principled and prepared, but reasonable, and if there wasn't a problem, we weren't going to insist there was one. If there was one, we were going to make sure they worked with us to try and minimize the damage.

F.M. Clearly the Fish and Wildlife Service had to get rid of the likes of you. How did they do it?

M.B. They transferred me. "We want you at headquarters," they said. "You are too valuable to be out in the bush." I knew what that meant – you are either going to do it our way or you are going to suffer the consequences. I decided it was time to leave. That was in 1982, and I guess that was really the genesis of the Harmony Foundation.

Through my experiences as a wildlife biologist I had by now come to realize that we were always focused too tightly on specific problems. I came to the conclusion that as government employees we were putting so much effort into fighting little bush fires that we really weren't making much progress. And there was the notion out there amongst the public that since industry and government were the problem, they should find the solution.

But I was concerned that the public, too, was at fault. The public professes concern about contamination of the environment and what the future is going to be like for their children, the disappearance of wildlife, agricultural problems – we could craft a pretty long list – but most people really haven't changed their own behaviour significantly. While they are being concerned about toxic wastes in the Great Lakes, they put Draino down their sinks, and use toxic chemicals in their gardens, and leaded fuel, and toxic paint thinners. They are consuming the kinds of products that are causing contamination, either in production or waste disposal, and they go to the grocery store and take home six non-bio-degradable plastic bags, and so on.

We need the environmental advocates and regulations, but we also have to start doing damage control with adults, and translate the growing public concern for the environment into mass action. A recycling programme is a tiny example of where people's concern can be turned into applications in their daily lives. We have to get more individuals doing more things supportive of the environment rather than just wringing their hands in concern.

That's going to take an enormous increase in public awareness and public education. While we have to continue to insist that companies meet their obligations, and governments do a better job in regulating and developing policies and programmes to clean up and protect the environment, we also have to start intensive training of the public. We have to really give individual people the skills to judge the environmental consequences of actions in their personal and professional lives, and also develop the kinds of goals and values that are more compatible with a healthy environment.

That's what the Harmony Foundation is all about. It is advocating a cradle-to-grave programme of environmental education, but for practical reasons we want to start by getting the message into school and university programmes.

We have to take the environmental ethic and understanding and knowledge and infuse it into university disciplines so that it is required curriculum for engineers and agriculturalists and teachers, lawyers, business people and so on who will be making critical decisions affecting the environment.

We also have to maintain an ongoing programme of professional education because our environmental competence erodes so quickly. Five years after you graduate from university, your knowledge is obsolete. We have to have continuing education in environmental subjects so that people can stay current. The twenty-year-olds of today are going to become less and less open to new ideas as they get older, unless the stimulus is maintained.

The intention is to have successive waves or age groups which have a better understanding of the human place in nature and the impact of human populations and technology on the environment, and are committed to environmentally sound life styles and goals. We are trying to get people to unlearn many of the bad habits of consumption and exploitation, such as the notion that the solution to pollution is dilution. We have to recognize that it is not only a worthy thing to be environmentally committed, it's a responsiblity day in and day out – an *individual* responsibility, something I think many people now are avoiding. So the purpose of the Foundation is to get people to live as if nature matters, to get that concept infused throughout our society – expose every individual to this way of thinking. Whether it's buying a product, or taking a holiday, making a decision on where to live, or what kind of economic system we are going to favour. It must be all-pervasive that we understand nature as the basic reality – not as art appreciation, some place where you go to admire the birds two weeks on holidays and then go back and foul your own nest for the rest of the year.

F.M. You intend to penetrate the university system, but surely it is even more essential to work with children in the formative age.

M.B. Yes. The same way that we are sending our children in droves to French immersion schools, maybe we need to put them into nature immersion schools. We have to get into their minds and hearts. Tongue-in-cheek on occasion, when parents have resisted the notion of environmental concern and protection, I tell them, "We may miss you but we'll get into the minds of your kids and that's where we'll take over." Of course they don't like the prospect. Somehow we have to make it not seem threatening to people to learn a new way of living or relearn an old way.

Short-term damage control is where the environmental movement has tended to operate, probably out of necessity, as opposed to a long-term strategy that changes people's attitudes and values. It's a little difficult to talk to people sometimes in this context because they are not sure if it means we have to abandon technology, creature comforts and all the advantages with which the industrial revolution has provided us. We have a serious problem in persuading some people that good environmental practices can ensure that we not only remain comfortable but can live in a healthy environment without encroaching on every other life form and squeezing them out of existence. It doesn't seem to me, for instance, that the quality of life will diminish by driving our cars a little less, and taking mass transportation a little more often.

F.M. You and I may accept that, but most inhabitants of the modern consumptive world – I like to call it that because of the old connotation of "consumptive" meaning dying of consumption, as tuberculosis used to be called – would reject it as being retrogressive, since they believe any reduction in the "growth" of the automotive industry, for example, would lead to economic depression. How are you going to deal with that? And with a government dedicated to destroying *the* most efficient form of mass transportation – passenger rail?

M.B. There are a lot of people who are crying that the sky is already falling, that it's pretty well over anyway, so you may as well accumulate all the material possessions you can and use up resources as if they are going out of style. That's one of the rationalizations of those who want to believe that the prime purpose of life is the acquisition of material wealth. Instead of trying to convert people who can't be reached, because they defend themselves with rationalizations like these, our job is to find those who *do* care, and broaden the base from there. You'd be surprised how many average people low down on the economic totem pole are approachable on the environmental issue. I think this has been one of the problems with the environmental movement – we've been a little too elitist. Most of us are well educated. We tend to be from urban communities and are perhaps a little too judgmental in some respects, so it's difficult for the average person to enter our fortress.

Another thing I've found over the last couple of years in putting together Harmony Foundation and its programme is that the sixties revolution is not dead; it's just gone to live somewhere else. I find a fair number of senior executives in banks, publishing houses, the educational system and in industry who were once activists but are inactive now, mainly because they are fearful for their standing in the community. By giving these people an opportunity to express their concerns by helping to build a programme that's going to provide environmental education for their kids and others – which is a perfectly respectable activity – we obtain support from highly placed people.

F.M. But won't you still have most of the vested interests opposed to you?

M.B. They aren't in nearly such a good position to oppose the environmental movement as they used to be. I made a presentation to the board of directors of a major corporation not long ago, which was fascinating for me because I don't dress or think like them, or know any of them. What really got through to them was when I pointed out the interesting phenomenon that's taking place. Ten or twenty years ago, I told them, the environmental movement was at the outer fringe of society and you guys were at the centre. In those days people listened quite carefully to what industrialists were saying about the future of Canada and the world. Environmentalists were just a rag-tag band that could easily be disregarded. Now the tables have been turned. Public-opinion surveys suggest that few people *believe* what big business is telling them about where the future should be, or how we are going to get there. Somewhere between seventy-five and eighty per cent of Canadians have now identified the environment as one of their highest concerns. I challenged them to deal with that. "How does it feel now *you* are at the fringe of society? You may have an enormous economic empire, but you are prisoners of your own making because you have lost the public's trust." I think that's the challenge we have to take to them.

F.M. It has its dangers, of course. If it makes them feel beleaguered, and engenders a siege mentality, it may reduce their ability and willingness to come to terms with reality.

M.B. I always try to keep a dialogue going. The corporate executives are making critical decisions on what's going to happen to the environment. Even if we don't like what they are doing, we have to keep on talking terms. We have to keep the message in front of them, and keep the heat on.

I have to emphasize that the scenario isn't going to be rewritten overnight. The boss of one major resource company has now become an ardent environmentalist, so the public-relations people from his company tell us. Chances are, however, that it is lip-service environmentalism, without inner conviction. We have to get to Mr. Bigshot Junior, if there is one, and work a lot harder with him. But it's Mr. Bigshot III or perhaps the IVth, where the real changes will appear.

F.M. How does Harmony intend to accomplish that?

M.B. We couldn't muster enough people to go into *all* the schools regularly enough for it to have any impact with the kids, so what we intend to do is develop a programme to bring teachers from all over the country to seminars where we can clarify the environmental issues. We will be starting an in-residence summer programme in 1990. Environmentalists, business people and government people who have something to contribute in a progressive and constructive way will teach the teachers how to address environmental issues and enlighten and involve their students. These teachers, with the blessing of their school boards, will then do professional development with other teachers and so start building a network of teachers who are not only working within the schools but, hopefully, will also participate in a programme of public awareness and education.

F.M. I can't see how you can achieve your goal unless you get the North American school system to include environmental studies in the curriculum.

M.B. You're right. We have to get it into the curriculum – either required curriculum or, at the very least, supplemental curriculum. It has to be taught as a general subject, not as a science subject, because we want those kids who are going into law, the arts and business to be just as well versed and committed and concerned as those who are going to carry on with science. We want teachers from all these disciplines, and the programme is designed that way.

F.M. How will you fund the course for teachers?

M.B. We hope business will help by sponsoring the students. We have already found companies which will give us the money to sponsor two teachers from their community. Some school boards and private foundations will sponsor teachers from their districts. We will do our own selection, with the assistance of teacher organizations, on the basis of having a good cross-section of teachers from different parts of the country. People of different experiences – rural/urban, arts/science – who can come and in the first couple of weeks be students again and be exposed to the Farley Mowats of the world and the Robert Batemans and David Suzukis who can contribute something really substantial to their environmental awareness and knowledge. We'll also have professional educators involved who will examine curriculum development and how to incorporate these issues into existing curriculum. In the third week of the summer programme, the plan is that some of the teachers will become teachers again, and will use the skills they've developed to help students who have come from all across the country to be involved in an in-resident students' programme for environmental values education.

F.M. What other projects will Harmony be initiating?

M.B. Some of the most critical environmental decisions are being made by municipal politicans who have little or no environmental competence and are taking advice from people who may have vested interests. When they realize they've been had, they often have a hard time standing up in public and saying, "I made a mistake. I am going to change my vote." We believe if we can spirit them away to a place where they can loosen their ties and put on comfortable shoes, and bring them up to standard on environmental requirements, we can improve the quality of the decisions they make.

I like to think of politicians – especially local ones – as people standing in mine fields. If you don't have a map, you're going to stay put because you know it's safe. That's by and large how they behave. If we can give them a map and, even better, disarm some of the mines, then we may get better community-based decisions about waste disposal, industrial development, growth in communities.

We may also get engineers together for teaching seminars on environmental values, because they certainly need to be exposed to them. These are parts of what we are calling an Environmental Leadership Programme. We are working with several universities now to encourage a lot more environmental content in the curriculum of business and law and other disciplines.

We hope shortly to have established a public environmental learning and resource centre that can be a clearing house for information, expertise, contacts, for people and communities who are struggling with issues. If you are living in Toronto and concerned about solid waste disposal, you have an enormous wealth of information and resources available to work through the problem, but if you are living in Kirkland Lake, Ontario or Red Deer, Alberta or Sydney, Nova Scotia, your resources diminish.

Another thing we've already done is to host a forum on sustainable development at Trent University in Peterborough, Ontario. One hundred and thirty-five people attended from across the country from environment, labour, business, government and native groups – a cross-section of Canadian society who are concerned about these things, working in their own areas and having something constructive to contribute. We designed a programme that had people wrestling with the issues. They came up with some good solid discussion and hard recommendations as to how Canada can start turning itself in the direction of environmental survival.

F.M. How did the Foundation come about?

M.B. I started to realize that I was becoming an observer of nature's death, rather than a wildlife biologist. I was just recording the disappearance of caribou and grizzly bear and others. That wasn't good enough, so I began to think of what I could do that would be effective at reversing the tide. Education seemed to me to be the answer. I began looking for people who shared the commitment to resolving environmental problems through education and co-operation. I found a number of them and we put the Foundation together.

Funding was a problem. One of the significant developments was when Robert Bateman involved himself. He gave us the proceeds from a print produced on behalf of the Foundation. We've had some support from the Ontario government; and a number of individuals, large and small; a few other foundations have provided small amounts of assistance; similarly a few businesses have either provided in-kind support or financial donations.

We have a board of eight people who are in business, law, academia, with the managerial skills to make sure the organization operates as it should. They don't involve themselves in the programme content. There is an advisory council to the Foundation – about fifty people in agriculture, technology, wildlife, business, etc.; people like Stan Rowe, Stuart Hill, John Livingston, who can really contribute something to the kind of programmes we are trying to develop.

F.M. Can the general public participate directly in Harmony Foundation?

M.B. Yes. But we are not a member-based organization and we made that decision for a key reason. There are a number of organizations which unfortunately spend much of their time and resources just building membership lists. A very large percentage of their funds goes into mass mailings to get more members, and we aren't comfortable with this. Talking conservation and waste management, and then producing an avalanche of expensive fund-raising material that pours into people's homes unsolicited doesn't seem consistent with the message we are trying to get across.

As for public involvement – there are a number of communities where Harmony groups have now started up. These are learning and support groups. Montreal, Toronto, Ottawa and Calgary are already operating. They are trying to advance the Foundation's goals, to find the financial support or the people to become involved so that the effort can expand. At the same time, we make sure we have educational programmes for these people, because they want to learn as much as they want to give.

F.M. Can the general public join these groups?

M.B. Yes. We are hoping the groups will expand so that more people will be involved, not only to help the Foundation but to learn how to organize education programmes on behalf of the environment. We would like to see many clones of the Foundation, and hope people will take the initiative. We would like to see a public environmental learning and resource centre in every community, where teachers, parents, politicians, business people could find good hard information on issues; where they could meet, hopefully with some congeniality, to deal with community problems. We have to put a human face on the whole process.

F.M. You clearly see the Foundation as becoming an international organization?

M.B. The issues and approach *are* international. We have had interest already from a number of countries that would like to exchange information and see about programme development there.

F.M. But you are not in the business of empire-building.

M.B. No! We are not trying to raise money all the time to keep twenty or eighty people employed. I think you get more done by seeding opportunities and finding creative people who will take the initiative with your assistance, rather than creating bureaucrats. I didn't put this kind of personal risk and effort into bringing the Foundation to life because I wanted to be comfortable. I want to do something that's constructive and meaningful. If we can put as much of our energy as possible into environmental education programmes, cradle to grave, for children, students and adults, including those who have been professionally active for some time, then we are really going to contribute something. If we are true and consistent with that approach, then we should find more ready access to the people we need to influence.

F.M. What do you think our chances are of avoiding massive ecological disaster?

M.B. I never think in those terms because they are disabling. You are either part of the problem or part of the solution. Until the final curtain falls, there's still some glimmer of hope. We're probably in intensive care now, if not in critical condition, but the prognosis is we *can* recover if there is really serious and long-standing commitment.

I can't predict whether we will succeed. I'm going to argue like hell that it had *better* happen, and sooner rather than later. I temper my optimism by keeping my feet firmly planted and asking others to do the same. You talk to twenty- and even twelve-year-olds and many of them are quite negative about the prospects. They need optimism, but you also have to give them the straight goods and tell them it's going to be pretty tough. We have a lot of work to do, and we are the ones who have to do it. The future is now. We must actively incorporate sound environmental practices into our homes and workplaces. If we want the future to include a healthy environment, we, not someone else, must take the reponsibility.

Green Power:

Stephen Best and the International Wildlife Coalition

Now in his early forties, Stephen Best is a new-age environmental activist. Although totally committed to the cause, he is not encumbered by the romantic illusions which afflicted some of his predecessors. He is a realist who, having learned how power can be acquired, acquires it, then puts it to good use. There are those in the environmental movement who choose to try to penetrate the inner councils of the ravagers of natural life in order to *persuade* them to take a better course. Best is not one of these. He prefers to wrest power away from the spoilers and then turn it against them. The instrument with which he does this is called the International Wildlife Coalition.

S.B. I was born in Victoria on St. Patrick's Day in 1948. Later we moved to North Vancouver where we had an uneventful family life with the usual run of divorces and things like that.

I was a normal, suburban kid. We tried to buy booze when we weren't supposed to, get into bars when we weren't twenty-one, and all that. Kind of lower-middle class or upper-lower class. We would go around and hassle people on Indian reserves and in the Roman Catholic schools; they would come and hassle us in the Protestant school. We would hop trains. Russian boats would come in and you could go down and get on them. The Russian sailors took delight in trying to get these young kids drunk, and we took delight in trying to get drunk. We used to trade them our money for their money.

F.M. Were you doing anything with animals at that point?

S.B. Killing them. Usual sort of kid stuff. BB guns. There wasn't any organized hunting, but BB guns were there to kill birds and small animals with; that's what they were for. Something went by, and you would try to kill it. The idea of having any respect for wildlife was just not in the cards at all. I was more interested in getting drunk and getting laid. I had no insight into anything.

F.M. Did you watch birds? Did you have any interest in being an observer?

S.B. Nothing. I was a straight suburban teenager.

F.M. So what eventually brought you around?

S.B. I got into film production. After three or four years at the CBC I left to go freelance film editing. Then I got interested in cinematography and bought a small Arriflex 16mm camera and started practising. I got good enough at it to farm out my talents, and did some work in South America and then started producing and directing on a small scale.

Then, in 1972, Brian Davies of the International Fund for Animal Welfare wanted a film made of the harp seals, and I got the job because I was the cheapest they could find. Brian didn't have much money and I could do everything. I could go and shoot it, direct it, everything. I was a walking film studio, which was the nature of film production in those days.

This was my first experience with wildlife. The seal hunt had been roaring along for decades prior to that, and I didn't even realize there *was* a seal hunt. It sure was an eye opener for me. The first week, we went out to the Gulf of St. Lawrence herd and camped on the ice. I was supposed to get shots of the live seals, so I ran all over the place chasing after them. Finally, after fatigue set in, it dawned on me that the best thing to do was to sit down and let them come to me.

I set myself up at the edge of a blow-hole, got nice and warm and bundled up, and waited. Pretty soon the seals began to come up and look at me; inspect me; do water dances in front of me; and play games, like trying to get me wet. It was really clear after a few days that they were dog-like in terms of sociability and trust of people. One insisted on going into my little tent and I had to shoo her away. The pups would come up to me and want to be nursed. They were an absolute delight.

Also, the place was unbelievable. I had a real appreciation for images at this time, from filmmaking, but I had not seen anything that could compare to the ice, day and night. There would be fabulous sunsets, and then the Aurora. The water in the open leads turned to molten gold, with the seals' sleek heads popping up in it. Absolutely unbelievable. It really gave me a sense that I was a part of something I'd never encountered before. All of a sudden I realized there was something real here.

Nothing is more artificial than television and film production. It is the greatest con the world has ever seen. Working in that business you think you are the centre of the universe because everything swirls around you, and you are an official observer. You think what you are is important. Then to go and live with those seals in *their* world was to realize that the film world was completely unimportant.

F.M. This sounds like a conversion.

S.B. Total and instant. I could have died then. As far as I was concerned, it would have been fine. I realized at that point that all the things I had been thinking and doing and all the values I had were up for grabs. All of a sudden everything opened up. It was the sense of oneness – a sense of being a part. It then became an absolute joy filming these animals and being part of it. I stopped thinking of them as just animals I could get some shots of, and it was as if a rapport started to develop. It wasn't that we were communicating, but there was no antagonism between us. I wasn't out to bother them and they weren't the least bit concerned about me. Maybe the highest compliment you get from animals is when they ignore you and totally go about their business. As the days wore on, they knew who I was; they had it figured out, and I was a recognized part of their scene.

Then we went to Newfoundland to film the so-called hunt at the Front ice. Brian flew us in his helicopter to Mary's

Harbour first, but we couldn't get out to the ice because of fog and bad weather. Finally we worked our way down to Lewisporte and flew out from there, and a hundred miles offshore found a sealing ship in the pack ice and the seal hunt.

We took their mail out to the sealers. There was no fighting between sealers and the protesters in those days. We flew out to the ship, had lunch aboard and gave the mail to the guys, then went out on the ice and photographed them killing seals.

When I saw the first seal being killed up close, it hit me hard that these were the same animals I had been with for a week on the ice in the Gulf. I knew nothing about seal science at this point. I knew nothing about the economic or cultural significance of the hunt. I knew nothing about all the arguments people put forth about why you should and shouldn't kill seals. But I knew there was something deeply wrong about this. Something *felt* wrong. There was no rationale. Since then, I've constructed all sorts of rational arguments against sealing, but they just reinforce what I *know* to be the truth of the matter.

F.M. This was a purely subjective feeling?

S.B. Totally. To me it's at the core of being. If we were talking about God, I'd call it a religious experience. But it's even beyond that because there's no artificiality to it. It's a real thing. This creature here killing that creature there for no good, *natural* reason. I wouldn't have had trouble if it was a killer whale that came up and ate the seal. That is a direct and natural relationship based on essential need.

F.M. Would you have had any trouble if you had been out on the ice with an Inuit and he was hunting seals?

S.B. It would depend on the situation. I wouldn't have any trouble if he and I were out on the ice hungry and had to eat seal. But I have real trouble when the Inuit take seals to be sold into the fur fashion market or trinket market.

We are each of us biological entities. We are as much a part of the system as plants and bacteria. Every biological entity eventually displaces another. I don't care if you are vegetarian or if you are into a macrobiotic diet and only eat rice;

some land got cleared away to grow some rice. I don't care if you're a hunter-gatherer, that you are just grubbing for roots; something else didn't get the root you got. The question is how much displacement are we entitled to engage in and, to me, shouldn't modern man be moving towards as little displacement as possible?

If you don't *have* to kill, *don't* kill. I would even go further. I would say we, as humans, should work to develop the knowledge and wisdom to *enhance* the lives of other animals. A while ago I was going through Genesis on the question of man having "dominion" over other animals. That is often used to excuse what we do to exploit nature – but if you think about it, if indeed we *were* given dominion, that to me means care. If I'm given dominion over IBM, that doesn't mean I'm given the right to exploit the people who work there; in fact, quite the contrary. The responsibility of having dominion over something is to protect and improve its existence.

F.M. It should imply being a guardian?

S.B. A guardian and enhancer of the quality of the lives of those things. If you are a parent and have dominion over your children, your job is to make their lives as full as you can – not to exploit them. And as a species, I think that's what we should be moving towards in relation to other species that share this planet. That gives *us* value as a species. What value do we have if our main object is to rape everything we can; go for maximum sustainable yield; turn everything into Sony TV sets and Rolex watches. We don't have worth when we become destroyers of other species. It seems to me that one of the higher callings we can aspire to is to make our presence on the planet of value to all living things. Is that altruism?

F.M. If our presence on the planet benefits all of life, then we are ultimately benefiting ourselves as well.

S.B. It can also give the individual tremendous self-respect and enrich a sense of worth. It's truly important for life on earth that I am here is something we have to be able to say as individuals and as a species. Clearly we spend too much time killing other forms of life and each other, just to *physically* enrich ourselves.

F.M. Mindless production for witless consumption, and the hell with the consequences.
S.B. That's exactly what it is. If we think we've got trouble now, wait until a billion and a half Chinese come on line, and they all want Hyundais.
F.M. What did you do after the experience on the ice?
S.B. There was still a tremendous amount of inertia in me so I continued making films, but I helped out Brian and IFAW whenever I could. The idea of actually going out and doing something overt, becoming a mover and shaker, never even dawned on me. Then, in 1980, I was asked by Brian to put together some sort of strategies I thought might work, because the seal hunt was still going full tilt, and asking people to write to the prime minister or painting seal pups green as Greenpeace was doing was all rather unproductive.

The bottom line was that the same number of seals were still being killed. An awful lot of people had gone out to see the slaughter, and a lot of film had run through cameras, but the body count remained the same. So I started looking around at things that had worked on other types of issues, and it slowly became clear to me that the way you make things work is by acquiring power. You do this in one of two ways – putting aside the third way, building a standing army. You either do it economically or you do it through politics.

The International Fund for Animal Welfare had by that time developed some economic clout – membership had been increasing – but they had no political clout. I recommended they start getting involved in electoral politics by making sealing an electoral issue. You didn't have to defeat a candidate necessarily, but if you can sway the vote by maybe two per cent, in some constituencies you can actually change the outcome; but you have to target the ones you are going to affect. You don't need a mandate from the whole public. You only need to affect a small number of candidates, and only in selected constituencies.

I made up quite a long document on this, and Brian asked me if I wanted to work for them full time. I agreed and started putting together a political machine for IFAW by getting in touch with political consultants, media people who were involved in politics; learning about polling, all the ways modern political campaigns and politics are run, which is far removed from what the average voter thinks is happening. It's really an industry in its own right, the manipulation of the political process. And it works.

However, the ruling political parties didn't like anyone else playing that game, and the federal government proposed new laws to stop groups that weren't registered political parties being involved in political campaigns. We went through the process of registering as a political party – but then the government proposals were struck down by the Supreme Court. Meantime, we were also learning about direct-mail campaigns as a means of filling our war chest in preparation for the next federal election.

Then in November 1981, we heard that Stanley Johnson, a British member of the Parliament of the European Community, had put a proposal in the European Parliament to ban the importation of seal products into Europe. We obviously had to support Johnson, and this was a good chance to try out our new electoral gambit. We started by getting an ad campaign together, and a lobbying campaign, and collecting the names of the members of the European Parliament. Then we went off to Europe and presented Stanley Johnson and various other MPs involved with a complete plan to get his proposal through.

Bear in mind Europe was eighty-nine per cent of the market for seal skins; if you killed that, it would be very dramatic. We knew when the ban was going to come up in the European Parliament. We also had information that the Canadian government was going to do a big, fancy, pro-sealing campaign during the week before the vote, so *we* decided to do *two* campaigns. The first would be a pro-ban campaign a month before the vote, when we would have the attention of the Parliamentarians to ourselves, because no one would be opposing us. The second campaign would be timed for the vote week and aimed at discrediting what the Canadian government was doing.

We pulled in all sorts of people and groups under our umbrella, while other environmental groups went at it on their own. We called everybody I could think of who knew anything about seals, and eventually had four hundred people lobbying the parliamentary delegates.

Now, obviously, you don't do all that with one person sitting in an office. We had to open bank accounts, and get stuff printed and so forth. We took over ten rooms at the Hilton Hotel in Strasbourg where the parliament met. We had video equipment to show people films of the seals. We had scientific experts like Dr. Dave Lavigne and Dr. Sidney Holt. We had really good people lobbying – people who cared – and a politician is hard-pressed not to give time to someone who cares about something in a legitimate way.

We also had a huge direct-mail campaign going in the United Kingdom, and an ad campaign going all over Europe to get people to write to their European Parliamentary representatives. Normally the reps would get maybe eight letters a week – now they were getting eighty or more a day, just about seals. There was tremendous grass-roots pressure.

Then in the last week, the Canadian government sent in their team which included an Inuit delegation sent over by the Hudson's Bay Company, people from Newfoundland and so on. They had a very bad programme. A lot of the success we had was because the Canadian government contingent was so inept – particularly the Department of Fisheries and Oceans.

In dealing with the government's campaign, we made a point of only using information to counter it that came from official sources. We used Government of Canada documents to discredit what they were saying, because what they were saying wasn't true. When they would claim the seals were eating all the fish, we would have documents from the North Atlantic Fisheries Organization presented by Federal Department of Fisheries scientists, proving the seals don't eat all that much commercial fish. Or when the government would say the Humane Society of the United States and the Audubon Society all supported the seal hunt, we would produce letters *to* the government from those organizations saying they did not support the hunt. We discredited them all the way through, until it got to the point where the European parliamentarians just didn't believe the Canadian government delegation. When the vote was taken, the European Parliament voted to ban the import of seal products by something like 160 to 10.

But this was only the first step. The next was to convince the European Commission.* That was fairly routine. They just drafted the regulation in accordance with the vote of the Parliament.

The next step was a tight one. This was the Council of Ministers of the European Economic Community. This was the final administrative level necessary to validate the parliamentary vote. We had two countries that were opposed to the ban – Britain and Germany – and you only need any two of France, England and Germany to veto a proposal from the Parliament.

All the reports we were getting were that it wasn't going to go through the Council. We poured mail into Mrs. Thatcher, but she was opposed to any ban. However, in Germany there was an election coming up. German politics are often won or lost by a fraction of a percentage. Marginal votes. Brian decided to concentrate on Germany. We set up a budget and campaign for what promised to be a dirty fight. Canada threatened Germany with fishing sanctions in our territorial waters if she supported the ban, so we ran a campaign saying Helmut Kohl was caving in to Canadian pressure.

The campaign was big, broad and unique enough to get carried in all the media. To top that off, we were putting full-page ads in all the German papers. Newspapers in Europe are quite different from here; they have some real impact. And the polls began shifting. A significant number of people began saying they would vote against Helmut Kohl if he vetoed the seal ban. The days before the vote, I recall sitting

*The European Commission, headquartered in Brussels, is the legislative and administrative power of the European Community.

in Brussels with Brian and Stanley Johnson and getting one report that the Germans were going to vote for the ban, then another report that they were going to vote against it. It was that close, but in the end they voted for it. The only compromise that was made (and it has come back to haunt us) was it would ban whitecoats only. We were hoping for all seals; failing that, young of the year. But the ban went through and it was that tight right up to the last minute.

After that I went to England and did a boycott of Canadian fish products right away, because we didn't want the Canadian government to subsidize an ongoing seal hunt, which is what they intended to do now that the biggest part of the market was gone. We needed to bring pressure directly on Ottawa, and we did that with a boycott of Canadian fish products in the U.K.

Everyone laughed at the idea until some stores stopped buying Canadian fish. You only need a few major retailers to do that to start a chain reaction. The same quantity of Canadian fish as ever was going into Britain, but the price dropped. Fresh fish are a perishable item and, if they are frozen, they cost money to store. They have to move them, so down goes the price. The beauty of a boycott isn't that you stop the product being sold, it's that you lower the price, and that means lowering the profit. That's the real power of the boycott. So now the pressure was on the Canadian government from Canadian fish producers to *not* subsidize the seal hunt.

It was a good campaign. We had fish-and-chip shops all over the U.K. with signs saying "We do not carry Canadian fish." We had a twenty-foot-high inflatable figure of a sealer that did the tour of all the towns. Something like that always gets in the press. We had posters everywhere of someone killing seals, and Canadian fish attached to it.

F.M. You also tried the fish boycott in the U.S.A. but it was much less effective. Why?

S.B. The biggest Canadian fish market was the U.S., but going into the U.S. with a boycott was too big an undertaking for us to handle. The U.K. was manageable. It was also self-financing – and that is one of the keys to fighting effectively for wildlife. Although we spent roughly $3 million on the seal issue in Europe, we came out of it in the black. The boycott of Canadian fish products in the U.K. increased the U.K. membership until the whole thing became self-financing. That is the only way to go. If you put a certain amount of money into a campaign, then when that money is gone, the campaign is over. So all the opposition has to do is wait you out. If you run your campaign with an ongoing fund-raising component through direct mail, constant membership or people buying a product, then it can go for ever.

After the boycott came a political campaign. The Thatcher government was acting as Canada's surrogate in the European Community and there was real fear that by working behind the scenes, they were going to undermine a renewal of the ban on the import of whitecoats. Brian Davies wanted to "give Mrs. Thatcher a bloody nose" in the upcoming British election, so I went to the U.K. and we put together a full-blown campaign. We targeted fifty or sixty ridings, out of the six hundred-odd, which were clearly marginal. They were also in areas where people were interested in animals. We distributed publications that claimed Mrs. Thatcher (the polls were showing that she was weak on national health, unemployment and the environment) was uncaring. We had ads on this theme running in cinemas, newspapers and magazines.

Some people – even some of our British supporters – were absolutely scandalized by all this. Our office got two thousand letters of complaint for going after Mrs. Thatcher. Our English staff said I had to stop. Ian MacPhail, the national co-ordinator in England, was getting letters from Prince Philip's secretary asking what was the meaning of this terrible campaign. Ian came banging on my door saying Prince Philip was furious, but I said, "It's okay, Prince Philip can't vote." The bottom line was that a couple of Labour MPs later said they got elected because of it, and about three weeks after the election I got a call from the central office of the Conservative party wanting to know if we could have a little chat. So we had one of those wonderful, warm, heart-to-heart chats during which they said they thought our campaign had been disgraceful – that this sort of thing should not be done – and you couldn't win or lose an election on this sort of issue anyway. But since animals *were* on the political agenda, what was it that we wanted?

I said I thought they should speak to Brian, but what we would like was to have the government of the U.K. become supportive to the protection of marine mammals, and that they support the ban in Europe on the seals, and that they support campaigns to protect whales. We didn't get into fox hunting and all that.

Britain is now one of the major supporters of the sealing ban and is totally supportive of the International Whaling Commission. When the pilot whale slaughter in the Faeroe Islands recently became a major conservation issue, it was Britain who stood up and said you can't kill animals this way. When you see a minister of the Crown on BBC saying harpooning whales is cruel, and you might as well throw a spear into a cow and drag her across a field, you know that somebody has drawn the right conclusions.

F.M. In 1985 you left IFAW with two other IFAW senior people to form a new organization. Originally called IKARE – Individuals Against Killing Animals for Recreational Enjoyment – which is one hell of a mouthful – it was renamed the International Wildlife Coalition. Does this mean you and Brian Davies have gone separate ways in the environmental movement?

S.B. In March 1988 we at IWC were getting geared up again for the seal issue. We were absolutely convinced the seal hunt was on the increase and that the reports of its demise were wrong. We were considering another boycott of Canadian fish products – or a pledge to boycott – when Brian dropped into our office to talk to us.

He said that the Department of Fisheries and Oceans had assured him they were going to ban the whitecoat hunt entirely, together with the offshore hunt of all seals by large vessels. So he felt that a boycott would have a counter-productive effect on government policy at this juncture, and that if we all kept cool, the seal hunt would eventually dry up and vanish. Well, the discussion was very amicable, but we didn't see it his way. Frankly, we thought he had been conned. My experience is that your ability to win conservation battles is geared to how much pressure you can bring to bear. That isn't done by having coffee with the opposition. They've got to know you can call a boycott, can change votes, or something like that. But Brian felt he had a good rapport with them now, and that they really wanted to defuse the issue.

We remained skeptical, but agreed to wait and see what happened. Meanwhile, we sent a team of researchers and investigators to Newfoundland to check things out, and the reports they sent back were not consistent with a real decline in the seal hunt. So we took a harder look and, amongst other things, found there were plans to start processing seals into meat for ranch-raised mink and foxes. We also uncovered evidence of a slaughter of harp seals apparently undertaken solely to collect male sex organs for sale to the Oriental aphrodisiac market. It was clear to us that the seal hunt was far from over. Despite the public perception that it had ended in 1985, it had continued through '86, '87 and '88, increasing every year. In 1988 over 70,000 seals, mostly harps, were killed. That was about 40,000 more than in 1987. The evidence we had from everyone we talked to in Newfoundland was that the Federal Department of Fisheries and the maritime provincial departments and an industrial pro-sealing group were working to get it up even more, and were hoping eventually to reach the 1970s' quota which still stands officially at 186,000 seals per year. They thought if they didn't kill whitecoats but killed raggedy jackets and beaters, which is what young harps only a few weeks old are called, they could slip what they were doing past the media. And in fact it worked, and the public hasn't been told that the seal hunt is heating up again.

So we've made the commitment that we are going to shift a lot of our effort back onto the seal issue. Brian called recently to find out what was going on. I gather that although he'd been telling people the seal hunt was over, he now realizes it is not. We are gearing up for an on-going fight.

F.M. Not without cause! I predict that the collapse of North Atlantic cod stocks, due to our ruthless over-exploitation of them, will be blamed on the seals. So you can expect Ottawa to fund a massive slaughter of the ice seals, whether or not there is any market for them.

S.B. We're prepared to fight the seal slaughter, no matter how it gets disguised, as long as we have public support to do so. To us, seventy thousand is a full-blown seal hunt. Had it been declining in the past few years, we would have walked away and done work for elephants. But as long as the hunt continues, *and* continues to grow, we'll be in there slugging. I won't make any deals with the government.

As I see it, I represent a couple of constituencies. One, I represent a constituency of wildlife that doesn't want to be killed, and, two, I represent roughly one hundred thousand people who support the International Wildlife Coalition and who don't want seals killed. As long as the support is there, why would you not fight it? What would you make a deal for?

F.M. The theory might be that if you can make a deal, you can switch your resources to some other problem.

S.B. That's no advantage. The more issues you are involved in, the more people you can train. And the movement badly needs a larger body of trained people. That's crucial. Also, if the issues are formed properly, they fund themselves. It's from the issues that you build your membership list, your trained people, the infrastructure, the research structure to fight all those things. Issues are our product line. Give us the resources; we will solve the issue. Service industry.

F.M. Some people are bothered by that approach. They say it's too crass.

S.B. My attitude is that if I've got a cheque book and I'm reading my paper and there's something that really disturbs me that's happening to animals and I can't do anything about it personally, I *can* pay somebody else to do it for me, and far better that I should pay a professional than send my money to an amateur, no matter how good his intentions. That's my approach and I don't hide it. I really want to turn the animal welfare movement into a huge industry. We have a health industry to fix people, a social welfare industry to care for people. I don't see any reason for not having an animal welfare industry to care for animals. "Managing" wildlife is big business now because slaughtering wildlife always *has* been big business. So to me that's the only way to go. You need to approach the organization of an effective conservation movement from a business standpoint. When you see the array of talent lined up against you in direct, paid lobbying of government by animal exploiters, when you see the millions and millions of advertising dollars put into marketing of these wild animal products, you get some idea of what we are up against and why we have to hustle money.

F.M. There's a distinction here that too few people make. The money spent on lobbying and propagandizing by animal *exploiters* doesn't come out of their own pockets – it comes out of their customers' pockets, and the customers have no say in the matter. On the other hand, if someone *chooses* to give money to an animal *protection* organization, that is an act of conscious and informed volition. Doesn't it bother you when, say, fur industry spokesmen accuse groups like yours of milking the public to raise funds?

S.B. My feeling is that the fur industry, and all animal product industries, sell dead animals for us to eat or put on our backs or otherwise consume. I sell live animals that are going to go on living in the natural world. That's the difference. The techniques both sides use are much the same. I'm not worried if someone says I shouldn't be using direct marketing techniques, advertising, television, P.R. techniques, talented lawyers, graphic artists, advertising people and so on. All I am interested in, in the short term, is the body count. If there are more dead animals today, I'm not doing my job right. You have to go by real results. Did you get a conservation law passed? Fewer animals killed?

My experience has been "hire good people." I remember getting criticized in Europe about spending so much money. But we got what we paid for. I have difficulty with the Better Business Bureau. They ask us all kinds of questions about

finances that they'd never think of asking the Ford Motor Company. They ask Ford about their product and the service they give. Why don't they ask me that? Charities often get asked the wrong sort of questions.
F.M. How big is your staff?
S.B. We have about thirty people working for us, of whom half are involved in administration. We need that many, partly because of all the paper crap government demands from us. But the big job is maintaining the relationship with supporters. We thank every donor, which takes time, but it keeps the donors with us. Nothing is more important to us in terms of our ability to do the work than those supporters. From an ethical standpoint and from a business standpoint, you try for as close as you can get to a one-to-one relationship. You are representing them; they are your customers; you have to treat them with the courtesy that trust deserves. Everybody on our staff earns his keep, and that's the key. There's no money at the end of the year; it all comes in and it all goes out.

Decisions at the IWC concerning issues, strategy, etc. are for the most part made by the people working in the field. The Board of Trustees, made up of Dan Morast, Donna Hart and me, is responsible for insuring the organization conforms to the requirements of numerous regulatory agencies and is managed in an efficient and effective manner, and for determining how resources are to be dispersed to various projects. Obviously there are never enough funds or personnel available for all of the programmes that the field people can identify as needing attention.
F.M. You still haven't told me why you left IFAW.
S.B. Dan Morast, Donna Hart and I had the idea of pulling together into a coalition all the small environmental groups such as ARK II, the Kangaroo Protection Foundation, National Animal Rights Association, Care for the Wild, Cloverleaf Wildlife Rehabilitation Centre, and so on, bringing their mailing lists into one location and applying modern management and fund-raising techniques so they would have the money to do what they wanted to do. Our experience was

that there were many good folks around who were unable to get their organizations above that critical mass where they were not bogged down by day-to-day administration. It wasn't a project that fitted into the IFAW structure, so we set out to do it independently.

It has worked out very successfully in some areas. A classic example would be Mary Newman of the Kangaroo Protection Foundation. She had got herself really deep in debt with some direct-mail fund-raisers that didn't work, and was going to close the organization. We paid off her debt, put her on salary and gave her a budget so all she had to do was fight for kangaroos. We took over the administration stuff, the fund-raising aspect of it. So she's now in Washington working on bills banning kangaroo products, and also working on elephant protection in Africa.

In the U.K. we had the same situation with Care for the Wild. The organization actually had a fair amount of cash, but a declining mailing list, and they were losing money every month. We turned them around and they are now solvent and involved in the seal issue. In Canada, it worked out well with Anne Doncaster and the National Animal Rights Association. Anne now works full-time for our organization. Before, she was busy doing administrative work; now she is full time for animals.

Small organizations just get overwhelmed with the administration. That's what kills them. When they find they have to raise the money, give receipts for the money, have an audit and all this, they realize they are not doing anything for animals; they are doing administration all day long.

F.M. I wish IWC had been around when I was president of Project Jonah in Canada. Almost every nickel that came in went out in paperwork. We never had enough time or money to do much for the whales.

S.B. We systematize all that. You end up with really good activists who don't waste their time doing accounting, book-keeping, membership analysis – which most of them don't do well anyway.

F.M. What are the guiding principles of the IWC?

S.B. The philosophy is that we work to prevent the killing of wildlife; we work to prevent cruelty to wildlife; we work to prevent the destruction of wildlife habitat. We'll tackle any single issue we feel we can do, depending on what talent we have, what resources we can raise and so forth. In addition, we are involved in simple funding operations such as writing a cheque to people who are doing work to save flamingos in Bolivia, to reintroduce otters into the British countryside, to maintain a sanctuary in Kenya run by Daphne Sheldrake who takes care of rhinos and elephants whose parents have been killed by poachers, to a similar situation in Australia where a lady takes care of young kangaroos whose parents have been killed off, to a fellow in Montana to work with grizzly bears. We put money into trying to stop the wolf kill, and into things where we take a much larger commitment, like the grey seals on Canada's Atlantic coast which are being decimated. We are upgrading our campaign against the fur trade. We are working to have a ban on importation of kangaroo products into the U.S. We got a bill introduced in the U.S. to ban the importation of ivory. We are moving heavily into the elephant area. We have a whale adoption project to raise funds to protect whales. We produce a teacher's kit, which goes out free to schools, on humpback whales and whales in general. We are publishing a consumer's guide to what's being sold in the U.S. that has kangaroo products in it. We are doing a book on the fur trade. We have published a book in the U.K. which is a re-working of Bill Jordan's book, *Care for the Wild* – a handbook on how to care for wildlife, so if you have a bird hit your window you can help it.

Much of our work deals with international situations where the products come from third-world countries and are sold into western democracies. Hopefully we can alter the taste for wildlife products before the Asian market really opens up.

F.M. That *is* a terrifying prospect.

S.B. If you ever get all affluent people there wanting fur coats, you've got a real problem with animal survival.

Although we are fiscally conservative, our core supporters are radical and we do what they want us to do. They are essentially non-consumptive. They want animals to be *protected*. They are preservationists. I suspect that if many of the supporters of the World Wildlife Fund knew what it actually stood for, they wouldn't want to be part of it; the same applies to the Canadian Wildlife Federation. Greenpeace got nothing but flak from *their* supporters when they bailed out of the fur issue. People *want* animals to be protected. End of story. They don't want compromises, and that gives you hope.

On the other hand, the opposition is very powerful. The most powerful wildlife organization in the world is the National Wildlife Federation in Washington. It is all business from the word go, on a world-class scale. I would like to see *our* organization run like it. Unfortunately, they are the bad guys representing the hunting/fishing interests. They are the most powerful lobby in Washington. They make everybody else pale by comparison. They have millions upon millions of dollars, and really top, top people work for them. I have trouble with their ethics, but I don't for one minute question their efficacy. You are not going to find any other so-called conservation organization that even comes close to their effectiveness. The Canadian Wildlife Federation is Canada's version of the same organization.

F.M. How about Greenpeace? They had huge popular support and income at one time.

S.B. Greenpeace, for the most part, except on whales – they are extremely effective on whales – tends to go for publicity-stunt-type operations. Someone will camp on top of a smoke-stack or whatever, which is all well and good in exciting public opinion, but if you then don't use the public opinion in some constructive way it's a bit of a waste. Greenpeace did great publicity for the seals, and because Brian Davies was there to take advantage of all the publicity, it was very useful. But they don't begin to have the clout of the National Wildlife Federation, or even the clout the Canadian Wildlife Federation has.

F.M. What do you think a good wildlife *preservation* organization should be doing, and how should it do it?

S.B. To my way of thinking, a good wildlife organization has got to address the business aspects. The desire to fight for animals is a given. How do you do that effectively? You do it by having a large base of loyal support, large sums of money and really good people. That doesn't necessarily mean they have to live and die by what happens to wildlife. Your lawyers or ad people, etc. don't need to have a burning desire to protect the environment, but they must be top notch at what they do.

The organization has got to constantly expand. If it doesn't, people get frustrated and don't want to come to work any more. A good organization should think in international terms because there are virtually no purely *national* environmental issues any more. Even local issues are often international in essence. Hunting in Canada, for instance, is an international process with people coming from Europe and the United States to do much of the killing. We buy products internationally – including ivory and fur products.

The overall feeling I have about virtually every organization I have dealt with – even those you would think would be most radical – is that they are afraid of power. Afraid to use it. I think you've got to be very willing to use it. It's one thing being a protester and saying, "Don't do that"; it's another thing when you can actually *make* them not do it.

The main thing is, any organization worth its salt has to be willing to fight like hell. No pussy-footing. You have to acquire power, not to hoard for your own sake but to use for the sake of the animals. The world of man is based on power. The bureaucracy in Ottawa is based on power. If you have power and don't exercise it, it means nothing and you get nowhere.

F.M. How do you react to the pessimist's view that maybe we are already so far down the tube that there's no backing out?

S.B. I don't think we're that far. Human beings have a tremendous capacity to adjust and adapt and change, and ideas can have an amazing impact. Whether this one will or not, I don't know. But that's no reason for not giving it everything you've got.

F.M. You're a power-hungry optimist.

S.B. Exactly. But we're at a time when unique forces have come together. Not only have they come together to destroy the planet, another set has come together to try and save it.

The money and the educated following that are available in the western democracies are trend-setters. For a very short period of time we will be able to establish patterns about what will occur in the foreseeable future. All the tools – although not all easily accessible – are there. If they can be used effectively, we might be able to change things for the better. If we can change environmental attitudes in North America and Europe in the next few years, and if we can get *our* act together, it may be possible to do the same thing in the rest of the world.

The idea of care for other animals is a very new phenomenon in the West, but then the concept of universal human rights is relatively new too. So I think there's hope.

Gaia Women:

by Elizabeth May

Although titular leadership of most major environmental organizations had become a male prerogative by the end of the 1980s, it was not always so. The movement drew much of its initial energy and leadership from women. They were amongst the first to sound the call to arms, not because they had become rationally persuaded that the living world was in trouble, but because they *knew* it was.

On a summer day in 1973 on a flight from Halifax to Toronto, I found myself seated beside a young woman and we talked about the environment and the way things were going then. I do not recall her name, but I remember with great clarity what she said.

"When the womb of our Earth mother is being hurt, women feel it inside themselves. We feel the pain. And we know we have to try and defend and protect her if we or our kids are going to have a chance to survive."

Women provided much of the leadership (remember Rachel Carson) for the great crusade in its formative period, and, although men now dominate its upper ranks (having structured it to fit their logical perceptions), women continue to provide enormous impetus through their enduring passion - and compassion.

In addition to Vicki Miller and Elizabeth May, I had intended to talk with several other women who have been or still are in the forefront of the movement, but was prevented from doing so by factors I could not control. Perhaps it was just as well, for in desperation I asked Elizabeth May if she would do it for me. She responded with the *Gaia Women*.

During the late '70s and early '80s I was often asked: "Why are most of the leaders of the environmental movement women?" The reason for that question would not be readily apparent today, either in scanning the interviews in this book or in reviewing the mastheads of national environmental groups. The environmental movement is a fair mirror of society, so when an organization becomes established, incorporated, bureaucraticized and blessed with revenue, paid staff and an executive director, said executive director will usually be male.

However, in Nova Scotia at the start of the eighties, when almost all those working against herbicide spraying, uranium mining and other environmental threats were volunteers spending their own money and devoting huge amounts of unpaid time to the cause, society was mirrored once again – and the majority of identifiable "leaders" were women.

I was one of them. We buzzed around the province trying to keep up with the demand for environmental speakers. We appeared nightly in church halls and libraries, debating the salaried spokes*men* of industry and government. Although many men *were* involved in the environmental front, the public impression was of an army of Amazons – Donna Smyth, Gillian Thomas, Susan Holtz, Liz Calder, Gwen Phillips and me, to name but half a dozen.

In response to the question "Why are women in the forefront?" each of us had a different answer. The politically correct version was: "Men in Nova Scotia are worried about speaking out, for fear of losing their jobs." The practical version: "Women are a little freer to take on these issues. And, as mothers, we care about our children and so we get involved." And then there was my answer, for which I was roundly criticized by politically correct feminists.

My answer was and remains that women are essentially *different* from men. The things that *matter* to us are different.

We are the yin to their yang. We operate more from a left-brained intuitive thought process. We are biologically and spiritually connected to the cosmos, its planetary shifts, the earth's tides and the phases of the moon. We are more nurturing, more concerned with the flow and flux of life – people, plants, animals, rivers, even seas. Consciously or not, we feel ourselves part of Gaia, part of a living, planetary whole that nurtures all of us. It is to Gaia that we relate, to that universal life force which, given a chance, will heal itself of the wounds inflicted on her by *man*kind.

Women are, by nature, much more *selfless* than men. Although predominantly unpaid, or at least lower paid than their male counterparts, they tend to have the highest profile at the grass-roots where their most tireless labours are performed. They are generally unconcerned with competitive issues like whether taking on a certain cause will enhance their reputations or advance their careers. The women I want to tell you about would be baffled that anyone should think in such terms when we are faced with the problem of saving the planet. Our Gaia role models are women like Dr. Helen Caldicott from Australia, and Drs. Rosalie Bertell and Ursula Franklin from Canada. When we grow up, we want to be like them. Wise women.

We have sisters all around the globe. The Chipko movement in India was started by peasant women who could see what their husbands could not – that the loss of the forest meant no fuel for cooking, no water from the desiccated streams, and a harsh change to their climate. So they went out en masse and hugged the trees. When the tree cutters came, the women would not let go. "Chipko" literally means "to hug." The Chipko movement has spread to many parts of India, fighting the conversion of native mixed forest to commercial monocultures of imported eucalyptus. Men have joined the ranks, but women were the first to embrace the trees.

In Africa, women started the Greenbelt movement, the replanting of trees to fight the advancing desert. In the Philippines, Sister Ida Valesquez led the fight against a nuclear power plant which Marcos wanted to build, and she still fights the dumping of mine tailings into the rich fishing waters of the archipelago.

In Malaysia, a young woman lawyer, Meena Raman, was arrested and placed in solitary confinement for the crime of fighting the dumping of radioactive thorium by a subsidiary of Mitsubishi, and of defending the indigenous people of Borneo who had blocked logging roads in Sarawak in a desperate attempt to preserve their dwindling rainforest home. Meena did not *have* to endure such a fate. Her family was wealthy, and she was of the highest caste. But she chose to fight for the planet. After weeks in jail she was finally released – no specific charge ever having been laid. Within days she was back in court fighting the radioactive waste case. Her expert witness was Dr. Rosalie Bertell of Canada.

Rosalie Bertell is the bane of the nuclear industry. I once overheard two pro-nuclear legal flacks comparing notes about their experiences fighting the anti-nuclear movement in Canada. "You wouldn't believe it," one said to the other, "but when I got to court the other side was represented by a little old lady who was also a scientist, who was also a *nun*, for Chrissakes!" Exactly.

Rosalie started her career as a mathematician and was soon employed to help develop weapons systems. Thousands of people world-wide do such work. Developing better ways to kill people; better ways to poison them; better ways to destroy life with insecticides, herbicides, fungicides, rodenticides, algaecides. They are mostly decent people. They have wives or husbands, and children. Their friends do not think of them as monsters. They do not think of themselves as monsters. They have perfected the ability to disassociate themselves and their work from its ultimate purpose. If they did not do this work, they tell themselves, someone else would. Other people would still build bombs, pollute rivers, create toxic waste. This is called situational ethics. Personal responsiblity and morality is submerged in the vast, amoral anonymity of the "system," for whom *no one* bears responsibility.

Rosalie Bertell knew that this was not to be her life. She

became a sister in the Order of Grey Nuns and began what would become her life's work, the study of the effects of low-level radiation on the unborn, on children, on the elderly, on us all.

She now works out of the International Institute of Concern for Public Health in Toronto. She maintains an exhausting schedule, travelling to wherever she is needed to battle the dangers of nuclear pollution. She helped us in Nova Scotia, testifying about the dangers of uranium tailings and of radon gas. At the time of this writing, she was still commuting to Malaysia to provide expert evidence on the lethal effects of thorium being dumped by the subsidiary of Mitsubishi. She has been subjected to heavy intimidation and at least one attempt upon her life. But nothing deflects her from her work. She was recognized in *Harrowsmith* magazine in the spring of 1989 for her environmental dedication. And that was unusual, for she is rarely honoured. She is so self-effacing, so modest and gentle a warrior that she is often missed when the medals are handed out.

There are hundreds of Canadian women like her – largely unknown and unsung heroines, who work without reward or recognition in the cause of planetary survival. Maisie Schiell, in her seventies, has been campaigning against the excesses of Saskatchewan's uranium industry for decades. She even took the federal nuclear regulatory agency, Atomic Energy of Canada Limited, to court for its failure to impose safe guidelines. Supported by Grandma's Environmental Fund, she is unstoppable. Also in northern Saskatchewan, a beautiful young Métis woman, Vye Bouvier, organizes opposition to the spread of uranium mines. She lives for a good portion of every year in the bush, as her Indian ancestors have always done. Content with the simplest livelihood, she spends the vast bulk of her time and all her journalistic talents trying to protect the northern forest world from desecration and destruction.

In New Brunswick, the nuclear industry also has a female thorn or two in its side. One of them is Janice Harvey. When I first met Janice in 1979, she was a prim and proper young school teacher. She was born and raised on a blessed cluster of rocks known as Grand Manan Island. Her father was manager of Connor's fish canning plant, where most people on the island worked. When Janice was in her teens she joined the rows of ladies with hairnets and lightning quick fingers, who packed sardines at the plant. But eventually she left home to attend university and teacher's college. She got married and settled down, waiting to be promoted from substitute to full-time teacher.

In 1979 she had become concerned about New Brunswick's first-ever nuclear plant (then being built at Point Lepreau) after she read about the accident at Three Mile Island. Not content with the official line – "No one was killed – the accident just proves how safe nuclear power is" – she sought books on the subject, and the more she read, the more disquieted she became. She decided to attend the Maritime's first anti-nuclear gathering in December of that year, and this is where I met her.

Dr. Gordon Edwards, full-time volunteer head of the Canadian Coalition for Nuclear Responsibility (another unsung hero who deserves more than singing), had come from Montreal to brief us on the technical and political nature of the nuclear juggernaut. There were brain-storming sessions afterwards, and since a federal election campaign had just been announced, I suggested we should all run for Parliament as a way of publicizing our concerns. I talked Gordon Edwards into running against Prime Minister Trudeau in Montreal, and agreed to run against Allan J. MacEachen in my home riding of Cape Breton Highlands-Canso. One by one we committed ourselves to run in our own areas. All except Janice. As a product of generations of residents of Grand Manan, she was worried about what people would think. Neighbours always see everything in a small town and the last thing you want to do is to be controversial. It just isn't done. So she wrestled with herself. The conflict was written all over her face – the clash between conviction and personal peace. She chose conviction. "O.K. I'll do it. I'll run in Grand

Manan." Then she added with a laugh, "I can't believe I'm doing this!"

Once committed to the "Small Party," as we called ourselves, she ran one helluva campaign. She spoke at all-candidates meetings. She gave numerous television and radio interviews. She spoke in high schools. Reasonable, rational and persuasive, she had her facts straight and she impressed lifelong Grits and Tories alike. On election night, of the thirteen of us in six different provinces who ran, only Janice's name made it to the television reports. She was the only one of us to get more than one per cent of the vote.

For Janice, the campaign represented the point of no return. Although she continued to hope for that full-time teaching position, volunteer environmental work took up an ever-increasing amount of her time. Whenever the New Brunswick Electrical Power Commission issued a pro-nuclear press release, Janice would be ready with a devastating critique. Her name was in the news a lot. People with full-time teaching jobs, and the people who give them out, warned her, with the subtle tyranny of the well-meaning, that she was spoiling her chances for a permanent position. This just made her angry. She knew she was a competent teacher. She knew she had already waited longer than others for a permanent appointment. She did not really need people to tell her why she was being over-looked.

Her husband, a thoroughly nice person, agreed in general with the positions she took. At first he joined her on demonstrations. But the woman on television, the self-confident crusader who knew exactly what she was talking about, was not the woman he had married. Eventually they divorced. Janice Harvey was no longer living the conventional life she had assumed for herself. She had jumped off the career track, abandoning the safety of a marriage, a home, a job. This was not the liberated decision of an emancipated woman. This was a sacrifice for selfless conviction. In 1983 Janice became executive director of the Conservation Council of New Brunswick. The Council had existed for thirteen years before

Janice took it over and it had been politically very conservative. It had been slow to oppose such threats as budworm spraying, preferring to focus on safer issues like pointing out the energy savings from proper insulation. Janice brought tremendous change. Although she kept all that was best about it, she expanded the Council and herself to encompass an ever-increasing range of issues. The Council began championing safe groundwater and documenting the risk from leaking underground gasoline storage tanks. It started an organic gardening demonstration project on a farm outside Fredericton. It uncovered a local "Love Canal" – a grotesque, gooey mess of creosote, pentachlorophenol and other highly toxic wood preservatives – in a field near Newcastle. The Council stopped a major Domtar plant from re-opening on a new site until it had cleaned up the carcinogenic muck it had left behind at the old one. It challenged all manner of pesticide use, from the provincial government's annual chemical spray programme against spruce budworm to the use of herbicides by pulp and paper companies to kill hardwoods. The Council documented the presence of cadmium in lobsters and the contamination of drinking water in Newcastle. And it kept up the fight against a second nuclear power plant in New Brunswick.

The Conservation Council became, in effect, Janice Harvey and her assistant, David Coon. We wondered at her luck in being able to hire a bright, able researcher like David away from the glittering lights of Toronto and the environmental stardom of Pollution Probe. Janice and David became involved in more than a professional partnership. Their marriage more than doubled the strength of the New Brunswick environmental movement.

The New Brunswick Conservation Council gets my vote for being one of the best environmental groups in the country; for being consistently reliable, dedicated and perennially short of funds. Frequently Janice, as director, can't pay herself her own salary – a salary about equal to what a good waitress could expect.

She has changed in the ten years I've known her. Her hair is less perfectly coiffed. Her briefcase bulges at its seams. She is tougher – formidable even. I see her holding her own under cross-examination in energy hearings with the high-priced counsel of the nuclear industry doing his best to tie her in knots. I see her in meetings with giants of industry, with federal ministers and with senior bureaucrats. I see them react and they are impressed. They do not expect such unabrasive, business-like poise from the leader of some little environmental group in Fredericton. Janice gets more beautiful every year.

On the west coast, fighting other issues, is a woman who, like Janice, is happy to be described as "A Daughter of Copper Woman" – taken from the title of the feminist, ecological and native fable of Canadian writer Anne Cameron. Colleen McCrory is a natural phenomenon. As highly charged as an electrical storm, and harder to ignore, she has championed – and won – some of the hardest wilderness battles of British Columbia. She was foremost in saving the Valhalla Valley of the Kootenays, for which she was awarded the Governor General's Conservation Prize, and then she joined the crusade to save South Moresby.

One of nine children, she was born and raised in the tiny mining town of New Denver, cupped in a valley by the towering mountains and glaciers of the Valhalla Ranges. Her father was a prospector whose prospects never panned out. Colleen and her brothers and sisters attended the school immediately across the street from their tumbledown house. With only one minute's travelling time between her bedroom and the school doors, Colleen was nevertheless always late, honing her appearance of breathless expectation to perfection in those early years. She hiked in the mountains and swam in the crystal waters of the glacial lakes. She mothered goats, chickens, rabbits and sheep; perennially adopted strays – puppies, kittens and, later, hippy-newcomers. She learned that charity begins at home. Her mother took in three foster children, as if nine natural ones were not enough.

Colleen quit school after grade eleven, and was married by the time she was eighteen. It was all she ever wanted, to be married to a good man and to be the best mother in New Denver. While she wouldn't have been described then as an "activist," nevertheless, she was active. She volunteered at the hospital, helped with "Meals on Wheels," helped with homemakers' projects, and got elected to the school board. She had three children in quick succession, and helped her husband peel logs for the house they were building together. She gardened and baked, pickled and canned and preserved. Her first encounter with environmental work occurred when she was twenty-two. She led a campaign to stop plans to shoot the bears that haunted the New Denver garbage dump. She had an affinity for bears. Her older brother, Wayne, was a wildlife biologist, specializing in grizzlies. When she was a child, he had taken her on many hikes through the woods, pointing out "bear signs" and teaching her about their habits. On those hikes she had seen the devastation caused by clear-cut lumbering operations, the streams choking with debris, the hillsides wasted and barren, their good top soil flowing down to clog the little brooks that fed the mountain lakes. These things bothered her deeply. She was instinctively an environmentalist – one of those Gaia people for whom the umbilical cord between self and Mother Earth remains forever intact.

Colleen did not start the campaign to save the Valhallas from destruction by the so-called "forest industry" – but it is no exaggeration to say that she won it. It is often thus. Without one person who is prepared to sacrifice everything to the cause, who is prepared to put the rest of his or her life on hold until a million phone calls are made, until a hundred demonstrations are organized, until a thousand letters are written, all the earnest support of others devoting occasional effort to the cause will come to nothing. Every movement needs a workhorse-cum-martyr-cum-slave.

Colleen's involvement began, predictably, in cooking for

community fund-raising events supporting the work of her brother, Wayne, and others trying to save the valley from clear-cut logging. She organized dances with the "Pied Pumpkin," the local band, and she cooked Mexican food for three hundred people at a time. Gradually she became involved in other ways – organizing petition campaigns, convincing town councils and chambers of commerce to support a plan to have the region made into a provincial park, and travelling to Vancouver and Victoria to talk to the press and lobby politicians.

As her involvement deepened, she became more and more single-minded. One day while weeding her garden in front of the beautiful log house she and her husband had just finished building, she was struck with a thought, almost a command: "I have to leave all this." That same day she moved herself and her children down to the lakeshore to a small house heated only by a wood stove, a place which would offer no distractions to her dedication and would become her headquarters and battle-station for many years.

Victory in the long struggle to save the valley was won in 1983, with the establishment of a provincial park encompassing a region thirty miles long, with beauty to rival Banff. Colleen was euphoric. But she did not rest on her laurels. In the course of the Valhalla campaign, she had made friends with people fighting to save other wilderness regions across the province – the Stein, Meares Island, Stikine and South Moresby. Now she adopted the South Moresby cause. Though she lived over a thousand miles from the Queen Charlotte Islands whose lower third was referred to as South Moresby, she soon became crucial to the battle to save the region from clear-cut logging. She recruited the then-federal minister of the environment, Charles Caccia, and secured his commitment that the area should become a national park. She got so much attention from the news media that she began to achieve a national profile as an environmental fighter and for that she came under ferocious counter-attack from supporters of the B.C. forest industry.

After her marriage ended, Colleen ran her own little store in New Denver. She called it the Valhalla Trading Post, and it sold clothes and jewellery, camping supplies and books, as well as being the local outlet for Simpsons-Sears. Of course, the store did double-duty as the centre of environmental activity for the region. The enterprise was no more of a gold mine than the kind her father found, but it kept food on the table.

Then a very peculiar bird named R. L. Smith from the town of Sandspit – the pro-logging stronghold of the Queen Charlotte Islands – and editor of something called *The Red Neck News*, decided to make Colleen and the Valhalla Wilderness Committee the object of his attention. Previously he had attacked the Haida Indians of the Queen Charlottes and local members of the Islands Protection Society for their environmental stands, but Colleen was a bigger target. *The Red Neck News* attacked the Valhalla group with such venom and hurled such unfounded charges and vitriolic abuse at Colleen that local logging interests in the Valhalla Valley were incited to organize a boycott of her store. A rock was hurled through her front window and her children were threatened at school. Some members of the Valhalla Wilderness Committee were beaten up, others were threatened. In due course the store went bankrupt for lack of customers.

The pain and suffering Colleen endured at the hands of the semi-literate *Red Neck News* is difficult to imagine until you see the Valhalla Trading Post, all boarded up, the display counters dusty and empty, the Valhalla Park posters peeling from the wall. But South Moresby was saved from destruction, and that feat made everything worthwhile for Colleen.

I'll never forget the aftermath of saving South Moresby. Within a week of the signing of the agreement to protect nearly 1500 square kilometres of some of the most precious islands on earth, I had two phone calls. One was from Thom Henley, a towering hero of that same crusade, who had created the original South Moresby wilderness proposal fourteen years earlier. He was calling from the B.C. phone company office in Victoria. They had disconnected his home phone for the umpteenth time for late payment of the astronomical long-distance bills that fighting for the environment engenders. Even though he had the full amount in his hand, they refused to reconnect his phone without an additional one-thousand-dollar deposit. Environmentalists are a bad credit risk, according to the phone company.

I was, at the time, Senior Policy Adviser to the federal minister of the environment, so Thom figured I might be able to help. I explained to the phone company functionary that Mr. Henley was an international hero. "Look in this month's *National Geographic*!" I implored. I offered to cover the thousand-dollar deposit personally. She backed off, and started calling Thom "Mr. Henley," and finally apologized. The next call I got was from Colleen. *Her* phone was about to be disconnected and her electricity too. I made several calls for her, and although the recipients were not impressed by *her* stature as a heroine, they *were* impressed with my charge card numbers. Few people realize that working as a grass-roots environmentalist often means perpetual poverty, and our victories almost never bring any alleviations of that poverty.

Although campaigns of vilification against environmentalists are commonplace, none of my friends has ever launched a libel case against the perpetrators, for the dual reasons of wasted time and lack of money. The only time one of our number was embroiled in such a case, she was the defendant. In 1983 Donna Smyth was sued for libel by Dr. Leo Yaffe, a nuclear chemist. It happened in the middle of our campaign against uranium mining in Nova Scotia, which was also, more or less, in the middle of our battle against mass use of herbicides.

Donna Smyth is bright, funny, sweet and ferociously perceptive. She is also a talented writer. The book she wrote about the Nova Scotia uranium campaign is worth reading on many levels. It's called *Subversive Elements* and, if from time to time you see quotations as I write about Donna, it's because I have quoted from "*S.E.*"

She was born and raised in the shadow of the Rocky Mountains in southern British Columbia. Like almost every environmentalist I know, her life has been full of animal friends. "I keep dogs for company, cats for sensuality, chickens for comic relief (and eggs!) and goats for wisdom."* When she wrote that, she was teaching English at Acadia University in Wolfville, Nova Scotia, and managing a subsistence, back-to-the-land lifestyle in Ellershouse, some forty miles or so from Wolfville.

One day in the spring of 1981, a friend called to invite Donna to attend a meeting of the municipal council of West Hants. The Women's Institute planned to present a brief concerning uranium exploration and mining. Her farm was not far from a uranium "hot spot" that a French company called Aquitaine wanted to mine. So Donna attended the meeting, and some subsequent ones, and her blood began to boil at the patronizing, evasive dishonesty of the slick salesmen of the nuclear age. Like Donna, many other local residents couldn't swallow the assurances that a uranium mine and its radioactive wastes posed "no risk." "The Environmental Consultant . . . puts his hand on his heart and says that mining uranium presents no more risk than flying to Calgary and back. Every time people fly, he says, we absorb more cosmic radiation. Does that stop us from flying? The audience is skeptical. We all smell a rat. . . ."**

Donna and her neighbours formed a group to oppose uranium mining and whatever other environmental assaults might come their way. They called it C.A.P.E. – Citizens' Action to Protect the Environment. Donna embarked on a marathon of research on low-level radiation; energy alternatives; the international uranium market; non-proliferation treaties; weapons-grade plutonium; international uranium cartels; the Canadian government's illegal efforts to "fix" the price of uranium to protect the industry; corporate structures; the technology of tailings containment; half-lives; radon daughters; lung cancer among miners in Elliot Lake, Ontario, where the Serpent River system has been uranium-killed for miles downstream. Then Donna and others began storming

*Smyth, Donna E. *Subversive Elements*. Women's Press, Toronto, 1986, p. 9. **Ibid. p. 19.

speaking platforms across the province, debating geologists from the Nova Scotia Department of Mines and public relations/environmental affairs officers of the industry.

Slowly but surely Donna's band began to win the public debate. The provincial government, looking for a breathing space, then instituted a moratorium on further uranium exploration until a commission of inquiry could officially examine the pros and cons.

One morning I tuned in to the CBC Radio morning show from Halifax. A so-called nuclear expert was on the air, shooting down the arguments of the anti-nuclear, anti-uranium environmentalists. It turned out to be an interview with Dr. Leo Yaffe, a professor of nuclear chemistry from McGill. He was in Nova Scotia to deliver a lecture, "The Health Hazards of *Not* Going Nuclear," in Halifax, Wolfville and Antigonish.

His lecture was well reported throughout the province, without any suggestion that there was more than one side to the issue. Donna decided to right the imbalance. She wrote a well-reasoned opinion piece for the province's largest daily newspaper, *The Chronicle Herald*. Titled "That Desperate Attempt to Sell Nuclear," the piece opened by saying that Dr. Yaffe was "only one of many 'experts' that the nuclear industry will parade in front of us in their desperate attempt to sell 'nuclear' to Nova Scotia." The rest of the article dealt with the documented hazards of uranium mining and the nuclear fuel chain.

Donna soon received a letter from Yaffe's lawyers in Montreal threatening suit for libel. I was in law school in Halifax at the time, so she showed me the letter and I took it to my professors. None of them thought anything she had said could constitute libel. After another threatening letter in January 1983, nearly one year after the publication of her piece and just before the limitation period expired, Yaffe filed suit against Donna Smyth for defamation. The whole suit came down to her use of the one word "parade" and the quotation marks around expert. Yaffe sued Donna but, curiously, *not The Chronicle Herald*. Most defamation suits automatically include the offending publication as well as the author. But this wasn't to be like most defamation suits. This one came out like a morality play. For the next two years, Donna's time, energy and finances were consumed in the horrors of being dragged through the legal system. She had to take a year's unpaid leave in order to fight the case, supported by a local defence committee of dedicated environmentalists and friends and help from across the country. There were discovery examinations, witnesses to line up, and money to raise for swelling legal defence fees. Donna was forbidden to make any public comment on the issue. None of her articles could be circulated, thus effectively muzzling her. And there was the terrifying possibility that if she lost her case the media would be reluctant to disseminate the views of other environmentalists who dared to challenge the establishment. "Nuclear Critic Silenced" should have been somebody's headline. It wasn't.

The trial finally took place nearly two years after the papers were first filed and three years after the article appeared. Thank God, a defendant in a libel case in Nova Scotia has an absolute right to a jury instead of just a judge – and a jury was Donna's choice. Dr. Ursula Franklin, a colleague and friend of Leo Yaffe, testified. A grey-haired professor of metallurgy at the University of Toronto, she has fought tirelessly for decades past for the environment and for peace. If she could have done so, she told a startled court in her distinctive, motherly, German accent, she would have just given Leo a big hug so he would stop being upset with her other friend, Donna. On cross-examination, Yaffe's lawyer asked whether she would not agree that being identified with one side of a debate would damage a scientist's reputation. "I have a long and biased standing in favour of peace," she replied calmly, "and so I am very clearly identified with one side." He tried again. Would she not agree that her reputation would be damaged if it was alleged that she was in the pocket of the nuclear industry? "In that case," she said with a perfectly straight face, "the nuclear industry might sue *me* for libel."

It seemed as though the day was won, until the judge gave his charge to the jury. In summing up the "facts," he instructed the jury that Donna's article, which he characterized as "strident," in fact alleged that Dr. Yaffe was a "paid advocate, a hired gun" of the nuclear industry. Donna's lawyers were on their feet like a flash to object to His Lordship's interpretation of the evidence. The jury was shown out while her lawyers tried in vain to convince the judge that his instructions were prejudicial to their client's case. The judge didn't agree. The jury was recalled. The instructions stood. The jury went out again – for four hours – while Donna agonized over the verdict. If she lost, it meant an appeal. There were issues of the Charter of Rights here. But Yaffe would have a cash award against her. How much? She'd also owe him for all the legal costs of his prosecution of her. How much? Four hours seemed like an eternity after two years of torment.

Finally the jury of four men and three women returned their verdict. "Parade" was not defamatory. Donna had won. "I'm free," she told reporters. "We've got to live again." But she will never get those years back. She'll never recover the cost of that ordeal, financial or emotional.

In due course, the head of the uranium inquiry, Judge Robert McCleave, recommended that the moratorium on uranium exploration and mining in Nova Scotia be extended for five years. It has recently been re-extended for a further five years. This has been largely Donna's victory, but it isn't her only contribution to the environmental movement. In her book, radio programmes and other writings, she has been a powerful voice for truth and clarity. Here are a few of her thoughts.

"Environmentalists are often dismissed by industry and government as being too emotional or even hysterical. Women are familiar with this kind of accusation. Our cultural role is to be emotional, intuitive, imaginative, while the male is rational, scientific and intelligent. In this way, intellect is split off from the world. The female is body, the male the severed head. From this head has sprung the child Science who has no mother. . . .

"Scientists have cultivated this lopsided image of themselves with pride. Traditionally their laboratories have been shrines to the great god, Objectivity. In this world, 'scientific' becomes a talismanic word used to cleave the world into true/untrue; scientific/unscientific.

"This cleavage has filtered down into other levels of society. Even the media has adopted this model of objectivity, of the neutrality of the reporter, of the truth of the 'facts' as opposed to opinions and points of view. . . .

"By virtue of his education and training, he [the scientist] has set himself apart from the rest of us. He has called himself 'pure,' disinterested, a seeker after truth. . . . Because he is a Scientist, he declares he is not swayed by crass motivations. He may work for Atomic Energy of Canada, or Dow Chemical but his research and its results are absolutely objective.

"As a society we have swallowed this myth and its myth types holus-bolus. We worship in Science's Church and are rewarded with technological manna: microwave ovens, food-processors, electric toothbrushes, trail-bikes. These are the distractions of our consumer society, the offspring of capitalism mated to science.

"Not only capitalism. When Russian ships dock in Halifax Harbour, the sailors hurry ashore to buy designer jeans and hard rock records. They cannot wait to be distracted.

"The question is: from what are we distracted? . . .

"We are distracted from ourselves: we substitute one kind of boredom for another in front of the TV. . . . We save ourselves time with 'conveniences' only to realize that we don't know how to use this extra time. So we fill it up with more gadgets, more things. We hide our fear of death in our pursuit of eternal youth.

"We are distracted from each other: each household is a consumer unit. We all must have our snowblowers, our rototillers and our cars. We only share our individual resources at times of crisis. . . . We are distracted from essential realities:

we are poisoning our earth, our water, our air. We live on the edge of the nuclear abyss."*

Helen Caldicott calls this attitude of ours "collective death denial."

Of course, not all the people who see the world as an interlocking web of life are women. And not all women are prepared to recognize their affinity with Gaia. Nevertheless, the environmental movement owes an enormous debt to womankind – to Colleen and Donna, and to thousands of others ranging from Vicky Husband, saving wilderness and old-growth forests in coastal British Columbia, to Dr. Martha Kostuch, veterinarian, mother of three, spending every spare ounce of her strength fighting the Alberta government's plans to dam the Old Man River.

One of the first environmental activists in Nova Scotia was Teresa Boyd, now in her eighties. She knew Premier John Buchanan when he was an office boy in the coal company offices where she worked. Recently she accosted him about the dangers of the Point Lepreau nuclear power plant. He laughed in his charming way and said, "Don't you worry about that, Teresa. By the time that causes any trouble, you and I will be long gone!"

Men and women do *not* see the world in the same way. Women are fighting for enduring life; for the future of Earth and *all* her children. And as much as it would be nice to take a rest now and then, Gaia women don't have time.

---

*Smyth, Donna E. *Subversive Elements*. Women's Press, Toronto, 1986, pp. 146-8.

Epilogue:

The Prophetic View of John Livingston

John Livingston is a contemporary of mine, and we have had much in common as we struggled to understand the role mankind plays in the theatre of life on earth. We have pursued the same objectives, but followed different paths. Whereas I became something of a preacher, John developed into a phenomenally adept teacher and the prime philosopher of the environmental movement in this country.

The clarity of his insights, the breadth of his grasp of what ails this planet, and the ruthlessness of his conclusions combine to give him the stature of an Old-Testament prophet. Like one of those, he is revered by true believers but feared and rejected by those who are preoccupied with worldly self-interest.

I think it only fitting that he should have the last word in this book.

F.M. John, what brought you to an awareness of your indivisibility with other living beings?

J.L. There's a phenomenon which takes place in pre-adolescence that if one is exposed to other species – it doesn't matter particularly whether it's the dog or the cat, but better still if it is multi-species – results in a connection which is never lost.

Paul Shepard says youngsters literally ingest the experience of nature and it becomes part of them. I believe that this is so. In my case, it happened to be a fascination with newts and toads and frogs and stuff when I was a small child. Then I got interested in birds. I was a keen birder all my childhood.

F.M. What was your first intimation that all was not well between man and the natural world.

J.L. When I was a youngster in Toronto they decided to put a storm sewer through *my* ravine – Cedarvale – which meant ripping the heart out of the place. I remember weeping with rage, anger and frustration because it felt as if part of me was being cut out. It was like a piece coming out of my stomach, and I was only ten or twelve. I may have been a bit "bent" by that experience. But from then on I was committed to defending nature.

My first involvement in conservation work came in the early fifties when I was named executive director of the Canadian Audubon Society. That thrilled me because of all those magic names of great naturalists I had never met. Roger Tory Peterson, Alexander Sprunt, Alan Cruickshank were all on the Audubon staff at the time. It was as though heaven was here.

F.M. How lucky you were to have found a place so early on.

J.L. It *was* a place for me, and I mean "place" in the most profound sense, both social, physical and ideological.

I was involved in a lot of things there but most especially the protection of birds of prey, because they weren't protected under the Migratory Birds Act and were shot on sight as vermin by sportsmen and farmers alike. I spent an awful lot of time lobbying individual provinces to try to get them to enact protection for hawks and owls. Unfortunately the demands made on me by the Audubon head office in the United States were rather different from saving wildlife – they expected me to concentrate on administrative and financial affairs. There was a heavy debt to be realized, and I wasn't the guy to do that. So in 1962 I went to the CBC and began "The Nature of Things." I was the first producer, and I stayed there until 1968. Then I went to York University where I've been teaching ecology ever since.

F.M. When did your involvement with Pollution Probe come in?

J.L. The founders were my friends but I was never formally aligned with it. By that time I already suspected that the seat of the mischief was somewhat deeper than pollution. And, too, I was developing a terrible problem dealing with institutionalized beliefs, which had been so manifest in the Audubon Society way of perceiving and doing things. The conservation movement seemed to be becoming an alphabet soup of conflicting ideologies, none of which, I felt in my heart, had much to do with my frogs and toads and newts and warblers. By the mid-sixties I was becoming convinced that the roots of the difficulties between man and nature were cultural, as opposed to blaming government, industry and other such specifics. That's when I went to York University.

A university is a great refuge for a person like me. One can also make a modest contribution. If one can turn students on by slicing the onion in a different way, then one has done something useful. All of my work since 1969-70 has been in attempting to come to grips with and resolve the conflict between man and nature as I happen to perceive it.

F.M. You don't like being called a conservationist any more. Tell me why.

J.L. I'm *not* a conservationist. Shall we debate the semantics?

F.M. Aren't conservationists those who try to protect and preserve life on earth?

J.L. That isn't conservation as it is currently understood and applied. In practice, conservation is now resource development. The World Conservation Strategy holds that conservation is resource-oriented, and can only be defined in terms of human utility – in effect saying that everything was created by an almighty beneficence for human use. Therefore conservation becomes management – the "wise use" of these things in the long-term human interest.

F.M. It's generally short-term.

J.L. The rhetoric is long-term. The *fact* is short-term – economic horizons being what they are, and political horizons being even shorter.

F.M. In other words, the original meaning of conservation has been perverted to mean exploitation of nature for human gain?

J.L. Of course. Maximum economic return is what the word has come to mean. Conservation is resource development under intensive management. It is the antithesis of *preservation*.

The "preservation" meaning of the word is anathema from a technocratic point of view. As far as they are concerned, conservationists are those who use nature to pave the road for the technomachine, whereas preservationists are exemplified as stupid old ladies with their hearts on their sleeves who squat in the path of orderly progress. Preservationists are not to be taken seriously because they don't share in the ethos of the necessary primacy of human enterprise.

F.M. What do you think this book I'm writing is about, if not about conservation?

J.L. It looks as if it's at least partly a review of the institutionalized approaches to the perceived loss of natural resources, more than the loss of nature. But even the loss of nature is proprietory. *Our* birds, *our* endangered species, *our* woodlands, *our* swamplands are disappearing. *Our* natural heritage – I despise that attitude. Nobody in the respectable conservation movement is talking about nature for her own sake. Only individuals like you and me are weeping solitarily for nature for *her* sake.

It's hard to say whether the terrible sadness I feel is for the ongoing destruction of nature or for my own loss of the experience of nature.

F.M. I don't think you have to differentiate; it's all one.

J.L. I don't think so either. If anybody hurts my dog he hurts me. So both are damaged. That's not an easy concept to institutionalize in the technocratic society.

F.M. Isn't that what the animal welfare movement is trying to do?

J.L. Yes. Some of them. People like Stephen Best, Vicki Miller and Anne Doncaster are trying to articulate this, and are not embarrassed to say this. But no hard-line, middle-of-the-road conservationists would ever dream of uttering such things because of their terrible anxiety to be thought respectable and credible.

F.M. Read: rational and logical. Are they afraid of emotional, subjective attitudes because such things are not fashionable in a mechanistic world where the intellect has become the godhead?

J.L. There is a terrible paranoia in the neo-conservation community. Even within naturalist organizations, maybe especially these, there is paranoia about being seen as being emotional, and this fear has allowed them to mesmerize themselves right into the technocratic orbit. In order to appear respectable they permit themselves to become pawns of the Ministry of Natural Resources or whatever.

F.M. Are they being co-opted or are they co-opting themselves?

J.L. Both. Why don't naturalist groups, especially, have the guts to stand up and take a position against sport hunting and fashion fur? That would be too emotional. Can't do that, because we've got to play ball with the bureaucrats. This is the part that hurts more than anything else, that organizations begun by people with a deep and abiding love of nature are becoming indistinguishable from the conservation bureaucracy itself.

The only movement left that's speaking from the heart is the animal welfare movement.

F.M. What about Professor Peter Singer, the guru of animal rights? He is a very logical and rational human being – or appears to be.

J.L. He would almost professionally deny being an emotionalist because he has to be a proper philosopher. Don't forget that logic is technology. How to think, how to address a problem, how to define a problem, how to argue. The whole structure is so tyrannical, and it's part of technology. The philosophers get very angry when I say that they are part of the technomachine.

F.M. What *about* the business of hunting? Why *shouldn't* people hunt for sport?

J.L. I can't get around the idea of people getting their jollies by maiming and wounding and killing. Hunters deny they do this, of course. They say it's just like the bird watcher getting out and enjoying some kind of communion with nature. People have written whole books about hunters communing with nature. They say a mystical experience is derived from this bloodletting; which I simply cannot understand. "Man *is* a natural predator" is the rationale that's usually produced in scholarly circles in defence of sport hunting. They say we evolved as predators. I deny this. We evolved as gatherers, with a little bit of hunting on the side. The hunting instinct is no more ingrained in us than any other aberrant behaviour. The simple fact is that hunting has become an industrial enterprise – a very big one and a very big source of profit to any number of people. There's also the macho aspect in that most hunting, now, is carried on by urban folk because it's a "U" thing. Fortunately, hunters are becoming a shrinking minority, albeit a very vocal and powerful one. I think sport hunting is on the way out in spite of the hype it gets.

I once had to write an article about hunting, and I went to the local newspaper shop and bought the current issue of all the hunting magazines and read them all. What I found most informative was the advertisements. The language and style of the advertisements was so overtly sexual it was hard to believe.

A study Statistics Canada did a few years ago has the most compelling evidence I've seen that sport hunting is becoming passé. It was a review of the perceptions and uses made of nature by the general public – how many people like to watch birds, how many like to garden, how many like to go out in nature, hiking, visiting a conservation area, all that. Less than ten per cent said they liked to hunt! I suspect sport hunters are a dead-end expression of human domestication, of bad breeding, like the pit bull terrier.

I think it always was abnormal behaviour. It was the fullest expression of the commodification of nature. Animals are there to kill, and mount on a wall, or photograph yourself beside, and this is the ultimate form of consumption.

F.M. What about subsistence hunting? Don't you see any justification for that?

J.L. We've got a lot of historical revisionism going on these days about that. Subsistence hunting – what I call subsistence in its pure form – is ecologically circumscribed. You are hunting for your life. No problem there. But now the fur industry and its apologists in government and in several conservation organizations have redefined subsistence to include commercial hunting and trapping.

It's absolutely indefensible. There's no ecological, anthropological or economic basis for saying that the fur trade is part of the traditional aboriginal culture. None. It was the fur trade and the trade in animals of all kinds that *destroyed* the aboriginal cultures of North America. And to hear people today, including natives, claim the anti-trappers are going to bring down the native culture is bizarre.

I think the great change to the aboriginal cultures came when the native no longer saw the animal as part of himself, part of his environment, but as a source of cash. The animal was transformed into a cash symbol. The moment that happened, the aboriginal culture was gone.

One knows why they are making these statements now – because it's a part of the argument for land claims, and if one can claim one needs the land for aboriginal cultural purposes, then it's another little bit of support for one's case. However, proprietorship of land is just as foreign to aboriginal cultures as the taking of wildlife for cash.

F.M. What happens if we convert the wild-fur business to so-called fur ranching?

J.L. Captive breeding. I believe that the suffering of the captive-bred animals is infinitely greater than that of the wild-caught animal, because a wild animal shows very little psychological response to being attacked and killed if the action is done swiftly. But captive animals suffer over the whole duration of their lives. They live out their lives in terrible apprehension. These are not domesticated animals; they are captive *wild* animals, especially mink, weasels and foxes.

If there is anything wilder than those three predators, I'd like to know what it is. They all go crazy when you confine them. They can't be domesticated. The essence of domestication is social dependence, and there's no social dependence for them.

F.M. Would you say that a lot of the effort being expended against trapping and hunting might be better used elsewhere? That these problems are going to look after themselves?

J.L. Oh no. Commercial hunting and trapping will go on long after amateur recreational hunting has gone. So the money and effort is being well spent.

F.M. But aren't you being pretty hard on native trappers?

J.L. There's no money in it for the natives anyway. The money is all made at the wholesale, retail end. Native trappers average $200-300 in a year. It's aberrant behaviour for people to be wearing the furs of living beings for ostentation, for status symbols, as prestige goods.

F.M. Like having lampshades made out of tattooed human skin?

J.L. I don't think it's essentially any different. Can you imagine this sort of thing happening in nature? It is anomalous behaviour right from the top down. I see it as anti-social in a fundamental way because I firmly believe in inter-species social organization. I am absolutely convinced that inter-species relationships are the ultimate relationships. We start with individual selfishness, then our relationship sphere begins to expand. There's mother; there's family; there's the tribal self, and that eventually transcends to an inter-species self. At that stage, the essence of the feeling one has for nature is selflessness. The individual self dissolves in the overall relationship. A participatory relationship with nature. I don't want to stand outside and be a Cartesian observer; I want to participate, to feel. A man by the name of Morris Berman wrote a wonderful book called *The Re-enchantment of the World* in which he rejects the machine-like world of scientific objectivity. His goal is the retrieval of nature as sacred, as enchanted and as participatory at all levels, individual, group and so on. This is the kind of thing I am interested in.

F.M. How do we get rid of the mechanized world we have constructed and recapture awareness of where it is that we belong?

J.L. I know it sounds like a cop-out, but all I can say to that question is I have to understand it better and more deeply before offering a solution.

F.M. It may not require any conscious solution. The mechanical world may simply destroy itself, if not with nuclear devices, then through a collapse of the life-sustaining envelope as a result of our tinkering with it.

J.L. Leo Marx wrote a wonderful book called *The Machine in the Garden* about an image that originated long ago in Europe of the garden and the machine that kept invading and trying to subjugate it. True conservationists have always been out there fighting against the machine. This is his thesis. I don't pretend to comprehend why we should feel that way, except I suspect it is the pure expression of instinctive self-preservation.

I speculate sometimes with colleagues that true conservationists are analogous with the spruce budworm; it is the spruce budworm's job to prevent the overriding dominance by the spruce trees over the rest of the living community of the forest. Dominance in too great a degree makes for greater vulnerability of both the dominated *and* the dominator.

F.M. Technology *is* dominance for the human species, and it is clear that every technical advance since the invention of the hand axe, or before, has made us increasingly dominant, but also increasingly vulnerable to massive catastrophe by making us dependent on our artificial constructs. Our vulnerability as increasingly alien beings on Planet Earth has grown almost geometrically as technology has enabled us to become ever more dominant.

J.L. And so we have become increasingly dependent for survival, not on nature but on an external agent which we have ourselves created. Technology.

F.M. Perhaps we are becoming as vulnerable in our reliance on technology as is the cosmonaut in his tiny mechanical planet.

J.L. The space analogy is a good one. Technology is about nothing if it isn't about expertise, and narrow, compartmentalized expertise at that. Define the problem in terms of a solution is the name of the game. I think your average technocrat is a bladder stuffed with solutions, looking for ways to turn these into power. If the problem doesn't have a solution, then redefine the problem to fit the solution at hand. That is the essence of technocracy and of the cultivation of expertise. Matters of the heart and the being and the bone marrow don't have much to do with expertise. And expertise without these qualities of *living* things isn't going to solve the problem of how to save this planet.

Everything hinges on *preserving* – not conserving, mark you – quality habitat, whether it holds aquatic or terrestrial communities. Everything derives from quality habitat, and that means plants – without which there can *be* no animals.

F.M. Habitat protection seems now to be the main thrust of many conservation organizations.

J.L. It is – and that's good. But in many cases it still doesn't mean preservation – it means management. And what does that mean? It means sustainable development.

F.M. Setting aside "natural" regions to be used for a different kind of exploitation?

J.L. That's right. I don't like the expression "set aside." It's like dessert that we'll set aside for later consumption. The rhetoric of many neo-conservationists appals me.

F.M. There is a whole new language here. A kind of newspeak.

J.L. And one has to understand it. "Sustainable development," "maximum sustained yield," "resource conservation," "wise use" are in fact attempts to sugar-coat our ongoing intention to continue to exploit nature for our own, often indefensible, ends. Human utility remains the name of the game. I think many so-called environmental organizations have deliberately set out to demonstrate the utility of nature to the human enterprise as the most palatable way of selling conservation. And it has become so ingrained with them now to argue the cause of nature in terms of human requirements – real or otherwise – that they can no longer escape from it. To see conservation organizations like the World Wildlife Fund, the Federation of Ontario Naturalists, or other such who fundamentally stand for the interests of nature – to see them argue in terms of human utility nauseates me, because it is caving in to the demands of the technostructure. Instead of the consumer or commodifier having to *prove* the legitimacy of claims on nature, those who would defend nature have to prove a case for its protection. Unfortunately, the argument they use is inescapably utilitarian. This is a suicidal intellectual as well as emotional position. And this is what I dislike the most about the institutionalized conservation movement.

F.M. If you stand only on the defence in war, you court inevitable defeat. What we should be doing is demanding of the users or abusers of nature: "By what right do you do this?"

J.L. This is correct. And in this connection I have to add that "animal rights" – as opposed to "animal welfare" – is a stupid argument in my view because there is no way to argue rights outside the human enterprise. So by arguing for animal rights we are again anthropomorphizing nature and going on the defensive.

We are imprisoned by rational arguments. This is the part that hurts. You hear the most impassioned, eloquent arguments of all reduced down to nature's utility to man. Even the esthetic is a utility. Even the appeal to preserve nature for future generations is a utility. Leave it for future generations to utilize – that's what it boils down to. Somebody has to have the guts to fight for nature simply because it's in our marrow, and because we love it and can't live without it!

It is so sad to see conservation groups falling into that trap, becoming instruments of the very organizations and governments they are trying to oppose.

F.M. I wonder if there is any real alternative. Taking the subjective and emotional point of view automatically disqualifies you from a respectable hearing. Nobody is going to listen. So maybe you have to fight them with their own self-serving logic.
J.L. If you do, you're dead. And in the end, the living world will be dead too.

L'Envoi

We are like yeasts in a vat – mindlessly multiplying as we greedily devour a finite world. If we do not change our ways, we will perish as the yeasts perish – having exhausted our sustenance and poisoned ourselves in the lethal brew of our own wastes.

Farley Mowat
January 1990

Appendix

ARK II
Canadian Animal Rights Network
P.O. Box 687, Station Q
Toronto, Ontario M4T 2N5
(416) 588-0885

President: Robert Eastwood

Canadian Nature Federation
453 Sussex Drive
Ottawa, Ontario K1N 6Z4
(613) 238-6154

Executive Director: Paul Griss

Harmony Foundation of Canada
19 Oakvale Avenue
Ottawa, Ontario K1Y 3S3
(613) 230-7353

Executive Director: Michael Bloomfield

International Fund for Animal Welfare
P.O. Box 193
Yarmouthport, Mass. 02675
U.S.A.
(508) 362-4944

Executive Director: Richard Moore

International Wildlife Coalition
P.O. Box 461, Port Credit Postal Station
Mississauga, Ontario L5G 4M1
(416) 274-0633

Canadian Co-ordinator: Anne Doncaster

Nature Conservancy of Canada
794-A Broadview Avenue
Toronto, Ontario M4K 2P7
(416) 469-1701

Executive Director: John Eisenhauer

Sierra Club of Eastern Canada
2316 Queen Street East
Toronto, Ontario M4E 1G8
(416) 698-8446

Chair: Jane Eligh-Feryn

Sierra Club of Western Canada
620 View Street, Suite 314
Victoria, B.C. V8W 1J6
(604) 386-5255

Chair: Duncan Stewart

Toronto Humane Society
11 River Street
Toronto, Ontario M5A 4C2
(416) 392-2273

Executive Director: Kathleen Hunter

World Wildlife Fund Canada
60 St. Clair Avenue East, Suite 201
Toronto, Ontario M4T 1N5
(416) 923-8173

President: Monte Hummel

World Society for the Protection of Animals
215 Lakeshore Blvd. East, Suite 211
Toronto, Ontario M5A 3W9
(416) 369-0044

Field Rep: Michael O'Sullivan